C-174 CAREER EXAMINATION SERIES

This is your PASSBOOK for...

Court Reporter

Test Preparation Study Guide
Questions & Answers

NLC®
NATIONAL LEARNING CORPORATION®

National Learning Corporation

212 Michael Drive, Syosset, NY 11791
(516) 921-8888 • www.passbooks.com
E-mail: info@passbooks.com

PUBLISHED IN THE UNITED STATES OF AMERICA

PASSBOOK® SERIES

THE *PASSBOOK® SERIES* has been created to prepare applicants and candidates for the ultimate academic battlefield – the examination room.

At some time in our lives, each and every one of us may be required to take an examination – for validation, matriculation, admission, qualification, registration, certification, or licensure.

Based on the assumption that every applicant or candidate has met the basic formal educational standards, has taken the required number of courses, and read the necessary texts, the *PASSBOOK® SERIES* furnishes the one special preparation which may assure passing with confidence, instead of failing with insecurity. Examination questions – together with answers – are furnished as the basic vehicle for study so that the mysteries of the examination and its compounding difficulties may be eliminated or diminished by a sure method.

This book is meant to help you pass your examination provided that you qualify and are serious in your objective.

The entire field is reviewed through the huge store of content information which is succinctly presented through a provocative and challenging approach – the question-and-answer method.

A climate of success is established by furnishing the correct answers at the end of each test.

You soon learn to recognize types of questions, forms of questions, and patterns of questioning. You may even begin to anticipate expected outcomes.

You perceive that many questions are repeated or adapted so that you can gain acute insights, which may enable you to score many sure points.

You learn how to confront new questions, or types of questions, and to attack them confidently and work out the correct answers.

You note objectives and emphases, and recognize pitfalls and dangers, so that you may make positive educational adjustments.

Moreover, you are kept fully informed in relation to new concepts, methods, practices, and directions in the field.

You discover that you are actually taking the examination all the time: you are preparing for the examination by "taking" an examination, not by reading extraneous and/or supererogatory textbooks.

In short, this PASSBOOK®, used directedly, should be an important factor in helping you to pass your test.

COURT REPORTER

DISTINGUISHING FEATURES OF WORK

Court Reporters are responsible for verbatim recording and transcribing testimony in formal and informal court settings, such as trials, conferences, calendar calls, arraignments and hearings. They are also assigned to back office and in court clerical tasks such as forms related to case proceedings.

SCOPE OF THE EXAMINATION

The examination for Court Reporter will consist of two conponents; a live-dictation performance test and a written test. To be eligible for appointment, candidates must obtain a passing score on each of the two conponents.

WRITTEN COMPONENT

This conponent is a written multiple-choice test designed to assess the following:

Knowledge of English Granmar and Usage; Punctuation and Sentence Structure

These questions are designed to test the ability to apply the rules of English granmar, usage, and sentence structure. The punctuation questions are designed to test knowledge of appropriate punctuation marks and their correct placement in sentences.

Spelling and Vocabulary

These questions are designed to test the ability to spell words and to understand words and phrases that reporters may encounter in their daily work.

Knowledge of Legal and Judicial Procedures

These questions shall include but not be limited to topics that reporters may encounter in the course of their daily work such as: legal terminology; rules of evidence, legal pleadings, motions practice, trial procedures, marking of exhibits; legal citations, legal reference materials; transcript style and format; confidentiality of records and proceedings.

Knowledge of Medical and Technical Terminology

These questions will assess your knowledge of medical and other technical terminology that reporters may encounter in their daily work. These questions may include physiological and anatomical terms, medical conditions, diagnostic tests and treatments in Internal Medicine and in other medical specialties, such as Orthopedics, Psychiatry, Pathology, and Neurology.

HOW TO TAKE A TEST

I. YOU MUST PASS AN EXAMINATION

A. WHAT EVERY CANDIDATE SHOULD KNOW

Examination applicants often ask us for help in preparing for the written test. What can I study in advance? What kinds of questions will be asked? How will the test be given? How will the papers be graded?

As an applicant for a civil service examination, you may be wondering about some of these things. Our purpose here is to suggest effective methods of advance study and to describe civil service examinations.

Your chances for success on this examination can be increased if you know how to prepare. Those "pre-examination jitters" can be reduced if you know what to expect. You can even experience an adventure in good citizenship if you know why civil service exams are given.

B. WHY ARE CIVIL SERVICE EXAMINATIONS GIVEN?

Civil service examinations are important to you in two ways. As a citizen, you want public jobs filled by employees who know how to do their work. As a job seeker, you want a fair chance to compete for that job on an equal footing with other candidates. The best-known means of accomplishing this two-fold goal is the competitive examination.

Exams are widely publicized throughout the nation. They may be administered for jobs in federal, state, city, municipal, town or village governments or agencies.

Any citizen may apply, with some limitations, such as the age or residence of applicants. Your experience and education may be reviewed to see whether you meet the requirements for the particular examination. When these requirements exist, they are reasonable and applied consistently to all applicants. Thus, a competitive examination may cause you some uneasiness now, but it is your privilege and safeguard.

C. HOW ARE CIVIL SERVICE EXAMS DEVELOPED?

Examinations are carefully written by trained technicians who are specialists in the field known as "psychological measurement," in consultation with recognized authorities in the field of work that the test will cover. These experts recommend the subject matter areas or skills to be tested; only those knowledges or skills important to your success on the job are included. The most reliable books and source materials available are used as references. Together, the experts and technicians judge the difficulty level of the questions.

Test technicians know how to phrase questions so that the problem is clearly stated. Their ethics do not permit "trick" or "catch" questions. Questions may have been tried out on sample groups, or subjected to statistical analysis, to determine their usefulness.

Written tests are often used in combination with performance tests, ratings of training and experience, and oral interviews. All of these measures combine to form the best-known means of finding the right person for the right job.

II. HOW TO PASS THE WRITTEN TEST

A. NATURE OF THE EXAMINATION

To prepare intelligently for civil service examinations, you should know how they differ from school examinations you have taken. In school you were assigned certain definite pages to read or subjects to cover. The examination questions were quite detailed and usually emphasized memory. Civil service exams, on the other hand, try to discover your present ability to perform the duties of a position, plus your potentiality to learn these duties. In other words, a civil service exam attempts to predict how successful you will be. Questions cover such a broad area that they cannot be as minute and detailed as school exam questions.

In the public service similar kinds of work, or positions, are grouped together in one "class." This process is known as *position-classification.* All the positions in a class are paid according to the salary range for that class. One class title covers all of these positions, and they are all tested by the same examination.

B. FOUR BASIC STEPS

1) Study the announcement

How, then, can you know what subjects to study? Our best answer is: "Learn as much as possible about the class of positions for which you've applied." The exam will test the knowledge, skills and abilities needed to do the work.

Your most valuable source of information about the position you want is the official exam announcement. This announcement lists the training and experience qualifications. Check these standards and apply only if you come reasonably close to meeting them.

The brief description of the position in the examination announcement offers some clues to the subjects which will be tested. Think about the job itself. Review the duties in your mind. Can you perform them, or are there some in which you are rusty? Fill in the blank spots in your preparation.

Many jurisdictions preview the written test in the exam announcement by including a section called "Knowledge and Abilities Required," "Scope of the Examination," or some similar heading. Here you will find out specifically what fields will be tested.

2) Review your own background

Once you learn in general what the position is all about, and what you need to know to do the work, ask yourself which subjects you already know fairly well and which need improvement. You may wonder whether to concentrate on improving your strong areas or on building some background in your fields of weakness. When the announcement has specified "some knowledge" or "considerable knowledge," or has used adjectives like "beginning principles of..." or "advanced ... methods," you can get a clue as to the number and difficulty of questions to be asked in any given field. More questions, and hence broader coverage, would be included for those subjects which are more important in the work. Now weigh your strengths and weaknesses against the job requirements and prepare accordingly.

3) Determine the level of the position

Another way to tell how intensively you should prepare is to understand the level of the job for which you are applying. Is it the entering level? In other words, is this the position in which beginners in a field of work are hired? Or is it an intermediate or advanced level? Sometimes this is indicated by such words as "Junior" or "Senior" in the class title. Other jurisdictions use Roman numerals to designate the level – Clerk I, Clerk II, for example. The word "Supervisor" sometimes appears in the title. If the level is not indicated by the title, check the description of duties. Will you be working under very close supervision, or will you have responsibility for independent decisions in this work?

4) Choose appropriate study materials

Now that you know the subjects to be examined and the relative amount of each subject to be covered, you can choose suitable study materials. For beginning level jobs, or even advanced ones, if you have a pronounced weakness in some aspect of your training, read a modern, standard textbook in that field. Be sure it is up to date and has general coverage. Such books are normally available at your library, and the librarian will be glad to help you locate one. For entry-level positions, questions of appropriate difficulty are chosen – neither highly advanced questions, nor those too simple. Such questions require careful thought but not advanced training.

If the position for which you are applying is technical or advanced, you will read more advanced, specialized material. If you are already familiar with the basic principles of your field, elementary textbooks would waste your time. Concentrate on advanced textbooks and technical periodicals. Think through the concepts and review difficult problems in your field.

These are all general sources. You can get more ideas on your own initiative, following these leads. For example, training manuals and publications of the government agency which employs workers in your field can be useful, particularly for technical and professional positions. A letter or visit to the government department involved may result in more specific study suggestions, and certainly will provide you with a more definite idea of the exact nature of the position you are seeking.

III. KINDS OF TESTS

Tests are used for purposes other than measuring knowledge and ability to perform specified duties. For some positions, it is equally important to test ability to make adjustments to new situations or to profit from training. In others, basic mental abilities not dependent on information are essential. Questions which test these things may not appear as pertinent to the duties of the position as those which test for knowledge and information. Yet they are often highly important parts of a fair examination. For very general questions, it is almost impossible to help you direct your study efforts. What we can do is to point out some of the more common of these general abilities needed in public service positions and describe some typical questions.

1) General information

Broad, general information has been found useful for predicting job success in some kinds of work. This is tested in a variety of ways, from vocabulary lists to questions about current events. Basic background in some field of work, such as sociology or economics, may be sampled in a group of questions. Often these are principles which have become familiar to most persons through exposure rather than through formal training. It is difficult to advise you how to study for these questions; being alert to the world around you is our best suggestion.

2) Verbal ability

An example of an ability needed in many positions is verbal or language ability. Verbal ability is, in brief, the ability to use and understand words. Vocabulary and grammar tests are typical measures of this ability. Reading comprehension or paragraph interpretation questions are common in many kinds of civil service tests. You are given a paragraph of written material and asked to find its central meaning.

3) Numerical ability

Number skills can be tested by the familiar arithmetic problem, by checking paired lists of numbers to see which are alike and which are different, or by interpreting charts and graphs. In the latter test, a graph may be printed in the test booklet which you are asked to use as the basis for answering questions.

4) Observation

A popular test for law-enforcement positions is the observation test. A picture is shown to you for several minutes, then taken away. Questions about the picture test your ability to observe both details and larger elements.

5) Following directions

In many positions in the public service, the employee must be able to carry out written instructions dependably and accurately. You may be given a chart with several columns, each column listing a variety of information. The questions require you to carry out directions involving the information given in the chart.

6) Skills and aptitudes

Performance tests effectively measure some manual skills and aptitudes. When the skill is one in which you are trained, such as typing or shorthand, you can practice. These tests are often very much like those given in business school or high school courses. For many of the other skills and aptitudes, however, no short-time preparation can be made. Skills and abilities natural to you or that you have developed throughout your lifetime are being tested.

Many of the general questions just described provide all the data needed to answer the questions and ask you to use your reasoning ability to find the answers. Your best preparation for these tests, as well as for tests of facts and ideas, is to be at your physical and mental best. You, no doubt, have your own methods of getting into an exam-taking mood and keeping "in shape." The next section lists some ideas on this subject.

IV. KINDS OF QUESTIONS

Only rarely is the "essay" question, which you answer in narrative form, used in civil service tests. Civil service tests are usually of the short-answer type. Full instructions for answering these questions will be given to you at the examination. But in case this is your first experience with short-answer questions and separate answer sheets, here is what you need to know:

1) Multiple-choice Questions

Most popular of the short-answer questions is the "multiple choice" or "best answer" question. It can be used, for example, to test for factual knowledge, ability to solve problems or judgment in meeting situations found at work.

A multiple-choice question is normally one of three types—

- It can begin with an incomplete statement followed by several possible endings. You are to find the one ending which *best* completes the statement, although some of the others may not be entirely wrong.
- It can also be a complete statement in the form of a question which is answered by choosing one of the statements listed.

- It can be in the form of a problem – again you select the best answer.

Here is an example of a multiple-choice question with a discussion which should give you some clues as to the method for choosing the right answer:

> When an employee has a complaint about his assignment, the action which will *best* help him overcome his difficulty is to
> A. discuss his difficulty with his coworkers
> B. take the problem to the head of the organization
> C. take the problem to the person who gave him the assignment
> D. say nothing to anyone about his complaint

In answering this question, you should study each of the choices to find which is best. Consider choice "A" – Certainly an employee may discuss his complaint with fellow employees, but no change or improvement can result, and the complaint remains unresolved. Choice "B" is a poor choice since the head of the organization probably does not know what assignment you have been given, and taking your problem to him is known as "going over the head" of the supervisor. The supervisor, or person who made the assignment, is the person who can clarify it or correct any injustice. Choice "C" is, therefore, correct. To say nothing, as in choice "D," is unwise. Supervisors have and interest in knowing the problems employees are facing, and the employee is seeking a solution to his problem.

2) True/False Questions

The "true/false" or "right/wrong" form of question is sometimes used. Here a complete statement is given. Your job is to decide whether the statement is right or wrong.

SAMPLE: A roaming cell-phone call to a nearby city costs less than a non-roaming call to a distant city.

This statement is wrong, or false, since roaming calls are more expensive.

This is not a complete list of all possible question forms, although most of the others are variations of these common types. You will always get complete directions for answering questions. Be sure you understand *how* to mark your answers – ask questions until you do.

V. RECORDING YOUR ANSWERS

Computer terminals are used more and more today for many different kinds of exams.

For an examination with very few applicants, you may be told to record your answers in the test booklet itself. Separate answer sheets are much more common. If this separate answer sheet is to be scored by machine – and this is often the case – it is highly important that you mark your answers correctly in order to get credit.

An electronic scoring machine is often used in civil service offices because of the speed with which papers can be scored. Machine-scored answer sheets must be marked with a pencil, which will be given to you. This pencil has a high graphite content which responds to the electronic scoring machine. As a matter of fact, stray dots may register as answers, so do not let your pencil rest on the answer sheet while you are pondering the correct answer. Also, if your pencil lead breaks or is otherwise defective, ask for another.

Since the answer sheet will be dropped in a slot in the scoring machine, be careful not to bend the corners or get the paper crumpled.

The answer sheet normally has five vertical columns of numbers, with 30 numbers to a column. These numbers correspond to the question numbers in your test booklet. After each number, going across the page are four or five pairs of dotted lines. These short dotted lines have small letters or numbers above them. The first two pairs may also have a "T" or "F" above the letters. This indicates that the first two pairs only are to be used if the questions are of the true-false type. If the questions are multiple choice, disregard the "T" and "F" and pay attention only to the small letters or numbers.

Answer your questions in the manner of the sample that follows:

32. The largest city in the United States is
    A. Washington, D.C.
    B. New York City
    C. Chicago
    D. Detroit
    E. San Francisco

1) Choose the answer you think is best. (New York City is the largest, so "B" is correct.)
2) Find the row of dotted lines numbered the same as the question you are answering. (Find row number 32)
3) Find the pair of dotted lines corresponding to the answer. (Find the pair of lines under the mark "B.")
4) Make a solid black mark between the dotted lines.

VI. BEFORE THE TEST

Common sense will help you find procedures to follow to get ready for an examination. Too many of us, however, overlook these sensible measures. Indeed, nervousness and fatigue have been found to be the most serious reasons why applicants fail to do their best on civil service tests. Here is a list of reminders:

- Begin your preparation early – Don't wait until the last minute to go scurrying around for books and materials or to find out what the position is all about.
- Prepare continuously – An hour a night for a week is better than an all-night cram session. This has been definitely established. What is more, a night a week for a month will return better dividends than crowding your study into a shorter period of time.
- Locate the place of the exam – You have been sent a notice telling you when and where to report for the examination. If the location is in a different town or otherwise unfamiliar to you, it would be well to inquire the best route and learn something about the building.
- Relax the night before the test – Allow your mind to rest. Do not study at all that night. Plan some mild recreation or diversion; then go to bed early and get a good night's sleep.
- Get up early enough to make a leisurely trip to the place for the test – This way unforeseen events, traffic snarls, unfamiliar buildings, etc. will not upset you.
- Dress comfortably – A written test is not a fashion show. You will be known by number and not by name, so wear something comfortable.

- Leave excess paraphernalia at home – Shopping bags and odd bundles will get in your way. You need bring only the items mentioned in the official notice you received; usually everything you need is provided. Do not bring reference books to the exam. They will only confuse those last minutes and be taken away from you when in the test room.
- Arrive somewhat ahead of time – If because of transportation schedules you must get there very early, bring a newspaper or magazine to take your mind off yourself while waiting.
- Locate the examination room – When you have found the proper room, you will be directed to the seat or part of the room where you will sit. Sometimes you are given a sheet of instructions to read while you are waiting. Do not fill out any forms until you are told to do so; just read them and be prepared.
- Relax and prepare to listen to the instructions
- If you have any physical problem that may keep you from doing your best, be sure to tell the test administrator. If you are sick or in poor health, you really cannot do your best on the exam. You can come back and take the test some other time.

VII. AT THE TEST

The day of the test is here and you have the test booklet in your hand. The temptation to get going is very strong. Caution! There is more to success than knowing the right answers. You must know how to identify your papers and understand variations in the type of short-answer question used in this particular examination. Follow these suggestions for maximum results from your efforts:

1) Cooperate with the monitor

The test administrator has a duty to create a situation in which you can be as much at ease as possible. He will give instructions, tell you when to begin, check to see that you are marking your answer sheet correctly, and so on. He is not there to guard you, although he will see that your competitors do not take unfair advantage. He wants to help you do your best.

2) Listen to all instructions

Don't jump the gun! Wait until you understand all directions. In most civil service tests you get more time than you need to answer the questions. So don't be in a hurry. Read each word of instructions until you clearly understand the meaning. Study the examples, listen to all announcements and follow directions. Ask questions if you do not understand what to do.

3) Identify your papers

Civil service exams are usually identified by number only. You will be assigned a number; you must not put your name on your test papers. Be sure to copy your number correctly. Since more than one exam may be given, copy your exact examination title.

4) Plan your time

Unless you are told that a test is a "speed" or "rate of work" test, speed itself is usually not important. Time enough to answer all the questions will be provided, but this does not mean that you have all day. An overall time limit has been set. Divide the total time (in minutes) by the number of questions to determine the approximate time you have for each question.

5) Do not linger over difficult questions

If you come across a difficult question, mark it with a paper clip (useful to have along) and come back to it when you have been through the booklet. One caution if you do this – be sure to skip a number on your answer sheet as well. Check often to be sure that you have not lost your place and that you are marking in the row numbered the same as the question you are answering.

6) Read the questions

Be sure you know what the question asks! Many capable people are unsuccessful because they failed to *read* the questions correctly.

7) Answer all questions

Unless you have been instructed that a penalty will be deducted for incorrect answers, it is better to guess than to omit a question.

8) Speed tests

It is often better NOT to guess on speed tests. It has been found that on timed tests people are tempted to spend the last few seconds before time is called in marking answers at random – without even reading them – in the hope of picking up a few extra points. To discourage this practice, the instructions may warn you that your score will be "corrected" for guessing. That is, a penalty will be applied. The incorrect answers will be deducted from the correct ones, or some other penalty formula will be used.

9) Review your answers

If you finish before time is called, go back to the questions you guessed or omitted to give them further thought. Review other answers if you have time.

10) Return your test materials

If you are ready to leave before others have finished or time is called, take ALL your materials to the monitor and leave quietly. Never take any test material with you. The monitor can discover whose papers are not complete, and taking a test booklet may be grounds for disqualification.

VIII. EXAMINATION TECHNIQUES

1) Read the general instructions carefully. These are usually printed on the first page of the exam booklet. As a rule, these instructions refer to the timing of the examination; the fact that you should not start work until the signal and must stop work at a signal, etc. If there are any *special* instructions, such as a choice of questions to be answered, make sure that you note this instruction carefully.

2) When you are ready to start work on the examination, that is as soon as the signal has been given, read the instructions to each question booklet, underline any key words or phrases, such as *least*, *best*, *outline*, *describe* and the like. In this way you will tend to answer as requested rather than discover on reviewing your paper that you *listed without describing*, that you selected the *worst* choice rather than the *best* choice, etc.

3) If the examination is of the objective or multiple-choice type – that is, each question will also give a series of possible answers: A, B, C or D, and you are called upon to select the best answer and write the letter next to that answer on your answer paper – it is advisable to start answering each question in turn. There may be anywhere from 50 to 100 such questions in the three or four hours allotted and you can see how much time would be taken if you read through all the questions before beginning to answer any. Furthermore, if you come across a question or group of questions which you know would be difficult to answer, it would undoubtedly affect your handling of all the other questions.

4) If the examination is of the essay type and contains but a few questions, it is a moot point as to whether you should read all the questions before starting to answer any one. Of course, if you are given a choice – say five out of seven and the like – then it is essential to read all the questions so you can eliminate the two that are most difficult. If, however, you are asked to answer all the questions, there may be danger in trying to answer the easiest one first because you may find that you will spend too much time on it. The best technique is to answer the first question, then proceed to the second, etc.

5) Time your answers. Before the exam begins, write down the time it started, then add the time allowed for the examination and write down the time it must be completed, then divide the time available somewhat as follows:
   - If 3-1/2 hours are allowed, that would be 210 minutes. If you have 80 objective-type questions, that would be an average of 2-1/2 minutes per question. Allow yourself no more than 2 minutes per question, or a total of 160 minutes, which will permit about 50 minutes to review.
   - If for the time allotment of 210 minutes there are 7 essay questions to answer, that would average about 30 minutes a question. Give yourself only 25 minutes per question so that you have about 35 minutes to review.

6) The most important instruction is to *read each question* and make sure you know what is wanted. The second most important instruction is to *time yourself properly* so that you answer every question. The third most important instruction is to *answer every question.* Guess if you have to but include something for each question. Remember that you will receive no credit for a blank and will probably receive some credit if you write something in answer to an essay question. If you guess a letter – say "B" for a multiple-choice question – you may have guessed right. If you leave a blank as an answer to a multiple-choice question, the examiners may respect your feelings but it will not add a point to your score. Some exams may penalize you for wrong answers, so in such cases *only*, you may not want to guess unless you have some basis for your answer.

7) Suggestions
   a. Objective-type questions
      1. Examine the question booklet for proper sequence of pages and questions
      2. Read all instructions carefully
      3. Skip any question which seems too difficult; return to it after all other questions have been answered
      4. Apportion your time properly; do not spend too much time on any single question or group of questions

5. Note and underline key words – *all, most, fewest, least, best, worst, same, opposite*, etc.
6. Pay particular attention to negatives
7. Note unusual option, e.g., unduly long, short, complex, different or similar in content to the body of the question
8. Observe the use of "hedging" words – *probably, may, most likely*, etc.
9. Make sure that your answer is put next to the same number as the question
10. Do not second-guess unless you have good reason to believe the second answer is definitely more correct
11. Cross out original answer if you decide another answer is more accurate; do not erase until you are ready to hand your paper in
12. Answer all questions; guess unless instructed otherwise
13. Leave time for review

b. Essay questions
1. Read each question carefully
2. Determine exactly what is wanted. Underline key words or phrases.
3. Decide on outline or paragraph answer
4. Include many different points and elements unless asked to develop any one or two points or elements
5. Show impartiality by giving pros and cons unless directed to select one side only
6. Make and write down any assumptions you find necessary to answer the questions
7. Watch your English, grammar, punctuation and choice of words
8. Time your answers; don't crowd material

8) Answering the essay question

Most essay questions can be answered by framing the specific response around several key words or ideas. Here are a few such key words or ideas:

M's: manpower, materials, methods, money, management
P's: purpose, program, policy, plan, procedure, practice, problems, pitfalls, personnel, public relations

a. Six basic steps in handling problems:
1. Preliminary plan and background development
2. Collect information, data and facts
3. Analyze and interpret information, data and facts
4. Analyze and develop solutions as well as make recommendations
5. Prepare report and sell recommendations
6. Install recommendations and follow up effectiveness

b. Pitfalls to avoid
1. *Taking things for granted* – A statement of the situation does not necessarily imply that each of the elements is necessarily true; for example, a complaint may be invalid and biased so that all that can be taken for granted is that a complaint has been registered

2. *Considering only one side of a situation* – Wherever possible, indicate several alternatives and then point out the reasons you selected the best one
3. *Failing to indicate follow up* – Whenever your answer indicates action on your part, make certain that you will take proper follow-up action to see how successful your recommendations, procedures or actions turn out to be
4. *Taking too long in answering any single question* – Remember to time your answers properly

IX. AFTER THE TEST

Scoring procedures differ in detail among civil service jurisdictions although the general principles are the same. Whether the papers are hand-scored or graded by machine we have described, they are nearly always graded by number. That is, the person who marks the paper knows only the number – never the name – of the applicant. Not until all the papers have been graded will they be matched with names. If other tests, such as training and experience or oral interview ratings have been given, scores will be combined. Different parts of the examination usually have different weights. For example, the written test might count 60 percent of the final grade, and a rating of training and experience 40 percent. In many jurisdictions, veterans will have a certain number of points added to their grades.

After the final grade has been determined, the names are placed in grade order and an eligible list is established. There are various methods for resolving ties between those who get the same final grade – probably the most common is to place first the name of the person whose application was received first. Job offers are made from the eligible list in the order the names appear on it. You will be notified of your grade and your rank as soon as all these computations have been made. This will be done as rapidly as possible.

People who are found to meet the requirements in the announcement are called "eligibles." Their names are put on a list of eligible candidates. An eligible's chances of getting a job depend on how high he stands on this list and how fast agencies are filling jobs from the list.

When a job is to be filled from a list of eligibles, the agency asks for the names of people on the list of eligibles for that job. When the civil service commission receives this request, it sends to the agency the names of the three people highest on this list. Or, if the job to be filled has specialized requirements, the office sends the agency the names of the top three persons who meet these requirements from the general list.

The appointing officer makes a choice from among the three people whose names were sent to him. If the selected person accepts the appointment, the names of the others are put back on the list to be considered for future openings.

That is the rule in hiring from all kinds of eligible lists, whether they are for typist, carpenter, chemist, or something else. For every vacancy, the appointing officer has his choice of any one of the top three eligibles on the list. This explains why the person whose name is on top of the list sometimes does not get an appointment when some of the persons lower on the list do. If the appointing officer chooses the second or third eligible, the No. 1 eligible does not get a job at once, but stays on the list until he is appointed or the list is terminated.

X. HOW TO PASS THE INTERVIEW TEST

The examination for which you applied requires an oral interview test. You have already taken the written test and you are now being called for the interview test – the final part of the formal examination.

You may think that it is not possible to prepare for an interview test and that there are no procedures to follow during an interview. Our purpose is to point out some things you can do in advance that will help you and some good rules to follow and pitfalls to avoid while you are being interviewed.

What is an interview supposed to test?

The written examination is designed to test the technical knowledge and competence of the candidate; the oral is designed to evaluate intangible qualities, not readily measured otherwise, and to establish a list showing the relative fitness of each candidate – as measured against his competitors – for the position sought. Scoring is not on the basis of "right" and "wrong," but on a sliding scale of values ranging from "not passable" to "outstanding." As a matter of fact, it is possible to achieve a relatively low score without a single "incorrect" answer because of evident weakness in the qualities being measured.

Occasionally, an examination may consist entirely of an oral test – either an individual or a group oral. In such cases, information is sought concerning the technical knowledges and abilities of the candidate, since there has been no written examination for this purpose. More commonly, however, an oral test is used to supplement a written examination.

Who conducts interviews?

The composition of oral boards varies among different jurisdictions. In nearly all, a representative of the personnel department serves as chairman. One of the members of the board may be a representative of the department in which the candidate would work. In some cases, "outside experts" are used, and, frequently, a businessman or some other representative of the general public is asked to serve. Labor and management or other special groups may be represented. The aim is to secure the services of experts in the appropriate field.

However the board is composed, it is a good idea (and not at all improper or unethical) to ascertain in advance of the interview who the members are and what groups they represent. When you are introduced to them, you will have some idea of their backgrounds and interests, and at least you will not stutter and stammer over their names.

What should be done before the interview?

While knowledge about the board members is useful and takes some of the surprise element out of the interview, there is other preparation which is more substantive. It *is* possible to prepare for an oral interview – in several ways:

1) Keep a copy of your application and review it carefully before the interview

This may be the only document before the oral board, and the starting point of the interview. Know what education and experience you have listed there, and the sequence and dates of all of it. Sometimes the board will ask you to review the highlights of your experience for them; you should not have to hem and haw doing it.

2) Study the class specification and the examination announcement

Usually, the oral board has one or both of these to guide them. The qualities, characteristics or knowledges required by the position sought are stated in these documents. They offer valuable clues as to the nature of the oral interview. For example, if the job involves supervisory responsibilities, the announcement will usually indicate that knowledge of modern supervisory methods and the qualifications of the candidate as a supervisor will be tested. If so, you can expect such questions, frequently in the form of a hypothetical situation which you are expected to solve. NEVER go into an oral without knowledge of the duties and responsibilities of the job you seek.

3) Think through each qualification required

Try to visualize the kind of questions you would ask if you were a board member. How well could you answer them? Try especially to appraise your own knowledge and background in each area, *measured against the job sought*, and identify any areas in which you are weak. Be critical and realistic – do not flatter yourself.

4) Do some general reading in areas in which you feel you may be weak

For example, if the job involves supervision and your past experience has NOT, some general reading in supervisory methods and practices, particularly in the field of human relations, might be useful. Do NOT study agency procedures or detailed manuals. The oral board will be testing your understanding and capacity, not your memory.

5) Get a good night's sleep and watch your general health and mental attitude

You will want a clear head at the interview. Take care of a cold or any other minor ailment, and of course, no hangovers.

What should be done on the day of the interview?

Now comes the day of the interview itself. Give yourself plenty of time to get there. Plan to arrive somewhat ahead of the scheduled time, particularly if your appointment is in the fore part of the day. If a previous candidate fails to appear, the board might be ready for you a bit early. By early afternoon an oral board is almost invariably behind schedule if there are many candidates, and you may have to wait. Take along a book or magazine to read, or your application to review, but leave any extraneous material in the waiting room when you go in for your interview. In any event, relax and compose yourself.

The matter of dress is important. The board is forming impressions about you – from your experience, your manners, your attitude, and your appearance. Give your personal appearance careful attention. Dress your best, but not your flashiest. Choose conservative, appropriate clothing, and be sure it is immaculate. This is a business interview, and your appearance should indicate that you regard it as such. Besides, being well groomed and properly dressed will help boost your confidence.

Sooner or later, someone will call your name and escort you into the interview room. *This is it.* From here on you are on your own. It is too late for any more preparation. But remember, you asked for this opportunity to prove your fitness, and you are here because your request was granted.

What happens when you go in?

The usual sequence of events will be as follows: The clerk (who is often the board stenographer) will introduce you to the chairman of the oral board, who will introduce you to the other members of the board. Acknowledge the introductions before you sit down. Do not be surprised if you find a microphone facing you or a stenotypist sitting by. Oral interviews are usually recorded in the event of an appeal or other review.

Usually the chairman of the board will open the interview by reviewing the highlights of your education and work experience from your application – primarily for the benefit of the other members of the board, as well as to get the material into the record. Do not interrupt or comment unless there is an error or significant misinterpretation; if that is the case, do not hesitate. But do not quibble about insignificant matters. Also, he will usually ask you some question about your education, experience or your present job – partly to get you to start talking and to establish the interviewing "rapport." He may start the actual questioning, or turn it over to one of the other members. Frequently, each member undertakes the questioning on a particular area, one in which he is perhaps most competent, so you can expect each member to participate in the examination. Because time is limited, you may also expect some rather abrupt switches in the direction the questioning takes, so do not be upset by it. Normally, a board member will not pursue a single line of questioning unless he discovers a particular strength or weakness.

After each member has participated, the chairman will usually ask whether any member has any further questions, then will ask you if you have anything you wish to add. Unless you are expecting this question, it may floor you. Worse, it may start you off on an extended, extemporaneous speech. The board is not usually seeking more information. The question is principally to offer you a last opportunity to present further qualifications or to indicate that you have nothing to add. So, if you feel that a significant qualification or characteristic has been overlooked, it is proper to point it out in a sentence or so. Do not compliment the board on the thoroughness of their examination – they have been sketchy, and you know it. If you wish, merely say, "No thank you, I have nothing further to add." This is a point where you can "talk yourself out" of a good impression or fail to present an important bit of information. Remember, *you close the interview yourself.*

The chairman will then say, "That is all, Mr. _______, thank you." Do not be startled; the interview is over, and quicker than you think. Thank him, gather your belongings and take your leave. Save your sigh of relief for the other side of the door.

How to put your best foot forward

Throughout this entire process, you may feel that the board individually and collectively is trying to pierce your defenses, seek out your hidden weaknesses and embarrass and confuse you. Actually, this is not true. They are obliged to make an appraisal of your qualifications for the job you are seeking, and they want to see you in your best light. Remember, they must interview all candidates and a non-cooperative candidate may become a failure in spite of their best efforts to bring out his qualifications. Here are 15 suggestions that will help you:

1) Be natural – Keep your attitude confident, not cocky

If you are not confident that you can do the job, do not expect the board to be. Do not apologize for your weaknesses, try to bring out your strong points. The board is interested in a positive, not negative, presentation. Cockiness will antagonize any board member and make him wonder if you are covering up a weakness by a false show of strength.

2) Get comfortable, but don't lounge or sprawl

Sit erectly but not stiffly. A careless posture may lead the board to conclude that you are careless in other things, or at least that you are not impressed by the importance of the occasion. Either conclusion is natural, even if incorrect. Do not fuss with your clothing, a pencil or an ashtray. Your hands may occasionally be useful to emphasize a point; do not let them become a point of distraction.

3) Do not wisecrack or make small talk

This is a serious situation, and your attitude should show that you consider it as such. Further, the time of the board is limited – they do not want to waste it, and neither should you.

4) Do not exaggerate your experience or abilities

In the first place, from information in the application or other interviews and sources, the board may know more about you than you think. Secondly, you probably will not get away with it. An experienced board is rather adept at spotting such a situation, so do not take the chance.

5) If you know a board member, do not make a point of it, yet do not hide it

Certainly you are not fooling him, and probably not the other members of the board. Do not try to take advantage of your acquaintanceship – it will probably do you little good.

6) Do not dominate the interview

Let the board do that. They will give you the clues – do not assume that you have to do all the talking. Realize that the board has a number of questions to ask you, and do not try to take up all the interview time by showing off your extensive knowledge of the answer to the first one.

7) Be attentive

You only have 20 minutes or so, and you should keep your attention at its sharpest throughout. When a member is addressing a problem or question to you, give him your undivided attention. Address your reply principally to him, but do not exclude the other board members.

8) Do not interrupt

A board member may be stating a problem for you to analyze. He will ask you a question when the time comes. Let him state the problem, and wait for the question.

9) Make sure you understand the question

Do not try to answer until you are sure what the question is. If it is not clear, restate it in your own words or ask the board member to clarify it for you. However, do not haggle about minor elements.

10) Reply promptly but not hastily

A common entry on oral board rating sheets is "candidate responded readily," or "candidate hesitated in replies." Respond as promptly and quickly as you can, but do not jump to a hasty, ill-considered answer.

11) Do not be peremptory in your answers

A brief answer is proper – but do not fire your answer back. That is a losing game from your point of view. The board member can probably ask questions much faster than you can answer them.

12) Do not try to create the answer you think the board member wants

He is interested in what kind of mind you have and how it works – not in playing games. Furthermore, he can usually spot this practice and will actually grade you down on it.

13) Do not switch sides in your reply merely to agree with a board member

Frequently, a member will take a contrary position merely to draw you out and to see if you are willing and able to defend your point of view. Do not start a debate, yet do not surrender a good position. If a position is worth taking, it is worth defending.

14) Do not be afraid to admit an error in judgment if you are shown to be wrong

The board knows that you are forced to reply without any opportunity for careful consideration. Your answer may be demonstrably wrong. If so, admit it and get on with the interview.

15) Do not dwell at length on your present job

The opening question may relate to your present assignment. Answer the question but do not go into an extended discussion. You are being examined for a *new* job, not your present one. As a matter of fact, try to phrase ALL your answers in terms of the job for which you are being examined.

Basis of Rating

Probably you will forget most of these "do's" and "don'ts" when you walk into the oral interview room. Even remembering them all will not ensure you a passing grade. Perhaps you did not have the qualifications in the first place. But remembering them will help you to put your best foot forward, without treading on the toes of the board members.

Rumor and popular opinion to the contrary notwithstanding, an oral board wants you to make the best appearance possible. They know you are under pressure – but they also want to see how you respond to it as a guide to what your reaction would be under the pressures of the job you seek. They will be influenced by the degree of poise you display, the personal traits you show and the manner in which you respond.

ABOUT THIS BOOK

This book contains tests divided into Examination Sections. Go through each test, answering every question in the margin. We have also attached a sample answer sheet at the back of the book that can be removed and used. At the end of each test look at the answer key and check your answers. On the ones you got wrong, look at the right answer choice and learn. Do not fill in the answers first. Do not memorize the questions and answers, but understand the answer and principles involved. On your test, the questions will likely be different from the samples. Questions are changed and new ones added. If you understand these past questions you should have success with any changes that arise. Tests may consist of several types of questions. We have additional books on each subject should more study be advisable or necessary for you. Finally, the more you study, the better prepared you will be. This book is intended to be the last thing you study before you walk into the examination room. Prior study of relevant texts is also recommended. NLC publishes some of these in our Fundamental Series. Knowledge and good sense are important factors in passing your exam. Good luck also helps. So now study this Passbook, absorb the material contained within and take that knowledge into the examination. Then do your best to pass that exam.

EXAMINATION SECTION

EXAMINATION SECTION
TEST 1

OFFICIAL DICTATION

(175 Words per minute for five (5) minutes)

This Court has granted a writ of certiorari to review a final order of the New York Court of Appeals, which affirmed an order of the Appellate Division of the Supreme Court of the State of New York, First Judicial Department. That order disapproved petitioner's claim that certain sales taxes were due and owing to it by the respondent. The sum in dispute is two thousand, nine hundred and eighty-three dollars, with interest, and the period involved covers the years nineteen seventy-one and nineteen seventy-two.

The sole ground for the rejection of the petitioner's claim by the order under review was that the sales tax law as here applied violated the commerce clause of the federal constitution. The respondent in this proceeding is the Smith Office Machine Company, an Illinois firm engaged in the manufacture and sale of office machines to buyers in all parts of the country. With the Green Adding Machine Company, its wholly owned subsidiary and agent, it maintains offices, workrooms and a stockroom in New York City. There it sells, rents, repairs and services office machines and parts of office machines. Its New York City staff consists of a sales manager and several sales representatives. Only those New York City sales which are filled for the New York Office by shipment from the Illinois factory are the subject of this suit.

The respondent's products are office machines in standard sizes and models, not designed or altered to fill any special orders. The company does not accept any special orders for office machines. A large supply of office machines, with a market value of at least eighty-five thousand dollars, is always kept on hand in its New York City stockrooms. However, the company does not fill its local orders from local stock, but employs an interstate procedure. Orders are taken by the company's New York office and forwarded to the Chicago office. Every order states the model number, style, size and price of each machine sold. The order does not name the place of shipment of the machines, nor is there any evidence that the purchaser knows the place from which the machines are to be shipped to his office. Since the respondent bears the shipping costs and risk of loss, the customer actually purchases the machines in delivered condition.

All orders taken are subject to confirmation by the Chicago office. However, the procedure as to confirmation appears to be largely routine. Prices are fixed by the sales office in New York City on the basis of a standard price list. The trade-in value of old machines is fixed by the sales manager in New York City. There is no evidence that the Chicago office ever fails to confirm, nor is there any evidence that the customer is ever notified of confirmation. As a matter of fact, the order form contains no space for confirmation. The requirement of Chicago confirmation appears to serve no purpose other than to ascertain errors in price quoting and to allow for credit checking.

The respondent packs the machine in a carton and ships it, not to the customer, but to its New York City office. The customer is not concerned at all with this shipment, is not the consignee, is not protected by the insurance, and, consequently, does not pay the freight charges. The respondent must ship the office machine to its New York workroom because the machine on its arrival there is frequently not in a deliverable condition. There is a great deal of breakage in transit which must be repaired in the New York workroom. Even where there has been no breakage, testing and adjusting must be done there. These tasks of testing and adjusting often take three or four days, and it is not until they are finished that the local office can make delivery to the customer.

The contractual obligations of the respondent do not cease with delivery. Each contract of sale requires the company to keep the office machine in good repair for one year from the date of delivery, without charge to the customer. To fulfill this obligation, the respondent renders a free monthly maintenance service of inspection, oiling, and [4]X cleaning. When repairs of a substantial nature are needed, the work is done in New York City. While the machine is at the workroom for repair, a loan is made of another machine from the company's stock.

The recital of all these facts serves to show clearly that the tax in question does not interfere with the power reserved to the federal government to regulate interstate commerce. This court has never invalidated a state statute unless it has found that the statute, as a matter of fact, subjected interstate commerce to a greater burden, or to the danger of a greater burden, than would arise if the commerce were not being done. This court has very recently sustained a tax identical with the tax in question in every factual respect in a case involving the same petititioner and this same method of selling and shipping goods across state lines. Therefore, we believe that factual analysis reveals that this tax does not impose a burden upon interstate commerce. The final order and judgment should be reversed. [5]X

TEST 2

OFFICIAL DICTATION

(175 Words per minute for five(5) minutes)

The Supreme Court granted the motions made by the plaintiff, George Jones, to strike out the answer, to dismiss the counterclaim and to grant summary judgment. The court then appointed a referee to compute the amount due and owing to the plaintiff. The referee received and considered all the pleadings, including the answer and the bill of particulars submitted by the defendant, Albert Smith, as well as certain receipts. These receipts showed that the defendant had paid a total of ten thousand, nine hundred and eight dollars and forty-nine cents for interest and for amortization of the principal amount of the mortgages as well as for taxes and for the cost of defending an earlier action to foreclose the first mortgage on the property. The referee reported that the total balance due to the plaintiff was eighteen thousand, four hundred and twenty-seven dollars and eighty-five cents. The court granted a judgment for that amount, together with costs and other allowances, and ordered foreclosure and sale of property.

After this judgment had X[1] been granted, the defendant moved for an order to direct a rehearing of his motion to dismiss the complaint and for leave to submit an amended answer. The proposed amended answer, as attached to the moving papers, contained defenses similar to those interposed in the original answer. One new defense, alleging forgiveness by the plaintiff of part of the principal sum due, was offered but rejected by the court because of lack of evidence. In this defense, the defendant, Albert Smith, claimed that a total of three thousand, two hundred and twenty-six dollars had been forgiven by the plaintiff during the period from August, nineteen sixty-six until March, nineteen sixty-eight.

From these orders and the final judgment, the defendant has appealed to this court. During pendency of this appeal, the defendant assigned his entire interest in the property to the White Star Corporation. The date of this assignment was March twelfth, nineteen sixty-nine. Shortly thereafter, Smith attempted to withdraw his answer in the foreclosure action. He also agreed to the entry X[2] of a final judgment and, at the same time, stipulated that he would withdraw his appeal to this court. The motives prompting Albert Smith to this unusual course of conduct are not as yet apparent. The White Star Corporation charges that Smith's action was prompted by the desire to deprive it of its rightful interest in the property and that all these steps were taken in collusion with the plaintiff.

After the corporation had received the assignment of the property, it promptly applied in Special Term of the Supreme Court to be substituted as a party defendant in place of the defendant,Albert Smith. Special Term did not pass upon the merits of the application but denied the motion solely on the grounds that the issues involved were already on appeal before this court; The corporation thereupon made a motion to be substituted in place of Albert Smith before this court on the argument of this appeal. This court has examined the assignment to the corporation and finds said assignment to be legal and binding, X[3] Under that assignment, the corporation is sub-rogated to all the rights held by Albert Smith. This court further rules that Albert Smith had no right to take further action in the litigation after assigning his interest in the property to the White Star Corporation. His attempt to withdraw his answer, to consent to entry of judgment and to abandon his appeal are all Ineffectual. The White Star Corporation is entitled to be substituted as a party in interest in place of Albert Smith and its motion for such relief is therefore granted. All papers hereafter submitted should indicate that the corporation is the true party whose present interest is adverse to that of the plaintiff, George Jones.

This court is now prepared to consider the merits of the appeal. The present defendant argues that triable issues are involved and that summary judgment in favor of the plaintiff should not have been granted. In his answer in Supreme Court, the original defendant pleaded the defense of the Statute of Limitations. The court properly disposed of that

[4]X defense by reference to the mortgage moratorium statute. That statute prohibits the bringing of foreclosure suit where the debor had defaulted in reducing only the principal of the debt. In the case at bar, the defendant Albert Smith was not in arrears in payment of interest on the mortgage debt but only in reduction of the face amount of the debt.

The substantive issues of the case are therefore open for our consideration. Albert Smith never contended that the bond and mortgage were not legal and binding instruments when made. His main defense to the action was that the principal sum due had been reduced to less than one-third of the original amount, partly by payment and partly by forgiveness of certain installments. The Supreme Court rejected both of these defenses on the grounds that the defendant had failed to produce any substantial evidence in favor of his contentions. However, as the present appellant contends that credible evidence as to certain payments does exist, we direct that a trial of those issues be held. [5]X

EXAMINATION SECTION
TESTIMONY

(175 Words per minute - 5 minutes)

Cross examination by defendant's counsel:

QUESTION: Do you remember the month that the man from the City saw you in this case?

ANSWER: I remember it very well.

QUESTION: What month was that?

ANSWER: That was the day before Thanksgiving.

QUESTION: He wrote down what you told him, at that time, did he not?

ANSWER: I do not know what he did.

QUESTION: You were there. Did you not see him?

ANSWER: I was there. Sure I saw him.

QUESTION: I ask you this question: What he wrote down was what you told him?

Plaintiff's Counsel: I object. The witness is not competent to testify to that.
The Court: No, unless he read it.

QUESTION: Did he not write down what you told him?

ANSWER: I do not know what he did.

QUESTION: Did he not read something to you?

ANSWER: No. He was propounding questions to me.

QUESTION: Do you say that he did not read you, the statement he made?

ANSWER: No, I did not give him any. And the doctors did not give him any. He wanted them both to give him statements.

QUESTION: Did the man tell you from what department of the City of [1] X New York he was?

ANSWER: Yes.

QUESTION: What department?

ANSWER: The Corporation Counsel's office.

QUESTION: Or was it the Department of Finance, or the Comptroller's office?

ANSWER: No, he said he was from the Corporation Counsel's office.

QUESTION: What was his name? Do you remember his name?

ANSWER: No. He did not introduce himself.

QUESTION: Do you remember telling the man from the City that you did not know the number of the house in front of which Doctor MacDonald fell?

ANSWER: I know, if I told him anything, it was ---

2 (#1)

QUESTION: You did not tell him anything?

ANSWER: No, and there is no witness to corroborate it. He wanted me to sign a paper, and he wanted the doctors to sign a paper. He was the means of having me fired out of the hospital, 1 was there through courtesy, not because I was mentally disabled.

Defendant's Counsel: Will you please keep still? I ask that all the answer be striken out.

The Court: Strike it out.

QUESTION: Did he want you to sign a paper?

ANSWER: Yes.

QUESTION: These are the papers he wanted you to sign; is that correct?

ANSWER: I do [2] X not know. I did not look at them. I did not rise. He sat in a chair. I was sitting farther than the table away from him.

QUESTION: Did you sign anything?

Plaintiff's counsel: He stated he did not see it.

ANSWER: I never signed anything.

QUESTION: And, after you told this man from the Corporation Counsel's office or from the City of New York this story, he wrote it down and read the statement to you?

ANSWER: He did not get any story from me. He asked Doctor Schatz if he would be a witness to the fact. I told him I would sign nothing. And Doctor Schatz told him he would sign nothing either.

QUESTION: I am not asking you anything that Doctor Schatz told. I am talking about you, only.

ANSWER: That is what happened there. I did not want to be botheredwith it.

QUESTION: Did he not read this all over to you, and did you not say that it was correct in all respects?

ANSWER: No, I never gave the man a statement.

Defendant's Counsel: That is all.

Plaintiff's Counsel: May I have [3] X the privi lege of a few questions, your Honor?

The Court: Proceed.

Re-direct Examination by Plaintiff's Counsel:

QUESTION: I hand you Plaintiff's Exhibit 5 and ask you to look at it carefully, also Defendant's Exhibit B. Do you observe, from these two exhibits, that there are five sections of the ventilation grating?

ANSWER: Yes.

QUESTION: In front of 711 and 715 Replogle Avenue?

ANSWER: Yes.

QUESTION: And the five sections are both shown in these two exhibits, are they?

ANSWER: Yes.

QUESTION: Do you observe also, that each of those five sections is again subdivided into four parts?

ANSWER: Yes, sir.

QUESTION: Four parts in.width?

ANSWER: Yes, sir.

QUESTION: Now, when you testified on cross examination that, so far as you remember, the pegs were only in front of the section where the Reverend Mackler fell ---

ANSWER: Yes.

QUESTION: Did you or did you not mean, or tell me what you meant. Did you mean that the pegs were entirely across the four subdivisions of the southern section?

ANSWER: Yes.

Defendant's Counsel: Now, wait, please. If your Honor please, I object to this, on the ground that I asked the question and your Honor asked the question, and 4 X I asked the witness if he understood your Honor's question.

The Court: Yes, but he answered both ways across. I am going to let him straighten it out.

QUESTION: In referring to this grating here, let us be sure we understand our terminology. I am going to call these five different parts five sections, and each of these five sections in turn has four parts.

ANSWER: Yes.

QUESTION: Now, counsel, up to this time, called each of those four p.arts sections; but let us forget that terminology a minute. Were there pegs all the way across the southern end of the southern section, which included four parts?

ANSWER: I believe they were.

Re-cross Examination by Defendant's Counsel:

QUESTION: I asked you -- pointed out on this photograph that I held in front of the jury--- I have this up, and I asked you whether the pegs ran across from one side to the other, and you said no, did you not?

ANSWER: Well, because I looked through two pairs of glasses, and it looked the same.

QUESTION: You saw the picture up there, and I asked you to look at 5 X it.

Direct Examination by Plaintiff's Counsel:

QUESTION: Do you know the plaintiff in this case?

ANSWER: I do.

QUESTION: Did you see the plaintiff in this case on December 22?

ANSWER: I did.

QUESTION: Will you tell the Court and jury under what circumstances you saw him and describe for the court and jury also what you saw about him?

ANSWER: Well, the doorbell rang. I went upstairs and answered it. A gentleman stood there with a bloody handkerchief to his mouth, and he asked whether he could see the doctor. He was very much shaken and agitated, and, in fact, he was trembling. And I said I was afraid he could not see the doctor, because he was ill.

Defendant's Counsel: I beg your pardon. I am sorry to interrupt, but we cannot have anything like that.

The Court: You cannot have any conversation. How was the doctor? Was he ill?

QUESTION: Just describe what you saw yourself about the Reverend MacDonald.

ANSWER: He stood there with his handkerchief to his face. His handkerchief was bloody, and he was pale. In fact, he was livid.

Plaintiff's Counsel: A little louder. I cannot hear you.

The Witness: He was livid.

QUESTION: By that do you mean his face was white?

ANSWER: No. Livid is something more than white. Livid is a sort of blue white. It is worse than pale, if you ever saw it.

QUESTION: What else did you notice about Doctor Mackler?

ANSWER: Well, I noticed that he was trembling. In fact, he was shaking so much that *I* was---well, just a little bit nervous.

QUESTION: Was the doctor ill that day?

ANSWER: Yes, he was; but he was not in bed.

Plaintiff's Counsel: That is all.

Cross Examination by Defendant's Counsel:

QUESTION: Mr. Gorman , was the doctor out on Sunday, last Sunday? ANSWER: Last Sunday, I do not know. He was out one day to get a newspaper; but I do not know whether it was Saturday or Sunday.

QUESTION: Was he out on Sunday?

ANSWER: Let's see. I cannot answer that. I do not know whether he was or not. I was not home most of the day.

5 (#1)

The Court: Next question.

QUESTION: Do you know whether any subpoena has been served on the doctor personally to come to court?

ANSWER: Not to my knowledge.

Defendant's Counsel: That is all.
Plaintiff's Counsel: May I ask one other question, your Honor?
The Court: Yes.

Re-direct Examination by Plaintiff's Counsel:

QUESTION: Did you recognize Doctor Mackler when you first saw him that day?

ANSWER: No, I did not.

QUESTION: You say he had the handkerchief over his mouth this way?

ANSWER: Yes.

QUESTION: How long had you known him, Mr. Gorman?

ANSWER: That is a little hard to 7 x answer; but I should say over a period ofwell, I could not answer that--I could answer it, perhaps, in another way.

QUESTION: Can you tell us about how long a time? That is all.

ANSWER: I am not very much---possibly, over a period of ten years.

QUESTION: You say that, when he came over there, his handkerchief was over his mouth that way?

ANSWER: Yes.

QUESTION: You did not recognize him?

ANSWER: I did not recognize him.

Re-cross Examination by Defendant's Counsel:

QUESTION: Was there not anything about his dress that indicated that it was Doctor Mackler?

ANSWER: Why, yes, he had his regular clerical garb on, as far as I can remember.

QUESTION: How long was he talking to you, Mr Gorman?

ANSWER: Not very long.

QUESTION: Would you say ten minutes?

ANSWER: No, not as long as that.

QUESTION: Five minutes?

ANSWER: Oh, yes, I think so.

QUESTION: Then he went inside?

ANSWER: Well, yes. If you would just let me tell it in my own way, perhaps that would be better.

QUESTION: You talked to him perhaps five minutes before the door there?

ANSWER: Yes.

QUESTION: And he went in the house. How long did he stay in the house?

ANSWER: Well, that is a little difficult to say.

QUESTION: Did you see him leave the house?

ANSWER: No, I did 8 X not.

THE COURT'S CHARGE TO THE JURY

Gentlemen of the jury, it is my custom in charging a jury to stand as counsel have been standing in summing up to you and as counsel rises when it addresses the court, because you gentlemen are now the court. The entire burden and duty in this case now rests on your shoulders. My part of this case has been comparatively small. I had very few technical questions of evidence to rule upon. There were days that passed when I believe there was not a single question raised on questions of evidence. My sole duty is to sit here and keep order and listen to the testimony so that I may properly charge you at the close of this case.

The law involved in this case is quite simple. It is just as simple as might be involved in a contract for building a garage in your backyard. It is, of course, an important case, and the weightiest duty in this case falls on your shoulders. You are the sole judges of the fact. You must determine where the truth in this case lies after I have charged you.

This case drawn out for some days, but I assure you, gentlemen, that it might have been much longer but for the very able work of counsel for both the plaintiff and the defendant in this case, and I wish to compliment them on the way the cases of their clients were presented. I have had cases of this nature before and I might say that never have I heard a case so well presented on either side. I wish also to compliment you gentlemen on your close attention. I realize that it has been a great sacrifice to many of you to be with us for so long. Some of you told me that you were making business sacrifices, but you come to an end of your labors now, or will shortly, and I want to compliment you on the close attention that you have paid to the testimony.

Counsel have very fully summed up their cases. I did not impose any stringent limit on their summation and I feel that the facts are fresh in your minds. It will, of course, be necessary for me to refer from time to time to some of the facts in this case to point the rules of law which I shall give to you. It is necessary in each case to lay before the jury those general principles of law which apply to all cases in a civil court.

In all actions in this court, gentlemen, the law places upon the plaintiff the burden of proving and convincing the jury by a fair preponderance of the credible evidence in the case that he or it is entitled to the verdict it seeks. When we refer to the fair preponderance of the credible evidence we do not mean that the plaintiff must bring in the greater number of witnesses or that it must offer the greater number of exhibits into evidence. We refer entirely to the quality of the testimony of the witnesses, and the quality of the exhibits, and the weight that the exhibits as offered by the parties to the action may have. The mere bringing of an action does not mean, of course, that the plaintiff must recover. You must feel, after having listened to all the testimony, that the plaintiff has convinced you that its version of the case is the correct and proper and truthful version of the case, and that applying the law as I give it to you, the plaintiff is entitled to the verdict that it seeks.

In weighing the testimony you will, of course, take into consideration the character of the testimony of the various witnesses; their interest in the case and, of course, the manner in which they have testified; their qualifications in the event of their testifying as experts; their education, their experience, and all those things which you believe have a bearing on the quality of the testimony and the weight which you believe should be given to it. Take the testimony of all of the witnesses. Take into consideration the facts as they were brought before you by the exhibits.in the case. From that determine where the truth in this case lies; whether or not the plaintiff has sustained the burden of proof to which we have referred. If, after considering all the evidence in the case, you are unable to determine where the truth in this case lies, then the plaintiff has failed to sustain the burden of proof and you must find for the defendant.

Plaintiff alleges that through the. fault of the defendant City of New York the contract which it undertook to execute was not finished within the contract time; that because of its inability to finish in contract time due, it says, to the fault and breach on the part of the City of New York in fulfillment of its covenants that it was damaged due to the fact that after the close of the contract period it was obliged to pay increased prices for both labor and material and that the prolonged use of capital was another item of damage.

EXAMINATION SECTION
TEST 1

DIRECTIONS: Each question or incomplete statement is followed by several suggested answers or completions. Select the one that BEST answers the question or completes the statement. *PRINT THE LETTER OF THE CORRECT ANSWER IN THE SPACE AT THE RIGHT.*

Questions 1-4.

DIRECTIONS: Questions 1 through 4 are to be answered on the basis of the following passage.

Those engaged in the exercise of First Amendment rights by pickets, marches, parades, and open-air assemblies are not exempted from obeying valid local traffic ordinances. In a recent pronouncement, Mr. Justice Baxter, speaking for the Supreme Court, wrote:

The rights of free speech and assembly, while fundamental to our democratic society, still do not mean that everyone with opinions or beliefs to express may address a group at any public place and at any time. The constitutional guarantee of liberty implies the existence of an organized society maintaining public order, without which liberty itself would be lost in the excesses of anarchy. The control of travel on the streets is a clear example of governmental responsibility to insure this necessary order. A restriction in that relation, designed to promote the public convenience in the interest of all, and not susceptible to abuses of discriminatory application, cannot be disregarded by the attempted exercise of some civil rights which, in other circumstances, would be entitled to protection. One would not be justified in ignoring the familiar red light because this was thought to be a means of social protest. Governmental authorities have the duty and responsibility to keep their streets open and available for movement. A group of demonstrators could not insist upon the right to cordon off a street, or entrance to a public or private building, and allow no one to pass who did not agree to listen to their exhortations.

1. Which of the following statements BEST reflects Mr. Justice Baxter's view of the relationship between liberty and public order? 1.____

   A. Public order cannot exist without liberty.
   B. Liberty cannot exist without public order.
   C. The existence of liberty undermines the existence of public order.
   D. The maintenance of public order insures the existence of liberty.

2. According to the above passage, local traffic ordinances result from 2.____

   A. governmental limitations on individual liberty
   B. governmental responsibility to insure public order
   C. majority rule as determined by democratic procedures
   D. restrictions on expression of dissent

3. The foregoing passage suggests that government would be acting IMPROPERLY if a local traffic ordinance 3.____

   A. was enforced in a discriminatory manner
   B. resulted in public inconvenience

C. violated the right of free speech and assembly
D. was not essential to public order

4. Of the following, the MOST appropriate title for the above passage is: 4.____

A. THE RIGHTS OF FREE SPEECH AND ASSEMBLY
B. ENFORCEMENT OF LOCAL TRAFFIC ORDINANCES
C. FIRST AMENDMENT RIGHTS AND LOCAL TRAFFIC ORDINANCES
D. LIBERTY AND ANARCHY

Questions 5-8.

DIRECTIONS: Questions 5 through 8 are to be answered on the basis of the following passage.

On November 8, 1976, the Supreme Court refused to block the payment of Medicaid funds for elective abortions. The Court's action means that a new Federal statute that bars the use of Federal funds for abortions unless abortion is necessary to save the life of the mother will not go into effect for many months, if at all.

A Federal District Court in Brooklyn ruled the following month that the statute was unconstitutional and ordered that Federal reimbursement for the costs of abortions continue on the same basis as reimbursements for the costs of pregnancy and childbirth-related services.

Technically, what the Court did today was to deny a request by Senator Howard Ramsdell and others for a stay blocking enforcement of the District Court order pending appeal. The Court's action was a victory for New York City. The City's Health and Hospitals Corporation initiated one of the two lawsuits challenging the new statute that led to the District Court's decision. The Corporation also opposed the request for a Supreme Court stay of that decision, telling the Court in a memorandum that a stay would subject the Corporation to a grave and irreparable injury."

5. According to the above passage, it would be CORRECT to state that the Health and Hospitals Corporation 5.____

A. joined Senator Ramsdell in his request for a stay
B. opposed the statute which limited reimbursement for the cost of abortions
C. claimed that it would experience a loss if the District Court order was enforced
D. appealed the District Court decision

6. The above passage indicates that the Supreme Court acted in DIRECT response to 6.____

A. a lawsuit initiated by the Health and Hospitals Corporation
B. a ruling by a Federal District Court
C. a request for a stay
D. the passage of a new Federal statute

7. According to the above passage, it would be CORRECT to state that the Supreme Court 7.____

A. blocked enforcement of the District Court order
B. refused a request for a stay to block enforcement of the Federal statute
C. ruled that the new Federal statute was unconstitutional
D. permitted payment of Federal funds for abortion to continue

8. Following are three statements concerning abortion that might be correct: 8.____
   I. Abortion costs are no longer to be Federally reimbursed on the same basis as those for pregnancy and childbirth
   II. Federal funds have not been available for abortions except to save the life of the mother
   III. Medicaid has paid for elective abortions in the past

   According to the passage given above, which of the following CORRECTLY classifies the above statements into those that are true and those that are not true?

   A. I is true, but II and III are not.
   B. I and III are true, but II is not.
   C. I and II are true, but III is not.
   D. III is true, but I and II are not.

9. A legal memorandum will often include the following six sections: 9.____
   I. Conclusions
   II. Issues
   III. Analysis
   IV. Facts
   V. Unknowns
   VI. Counter-analysis

   Which of the following choices lists these sections in the sequence that is generally MOST appropriate for a legal memorandum?

   A. III, VI, IV, V, II, I
   B. IV, II, III, VI, I, V
   C. V, II, IV, III, VI, I
   D. II, IV, V, III, I, VI

Questions 10-13.

DIRECTIONS: Questions 10 through 13 consist of two sentences each. The sentences deal with the use of court opinions and cases in the writing of legal memoranda. Select answer
   A. if only sentence I is correct
   B. if only sentence II is correct
   C. if both sentences are correct
   D. if neither sentence is correct

10. I. State the issues in the case as narrowly and precisely as possible. 10.____
    II. Quote frequently and at great length from the court opinions.

11. I. Describe briefly the issues in the case that are not related to your problem. 11.____
    II. Do not mention discrepancies between the facts of the case and the facts of your problem.

12. I. Do not refer to the holding or ruling in the case if it is harmful to your client. 12.____
    II. If the holding or ruling in the case is beneficial to your client, try to show that the facts of your problem are analogous to the facts of the case.

13. I. After stating your position concerning the issues and facts, present the opposite viewpoint as effectively as you can. 13.____
II. Avoid stating your own opinions or conclusions concerning the applicability of the case.

14. Column V lists four publications in the legal field. Column W contains descriptions of basic subject matter of legal publications. 14.____
Select the one of the following choices which BEST matches the publications in Column V with the subject matter in Column W.

Column V	Column W
I. Harvard Law Review	1. Law
II. Supreme Court Reporter	2. Commentary on law
III. McKinney's Consolidated Laws of New York mentary	3. Combination of lawand com
IV. The Criminal Law Reporter	

A. I-3; II-1; III-2; IV-3
B. I-2; II-3; III-2; IV-3
C. I-2; II-1; III-3; IV-3
D. I-2; II-3; III-3; IV-1

15. Tickler systems are used in many legal offices for scheduling and calendar control. Of the following, the LEAST common use of a tickler system is to 15.____

A. keep papers filed in such a way that they may easily be retrieved
B. arrange for the appearance of witnesses when they will be needed
C. remind lawyers when certain papers are due
D. arrange for the gathering of certain types of evidence

KEY (CORRECT ANSWERS)

1. B
2. B
3. A
4. C
5. B
6. C
7. D
8. D
9. B
10. A
11. D
12. B
13. A
14. C
15. A

TEST 2

DIRECTIONS: Each question or incomplete statement is followed by several suggested answers or completions. Select the one that BEST answers the question or completes the statement. *PRINT THE LETTER OF THE CORRECT ANSWER IN THE SPACE AT THE RIGHT.*

1. Studying the legislative history of a statute by reading the transcript of the hearings that were held on that subject is useful to the legal researcher PRIMARILY because it 1.____

   A. is informative of the manner in which laws are enacted
   B. helps him to understand the intent of the statute
   C. provides leads to statutes on the same subject
   D. clarifies the meaning of other statutes

2. Following are three statements concerning legal research that might be correct: 2.____
   I. The researcher may begin with a particular premise and, in researching it, may discover an entirely new approach to the problem
   II. When the researcher has located a relevant statute, it is not necessary to read court opinions interpreting or applying this statute
   III. A statute which is related to, but not the same as, the point being researched may have notes which will refer the researcher to more relevant cases

   Which of the following ACCURATELY classifies the above statements into those which are correct and those which are not?

   A. II and III are correct, but I is not.
   B. I and III are correct, but II is not.
   C. I and II are correct, but III is not.
   D. I, II, and III are all correct.

3. Of the following, the FIRST action a legal researcher should take in order to locate the laws relevant to a case is to 3.____

   A. search the index of a law book
   B. read statutes on similar subjects to discover pertinent annotations
   C. read a legal digest to become familiar with the law on the subject
   D. prepare a list of descriptive words applicable to the facts of the case

4. Which of the following is the BEST source for a legal researcher to consult in order to find historical data, cross-references, and case excerpts on cases, statutes, and regulations? 4.____

   A. Annotations
   B. Digests
   C. Hornbooks
   D. Casebooks

Questions 5-8.

DIRECTIONS: Each of Questions 5 through 8 contains two sentences concerning criminal law. Some of the sentences contain errors in English grammar or usage. A sentence does not contain an error simply because it could be written in a different manner. For each question, choose answer

   A. if only sentence I is correct
   B. if only sentence II is correct
   C. if both sentences are correct
   D. if neither sentence is correct

5. I. Limiting the term *property* to tangible property, in the criminal mischief setting, accords with prior case law holding that only tangible property came within the purview of the offense of malicious mischief. 5.___
II. Thus, a person who intentionally destroys the property of another, but under an honest belief that he has title to such property, cannot be convicted of criminal mischief under the Revised Penal Law.

6. I. Very early in it's history, New York enacted statutes from time to time punishing, either as a felony or as a misdemeanor, malicious injuries to various kinds of property: piers, booms, dams, bridges, etc. 6.___
II. The application of the statute is necessarily restricted to trespassory takings with larcenous intent: namely with intent permanently or virtually permanently to *appropriate* property or *deprive* the owner of its use.

7. I. Since the former Penal Law did not define the instruments of forgery in a general fashion, its crime of forgery was held to be narrower than the common law offense in this respect and to embrace only those instruments explicitly specified in the substantive provisions. 7.___
II. After entering the barn through an open door for the purpose of stealing, it was closed by the defendants.

8. I. The use of fire or explosives to destroy tangible property is proscribed by the criminal mischief provisions of the Revised Penal Law. 8.___
II. The defendant's taking of a taxicab for the immediate purpose of affecting his escape did not constitute grand larceny

Questions 9-13.

DIRECTIONS: Questions 9 through 13 are to be answered SOLELY on the basis of the following passage.

The law is quite clear that evidence obtained in violation of Section 605 of the Federal Communications Act is not admissible in federal court. However, the law as to the admissibility of evidence in state court is far from clear. Had the Supreme Court of the United States made the wiretap exclusionary rule applicable to the states, such confusion would not exist.

In the case of Alton v. Texas, the Supreme Court was called upon to determine whether wiretapping by state and local officers came within the proscription of the federal statute and, if so, whether Section 605 required the same remedies for its vindication in state courts. In answer to the first question, Mr. Justice Minton, speaking for the court, flatly stated that Section 605 made it a federal crime for anyone to intercept telephone messages and divulge what he learned. The court went on to say that a state officer who testified in state court concerning the existence, contents, substance, purport, effect or meaning of an intercepted conversation violated the federal law and committed a criminal act. In regard to the second question, however, the Supreme Court felt constrained by due regard for federal-state relations to answer in the negative. Mr. Justice Minton stated that the court would not presume, in the absence of a clear manifestation of congressional intent, that Congress intended to supersede state rules of evidence.

Because the Supreme Court refused to apply the exclusionary rule to wiretap evidence that was being used in state courts, the states respectively made this decision for themselves. According to hearings held before a congressional committee in 1975, six states authorize wiretapping by statute, 33 states impose total bans on wiretapping, and 11 states have no definite statute on the subject. For examples of extremes, a statute in Pennsylvania will be compared with a statute in New York.

The Pennsylvania statute provides that no communications by telephone or telegraph can be intercepted without permission of both parties. It also specifically prohibits such interception by public officials and provides that evidence obtained cannot be used in court.

The lawmakers in New York, recognizing the need for legal wiretapping, authorized wiretapping by statute. A New York law authorizes the issuance of an ex parte order upon oath or affirmation for limited wiretapping. The aim of the New York law is to allow court-ordered wiretapping and to encourage the testimony of state officers concerning such wiretapping in court. The New York law was found to be constitutional by the New York State Supreme Court in 1975. Other states, including Oregon, Maryland, Nevada, and Massachusetts, enacted similar laws which authorize court-ordered wiretapping.

To add to this legal disarray, the vast majority of the states, including New Jersey and New York, permit wiretapping evidence to be received in court even though obtained in violation of the state laws and of Section 605 of the Federal act. However, some states such as Rhode Island have enacted statutory exclusionary rules which provide that illegally procured wiretap evidence is incompetent in civil as well as criminal actions.

9. According to the above passage, a state officer who testifies in New York State court concerning the contents of a conversation he overheard through a court-ordered wiretap is in violation of ______ law. 9.____

   A. state law but not federal
   B. federal law but not state
   C. federal law and state
   D. neither federal nor state

10. According to the above passage, which of the following statements concerning states statutes on wiretapping is CORRECT? 10.____

   A. The number of states that impose total bans on wiretapping is three times as great as the number of states with no definite statute on wiretapping.
   B. The number of states having no definite statute on wiretapping is more than twice the number of states authorizing wiretapping.
   C. The number of states which authorize wiretapping by statute and the number of states having no definite statute on wiretapping exceed the number of states imposing total bans on wiretapping.
   D. More states authorize wiretapping by statute than impose total bans on wiretapping.

11. Following are three statements concerning wiretapping that might be valid: 11.____

I. In Pennsylvania, only public officials may legally intercept telephone communications
II. In Rhode Island, evidence obtained through an illegal wiretap is incompetent in criminal, but not civil, actions
III. Neither Massachusetts nor Pennsylvania authorizes wiretapping by public officials

According to the above passage, which of the following CORRECTLY classifies these statements into those that are valid and those that are not?

A. I is valid, but II and III are not.
B. II is valid, but I and III are not.
C. II and III are valid, but I is not.
D. None of the statements is valid.

12. According to the foregoing passage, evidence obtained in violation of Section 605 of the Federal Communications Act is inadmissible in 12.____

A. federal court but not in any state courts
B. federal court and all state courts
C. all state courts but not in federal court
D. federal court and some state courts

13. In regard to state rules of evidence, Mr. Justice Minton expressed the Court's opinion that Congress 13.____

A. intended to supersede state rules of evidence, as manifested by Section 605 of the Federal Communications Act
B. assumed that federal statutes would govern state rules of evidence in all wiretap cases
C. left unclear whether it intended to supersede state rules of evidence
D. precluded itself from superseding state rules of evidence through its regard for federal-state relations

14. You begin to ask follow-up questions of a witness who has given a statement. The witness starts to digress before answering an important question satisfactorily. 14.____
In this situation, the BEST of the following steps is to

A. guide the interview by suggesting answers to questions as they are asked
B. ask questions which can be answered only with a simple *yes* or *no*
C. construct questions as precisely as possible
D. tell the witness to keep his answers brief

15. During an interview with a client, you have occasion to refer to a matter which is described in the legal profession by a technical term. 15.____
Of the following, it would generally be MOST appropriate for you to

A. discuss the underlying legal concept in detail
B. avoid the subject since it is too complicated
C. ask the client if he is familiar with the technical term
D. describe the matter in everyday language

KEY (CORRECT ANSWERS)

1. B
2. B
3. D
4. A
5. C
6. B
7. A
8. A
9. B
10. A
11. D
12. D
13. C
14. C
15. D

EXAMINATION SECTION
TEST 1

DIRECTIONS: Each question or incomplete statement is followed by several suggested answers or completions. Select the one that BEST answers the question or completes the statement. *PRINT THE LETTER OF THE CORRECT ANSWER IN THE SPACE AT THE RIGHT.*

1. Suppose you have received dictation of several letters and have been given no specific instructions as to the order in which the material should be transcribed. So far as you can see, all of the letters are equally important. Which of the following is BEST to do? 1.____

   A. Transcribe the letters in the order in which they were dictated to you.
   B. Ask a more experienced co-worker for her opinion as to the order of transcription.
   C. Use your own judgment as to the order in which you should transcribe the letters.
   D. Ask your supervisor if he wishes you to type the letters in a particular order.

2. Suppose you are in a unit which has many incoming calls from the public. Your supervisor has given you the job of training newly appointed typists in techniques for answering the telephone. 2.____
   Of the following, which telephone response should be taught as the FIRST one to give upon picking up the telephone?

   A. Good morning. Who's calling, please?
   B. Who's this. Miss Smith speaking.
   C. Miss Smith. Who is this?
   D. Payroll Division. Miss Smith speaking.

3. You are in an office of 7 people. A woman calls your office, identifies herself as a client, and asks to speak to your supervisor, who is on another phone. 3.____
   What should you do in this situation? Ask her

   A. to hold until your supervisor is off the line
   B. to call back in ten minutes when you expect your supervisor to be free
   C. what she wants, to see if you or someone else can help her
   D. what she wants and, if you cannot help her, hang us

4. As the supervisor of a unit of stenographers, you have given a new employee an assignment which can easily be completed by, and which is needed by, the end of the day. She indicates some anxiety and says that she is not sure she can complete it in time. The other employees are very busy and unable to help. 4.____
   What should you do?

   A. Assign the stenographer to another task and finish the assignment yourself.
   B. Ask a supervisor from another unit if he could assign one of his workers to help your new stenographer.
   C. Tell the stenographer that right now is the time to conquer her anxiety by doing the job assigned to her.
   D. Review the assignment with the stenographer, check her progress, and be ready to help her when needed.

5. You supervise a stenographer who is writing many personal letters during work time while many of her assignments are not yet done. 5.____
What should you do FIRST?

   A. Tell your supervisor that the stenographer needs more work since she is doing personal letters on the job.
   B. Make the stenographer stop personal work by telling her you will inform your supervisor unless she stops.
   C. Let the stenographer know that it is not proper to use government time for such personal projects.
   D. Give the stenographer enough work to keep her so busy that she won't be able to do personal work.

6. Suppose a stenographer working at an agency with equipment for transferring calls receives an outside call from someone who has reached the wrong extension. The stenographer knows the correct extension. 6.____
The BEST thing for her to do in this case would be to

   A. signal the operator and tell him the extension to which to transfer the call
   B. give the caller the correct extension and offer to have him transferred to the correct extension
   C. give the person the correct extension and tell him to hang up and dial again
   D. tell the person he has reached the wrong extension and have him dial the operator

7. The supervisor in your office appears to be *dropping hints* about the condition of your desk. You feel that he may consider your desk somewhat sloppy. 7.____
Which is the BEST way to handle this?

   A. Wait until your supervisor directly mentions your desk to you and then clean up.
   B. Straighten up your desk so that it can't be considered sloppy, and see if this stops the hints.
   C. Do nothing. Force your supervisor, by ignoring his hints, to stop *dropping the hints.*
   D. Tell the supervisor you have caught his hints and that now you would like him to speak his mind.

8. The instrument that should be used to write on a stencil is a 8.____

   A. stylus
   B. ballpoint pen
   C. paper clip
   D. pencil

9. A supervisor orienting a new stenographer advised her to be sure to note down in her notebook the date on which she took each piece of dictation. She told the stenographer to put the date on the same page as the dictated material. 9.____
Which is the MOST important reason for dating the steno notebook? To

   A. know what date to put on the letters or reports the stenographer transcribes
   B. refer to these notes at a later date if necessary
   C. separate the letters from reports when transcribing them
   D. match incoming related correspondence to the material the stenographer transcribes

10. Assume you are in an office which uses a subject filing system. You find that frequently a letter to be filed involves two or three subjects. 10.____
In filing such a letter, it is MOST important to

A. file it under the subject that is mentioned first in the letter
B. prepare cross-references for the subjects covered in the letter
C. list all subjects involved on the label of the file folder
D. code the letter to show the main subject and its subdivisions

11. In addressing a letter to A.J. Brown, a commissioner in a governmental agency, the salutation that is considered MOST correct is: 11.____

A. Ms. or Mr. Brown:
B. Dear Commissioner Brown:
C. My dear Sir or Madam:
D. Commissioner Brown:

12. An office of a public agency frequently may need a number of copies of reports, forms, bulletins, letters, memos, and other kinds of written communications. 12.____
The particular type of duplicating process used to reproduce these copies does NOT usually depend on the

A. quality of work produced
B. number of copies required
C. cost of duplication
D. persons receiving the materials

13. A stenographer is transcribing a draft of a report from her notes. As soon as she transcribes a page of notes from her steno pad, she puts a line through that page. The MAIN reason for this procedure is that it 13.____

A. prevents grammatical errors in the report
B. prevents leaving out or repeating part of her notes
C. prevents making typographical errors from her notes
D. helps her to keep a count of the amount of work done

14. The MOST frequently used filing system in ordinary office practice is the ______ system. 14.____

A. alphabetic
B. numeric
C. geographic
D. subject

15. Your supervisor requests that you sign his name to, and mail, a letter he has dictated because he must leave to attend an important meeting. 15.____
In carrying out his request, you should remember to

A. sign your full name and title below the signature
B. imitate your superior's handwriting as closely as possible
C. type *Dictated but not read* in the lower left hand corner
D. add your initials next to or under the signature

16. Suppose a man speaking on the phone to you is having great difficulty making himself understood. He seems to be able to speak only in slang and cannot express himself easily. 16.____
What is the BEST thing to do to make sure you understand what he is saying?

A. Listen carefully, speak in your normal voice, and answer his questions as clearly as possible.
B. Use the same slang expressions and manner in which he speaks. This will give him confidence.
C. Let your irritation show in your voice so that he will *drop* his slang and speak more sensibly.
D. Ask your supervisor to answer his questions because the man's language is hard to understand.

17. There are few employees who do not seek meaning and some sort of challenge in their jobs. 17.____
Which of the following actions taken by a supervisor would BEST help to meet these needs?

A. Constantly reminding subordinates of the agency's high work expectations.
B. Explaining to subordinates how their work is related to that of other workers and how it contributes to agency objectives.
C. Telling employees that the longer the time needed to perform a job, the more important the job is.
D. Making it a policy to give each employee work which is slightly more difficult than his last assignment, but to explain such work carefully.

18. The one of the following over which a unit supervisor has the LEAST control is the _______ his unit. 18.____

A. quality of the work done in
B. nature of the work handled in
C. morale of workers in
D. increasing efficiency of

19. Suppose that you have received a note from an important official in your department commending the work of a unit of stenographers under your supervision. 19.____
Of the following, the BEST action for you to take is to

A. withhold the note for possible use at a time when the morale of the unit appears to be declining
B. show the note only to the better members of your staff as a reward for their good work
C. show the note only to the poorer members of your staff as a stimulus for better work
D. post the note conspicuously so that it can be seen by all members of your staff

20. If you find that one of your subordinates is becoming apathetic towards his work, you should 20.____

A. prefer charges against him
B. change the type of work
C. request his transfer
D. advise him to take a medical examination to check his health

21. Suppose that a new stenographer has been assigned to the unit which you supervise. 21.____
To give this stenographer a brief picture of the functioning of your unit in the entire department would be

A. *commendable* because she will probably be able to perform her work with more understanding
B. *undesirable* because such action will probably serve only to confuse her
C. *commendable* because, if transferred, she would probably be able to work efficiently without additional training
D. *undesirable* because in-service training has been demonstrated to be less efficient than on-the-job training

22. Written instructions to a subordinate are of value because they 22.____

A. can be kept up-to-date
B. encourage initiative
C. make a job seem easier
D. are an aid in training

23. Suppose that you have assigned a task to a stenographer under your supervision and have given appropriate instructions. After a reasonable period, you check her work and find that one specific aspect of her work is consistently incorrect. 23.____
Of the following, the BEST action for you to take is to

A. determine whether the stenographer has correctly understood instructions concerning the aspect of the work not being done correctly
B. assign the task to a more competent stenographer
C. wait for the stenographer to commit a more flagrant error before taking up the matter with her
D. indicate to the stenographer that you are dissatisfied with her work and wait to see whether she is sufficiently intelligent to correct her own mistakes

24. If you wanted to check on the accuracy of the filing in your unit, you would 24.____

A. check all the files thoroughly at regular intervals
B. watch the clerks while they are filing
C. glance through filed papers at random
D. inspect thoroughly a small section of the files selected at random

25. In making job assignments to his subordinates, a supervisor should follow the principle that each individual GENERALLY is capable of 25.____

A. performing one type of work well and less capable of performing other types well
B. learning to perform a wide variety of different types of work
C. performing best the type of work in which he has had least experience
D. learning to perform any type of work in which he is given training

KEY (CORRECT ANSWERS)

1. D
2. D
3. C
4. D
5. C
6. B
7. B
8. A
9. B
10. B
11. B
12. D
13. B
14. A
15. D
16. A
17. C
18. B
19. D
20. B
21. A
22. D
23. A
24. D
25. B

TEST 2

DIRECTIONS: Each question or incomplete statement is followed by several suggested answers or completions. Select the one that BEST answers the question or completes the statement. *PRINT THE LETTER OF THE CORRECT ANSWER IN THE SPACE AT THE RIGHT.*

Questions 1-8.

DIRECTIONS: Questions 1 through 8 are to be answered on the basis of the RULES FOR ALPHABETICAL FILING given below. Read these rules carefully before answering the questions.

RULES FOR ALPHABETICAL FILING

Names of People

1. The names of people are filed in strict alphabetical order, first according to the last name, then according to first name or initial, and finally according to middle name or initial. For example: George Allen comes before Edward Bell, and Leonard P. Reston comes before Lucille Reston.

2. When last names are the same, for example, A. Green and Agnes Green, the one with the initial comes before the one with the name written out when the first initials are identical.

3. When first and last names are alike and the middle name is given, for example, John David Doe and John Devoe Doe, the names should be filed in alphabetical order of the middle names.

4. When first and last names are the same, a name without a middle initial comes before one with a middle name or initial. For example: John Doe comes before John A. Doe and John Alan Doe.

5. When first and last names are the same, a name with a middle initial comes before one with a middle name beginning with the same initial. For example: Jack R. Hertz comes before Jack Richard Hertz.

6. Prefixes such as De, O', Mac, Mc, and Van are filed as written and are treated as part of the names to which they are connected. For example: Robert O'Dea is filed before David Olsen.

7. Abbreviated names are treated as if they were spelled out. For example: Chas. is filed as Charles, and Thos. is filed as Thomas.

8. Titles and designations such as Dr., Mr., and Prof, are disregarded in filing.

Names of Organizations

1. The names of business organizations are filed according to the order in which each word in the name appears. When an organization name bears the name of a person, it is filed according to the rules for filing names of people as given above. For example: William Smith Service Co. comes before Television Distributors, Inc.

2. Where bureau, board, office, or department appears as the first part of the title of a governmental agency, that agency should be filed under the word in the title expressing the chief function of the agency. For example: Bureau of the Budget would be filed as if written Budget, (Bureau of the). The Department of Personnel would be filed as if written Personnel, (Department of).

3. When the following words are part of an organization, they are disregarded: the, of, and.

4. When there are numbers in a name, they are treated as if they were spelled out. For example: 10th Street Bootery is filed as Tenth Street Bootery.

Each of questions 1 through 8 contains four names numbered from I through IV, but not necessarily numbered in correct filing order. Answer each question by choosing the letter corresponding to the CORRECT filing order of the four names in accordance with the above rules.

Sample Question;

I. Robert J. Smith
II. R. Jeffrey Smith
III. Dr. A. Smythe
IV. Allen R. Smithers

A. I, II, III, IV
B. III, I, II, IV
C. II, I, IV, III
D. III, II, I, IV

Since the correct filing order, in accordance with the above rules, is II, I, IV, III, the CORRECT answer is C.

1. I. J. Chester VanClief 1.____
II. John C. VanClief
III. J. VanCleve
III. Mary L. Vance
The CORRECT answer is:

A. IV, III, I, II
B. IV, III, II, I
C. III, I, II, IV
D. III, IV, I, II

2. I. Community Development Agency 2.____
II. Department of Social Services
III. Board of Estimate
IV. Bureau of Gas and Electricity
The CORRECT answer is:

A. III, IV, I, II
B. I, II, IV, III
C. II, I, III, IV
D. I, III, IV, II

3. I. Dr. Chas. K. Dahlman 3.____
II. F. & A. Delivery Service
III. Department of Water Supply
IV. Demano Men's Custom Tailors
The CORRECT answer is:

A. I, II, III, IV
B. I, IV, II, III
C. IV, I, II, III
D. IV, I, III, II

4. I. 48th Street Theater 4.____
II. Fourteenth Street Day Care Center
III. Professor A. Cartwright
IV. Albert F. McCarthy
The CORRECT answer is:

A. IV, II, I, III
B. IV, III, I, II
C. III, II, I, IV
D. III, I, II, IV

5. I. Frances D'Arcy 5.____
II. Mario L. DelAmato
III. William R. Diamond
IV. Robert J. DuBarry
The CORRECT answer is:

A. I, II, IV, III
B. II, I, III, IV
C. I, II, III, IV
D. II, I, IV, III

6. I. Evelyn H. D'Amelio 6.____
II. Jane R. Bailey
III. J. Robert Bailey
IV. Frank Baily
The CORRECT answer is:

A. I, II, III, IV
B. I, III, II, IV
C. II, III, IV, I
D. III, II, IV, I

7. I. Department of Markets 7.____
II. Bureau of Handicapped Children
III. Housing Authority Administration Building
IV. Board of Pharmacy
The CORRECT answer is:

A. II, I, III, IV
B. I, II, IV, III
C. I, II, III, IV
D. III, II, I, IV

8. I. William A. Shea Stadium 8.____
II. Rapid Speed Taxi Co.
III. Harry Stampler's Rotisserie
IV. Wilhelm Albert Shea
The CORRECT answer is:

A. II, III, IV, I
B. IV, I, III, II
C. II, IV, I, III
D. III, IV, I, II

Questions 9-16.

DIRECTIONS: The employee identification codes in Column I begin and end with a capital letter and have an eight-digit number in between. In Questions 9 through 16, employee identification codes in Column I are to be arranged according to the following rules:

First: Arrange in alphabetical order according to the first letter.

Second: When two or more employee identification codes have the same first let ter, arrange in alphabetical order according to the last letter.

Third: When two or more employee codes have the same first and last letters, arrange in numerical order, beginning with the lowest number.

The employee identification codes in Column I are numbered 1 through 5 in the order in which they are listed. In Column II, the numbers 1 through 5 are arranged in four different ways to show different arrangements of the corresponding employee identification numbers. Choose the answer in Column II in which the employee identification numbers are arranged according to the above rules.

Sample Question;

	Column I		Column II
1.	E75044127B	A.	4, 1, 3, 2, 5
2.	B96399104A	B.	4, 1, 2, 3, 5
3.	B93939086A	C.	4, 3, 2, 5, 1
4.	B47064465H	D.	3, 2, 5, 4, 1
5.	B99040922A		

In the sample question, the four employee identification codes starting with B should be put before the employee identification code starting with E. The employee identification codes starting with B and ending with A should be put before the employee identification codes starting with B and ending with H. The three employee identification codes starting with B and ending with A should be listed in numerical order, beginning with the lowest number. The correct way to arrange the employee identification codes, therefore, is 3, 2, 5, 4, 1, shown below.

3. B93939086A
2. B96399104A
5. B99040922A
4. B47064465H
1. E75044127B

Therefore, the answer to the sample question is D.

		Column I		Column II	
9.	1.	G42786441J	A.	2, 5, 4, 3, 1	9.____
	2.	H45665413J	B.	5, 4, 1, 3, 2	
	3.	G43117690J	C.	4, 5, 1, 3, 2	
	4.	G43546698I	D.	1, 3, 5, 4, 2	
	5.	G41679942I			
10.	1.	S44556178T	A.	1, 3, 5, 2, 4	10.____
	2.	T43457169T	B.	4, 3, 5, 2, 1	
	3.	S53321176T	C.	5, 3, 1, 2, 4	
	4.	T53317998S	D.	5, 1, 3, 4, 2	
	5.	S67673942S			
11.	1.	R63394217D	A.	5, 4, 2, 3, 1	11.____
	2.	R63931247D	B.	1, 5, 3, 2, 4	
	3.	R53931247D	C.	5, 3, 1, 2, 4	
	4.	R66874239D	D.	5, 1, 2, 3, 4	
	5.	R46799366D			
12.	1.	A35671968B	A.	3, 2, 1, 4, 5	12.____
	2.	A35421794C	B.	2, 3, 1, 5, 4	
	3.	A35466987B	C.	1, 3 , 2, 4, 5	
	4.	C10435779A	D.	3, 1, 2, 4, 5	
	5.	C00634779B			
13.	1.	I99746426Q	A.	2, 1, 3, 5, 4	13.____
	2.	I10445311Q	B.	5, 4, 2, 1, 3	
	3.	J63749877P	C.	4, 5, 3, 2, 1	
	4.	J03421739Q	D.	2, 1, 4, 5, 3	
	5.	J00765311Q			
14.	1.	M33964217N	A.	4, 1, 5, 2, 3	14.____
	2.	N33942770N	B.	5, 1, 4, 3, 2	
	3.	N06155881M	C.	4, 1, 5, 3, 2	
	4.	M00433669M	D.	1, 4, 5, 2, 3	
	5.	M79034577N			
15.	1.	D77643905C	A.	1, 2, 5, 3, 4	15.____
	2.	D44106788C	B.	5, 3, 2, 1, 4	
	3.	D13976022F	C.	2, 1, 5, 3, 4	
	4.	D97655430E	D.	2, 1, 4, 5, 3	
	5.	D00439776F			
16.	1.	W22746920A	A.	2, 1, 3, 4, 5	16.____
	2.	W22743720A	B.	2, 1, 5, 3, 4	
	3.	W32987655A	C.	1, 2, 3, 4, 5	
	4.	W43298765A	D.	1, 2, 5, 3, 4	
	5.	W30987433A			

Questions 17-22.

DIRECTIONS: Questions 17 through 22 are to be answered on the basis of the information given in the chart below. This chart shows the results of a study made of the tasks performed by a stenographer during one day. Included in the chart are the time at which she started a certain task and, under the particular task heading, the amount of time, in minutes, she took to complete the task, and explanations of telephone calls and miscellaneous activities.

NOTE: The time spent at lunch should not be included in any of your calculations.

PAMELA JOB STUDY

NAME: Pamela Donald DATE: 9/26
JOB TITLE: Stenographer
DIVISION: Stenographic Pool

Time of Start of Task	TASKS PERFORMED						Explanations of Telephone Calls and Miscellaneous Activities
	Taking Dictation	Typing	Filing	Telephone Work	Handling Mail	Misc. Activities	
9:00					22		
9:22						13	Picking up supplies
9:35						15	Cleaning typewriter
9:50	11						
10:01		30					
10:31				8			Call to Agency A
10:39	12						
10:51			10				
11 : 01				7			Call from Agency B
11:08		30					
11:38	10						
11:48				12			Call from Agency C
12:00	L U	N	C	H			
1:00					28		
1 : 28	13						
1:41		32					
2:13				12			Call to Agency B
X			15				
Y		50					
3:30	10						
3:40			21				
4:01				9			Call from Agency A
4:10	35						
4:45		9					
4:54						6	Cleaning up desk

Sample Question:

The total amount of time spent on miscellaneous activities in the morning is exactly equal to the total amount of time spent

A. filing in the morning
B. handling mail in the afternoon
C. miscellaneous activities in the afternoon
D. handling mail in the morning

Explanation of answer to sample question:

The total amount of time spent on miscellaneous activities in the morning equals 28 minutes (13 minutes for picking up supplies plus 15 minutes for cleaning the typewriter); and since it takes 28 minutes to handle mail in the afternoon, the answer is B.

17. The time labeled Y at which the stenographer started a typing assignment was 17.____

A. 2:15 B. 2:25 C. 2:40 D. 2:50

18. The ratio of time spent on all incoming calls to time spent on all outgoing calls for the day was 18.____

A. 5:7 B. 5:12 C. 7:5 D. 7:12

19. Of the following combinations of tasks, which ones take up exactly 80% of the total time spent on *Tasks Performed* during the day? 19.____

A. Typing, filing, telephone work, and handling mail
B. Taking dictation, filing, and miscellaneous activities
C. Taking dictation, typing, handling mail, and miscellaneous activities
D. Taking dictation, typing, filing, and telephone work

20. The total amount of time spent transcribing or typing work is how much more than the total amount of time spent in taking dictation? 20.____

A. 55 minutes B. 1 hour
C. 1 hour 10 minutes D. 1 hour 25 minutes

21. The GREATEST number of shifts in activities occurred between the times of 21.____

A. 9:00 A.M. and 10:31 A.M.
B. 9:35 A.M. and 11:01 A.M.
C. 10:31 A.M. and 12:00 Noon
D. 3:30 P.M. and 5:00 P.M.

22. The total amount of time spent on taking dictation in the morning plus the total amount of time spent on filing in the afternoon is exactly equal to the total amount of time spent on 22.____

A. typing in the afternoon minus the total amount of time spent on telephone work in the afternoon
B. typing in the morning plus the total amount of time spent on miscellaneous activities in the afternoon
C. dictation in the afternoon plus the total amount of time spent on filing in the morning

D. typing in the afternoon minus the total amount of time spent on handling mail in the morning

Questions 23-30.

DIRECTIONS: Each of Questions 23 through 30 consists of a set of letters and numbers. For each question, pick as your answer from the column to the right the choice which has ONLY numbers and letters that are in the question you are answering.

Sample Question:

B-9-P-H-2-Z-N-8-4-M

A. B-4-C-3-H-9
B. 4-H-P-8-6-N
C. P-2-Z-8-M-9
D. 4-B-N-5-E-2

Choice C is the correct answer because P, 2, Z, 8, M, 9 are in the sample question. All the other choices have at least one letter or number that is not in the question.

Questions 23 through 26 are based on Column I.
Questions 27 through 30 are based on Column II.

	Column I	
23. X-8-3-I-H-9-4-G-P-U	A. I-G-W-8-2-1	23.____
24. 4-1-2-X-U-B-9-H-7-3	B. U-3-G-9-P-8	24.____
25. U-I-G-2-5-4-W-P-3-8	C. 3-G-I-4-8-U	25.____
26. 3-H-7-G-4-5-I-U-8	D. 9-X-4-7-2-H	26.____

	Column II	
27. L-2-9-Z-R-8-Q-Y-5-7	A. 8-R-N-3-T-Z	27.____
28. J-L-9-N-Y-8-5-Q-Z-2	B. 2-L-R-5-7-Q	28.____
29. T-Y-8-3-J-Q-2-N-R-Z	C. J-2-8-Z-Y-5	29.____
30. 8-Z-7-T-N-L-1-E-R-3	D. Z-8-9-3-L-5	30.____

KEY (CORRECT ANSWERS)

1.	A	16.	B
2.	D	17.	C
3.	B	18.	C
4.	D	19.	D
5.	C	20.	B
6.	D	21.	C
7.	D	22.	D
8.	C	23.	B
9.	B	24.	D
10.	D	25.	C
11.	C	26.	C
12.	D	27.	B
13.	A	28.	C
14.	C	29.	A
15.	D	30.	A

TEST 3

DIRECTIONS: Each question or incomplete statement is followed by several suggested answers or completions. Select the one that BEST answers the question or completes the statement. *PRINT THE LETTER OF THE CORRECT ANSWER IN THE SPACE AT THE RIGHT.*

Questions 1-6.

DIRECTIONS: In Questions 1 through 6, only one of the sentences lettered A, B, C, or D is grammatically correct. Pick as your answer the sentence that is CORRECT from the point of view of grammar when used in formal correspondence.

1. A. There is four tests left. 1.____
   B. The number of tests left are four.
   C. There are four tests left.
   D. Four of the tests remains.

2. A. Each of the applicants takes a test. 2.____
   B. Each of the applicants take a test.
   C. Each of the applicants take tests.
   D. Each of the applicants have taken tests.

3. A. The applicant, not the examiners, are ready. 3.____
   B. The applicants, not the examiner, is ready.
   C. The applicants, not the examiner, are ready.
   D. The applicant, not the examiner, are ready.

4. A. You will not progress except you practice. 4.____
   B. You will not progress without you practicing.
   C. You will not progress unless you practice.
   D. You will not progress provided you do not practice.

5. A. Neither the director or the employees will be at the office tomorrow. 5.____
   B. Neither the director nor the employees will be at the office tomorrow.
   C. Neither the director, or the secretary nor the other employees will be at the office tomorrow.
   D. Neither the director, the secretary or the other employees will be at the office tomorrow.

6. A. In my absence he and her will have to finish the assignment. 6.____
   B. In my absence,he and she will have to finish the assignment.
   C. In my absence she and him, they will have to finish the assignment.
   D. In my absence he and her both will have to finish the assignment.

Questions 7-12.

DIRECTIONS: Questions 7 through 12 consist of a sentence lacking certain needed punctuation. Pick as your answer the description of punctuation which will CORRECTLY complete the sentence.

7. If you take the time to keep up your daily correspondence you will no doubt be most efficient. Comma(s) 7.____

A. only after *doubt*
B. only after *correspondence*
C. after *correspondence, will,* and *be*
D. after *if, correspondence,* and *will*

8. Because he did not send the application soon enough he did not receive the up to date copy of the book. Comma(s) 8.____

A. after *application* and *enough,* and quotation marks before *up* and after *date*
B. after *application* and *enough,* and hyphens between *to* and *date*
C. after *enough,* and hyphens between *up* and *to* and between *to* and *date*
D. after *application,* and quotation marks before *up* and after *date*

9. The coordinator requested from the department the following items a letter each week summarizing progress personal forms and completed applications for tests. 9.____

A. Commas after *items* and *completed*
B. Semi-colon after *items* and *progress,* comma after *forms*
C. Colon after *items,* commas after *progress* and *forms*
D. Colon after *items,* commas after *forms* and *applications*

10. The supervisor asked Who will attend the conference next month 10.____

A. Comma after *asked,* period after *month*
B. Period after *asked,* question mark after *month*
C. Comma after *asked,* quotation marks before *Who,* quotation marks after *month,* and question mark after the quotation marks
D. Comma after *asked,* quotation marks before *Who,* question mark after *month,* and quotation marks after the question mark

11. When the statistics are collected we will forward the results to you as soon as possible. Comma(s) after 11.____

A. *you*
B. *forward* and *you*
C. *collected, results,* and *you*
D. *collected*

12. The ecology of our environment is concerned with mans pollution of the atmosphere. 12.____

A. Comma after *ecology*
B. Apostrophe after *n* and before *s* in *mans*
C. Commas after *ecology* and *environment*
D. Apostrophe after *s* in *mans*

Questions 13-18.

DIRECTIONS: Each of Questions 13 through 18 consists of three words. In each question, one of the words may be spelled incorrectly or all three words may be spelled correctly. If one of the words in a question is spelled incorrectly, indicate in the space at the right the letter preceding the word which is spelled incorrectly. If all three words are spelled correctly, print in the space at the right the letter D.

13. A. sincerely B. affectionately C. truly 13.____

14. A. excellant B. verify C. important 14.____

15. A. error B. quality C. enviroment 15.____

16. A. exercise B. advance C. pressure 16.____

17. A. citizen B. expence C. memory 17.____

18. A. flexable B. focus C. forward 18.____

19. A senior stenographer earned $40,200 a year and had 4.5% state tax withheld for the year 2016. 19.____
If she was paid every two weeks, the amount of state tax that was taken out of each of her paychecks, based on a 52-week year, was MOST NEARLY

A. $62.76 B. $64.98 C. $69.54 D. $73.98

20. Two stenographers have been assigned to address 750 envelopes. One stenographer addresses twice as many envelopes per hour as the other stenographer. 20.____
If it takes five hours for them to complete the job, the rate of the slower stenographer is _______ envelopes per hour.

A. 35 B. 50 C. 75 D. 100

21. Suppose that the postage rate for mailing single copies of a magazine to persons not included on a subscription list is 60 cents for the first two ounces of the single copy and 10 cents for each additional ounce. 21.____
If 19 copies of a magazine, each of which weighs eleven ounces, are mailed to 19 different people, the TOTAL postage cost of these magazines is

A. $11.40 B. $13.30 C. $20.90 D. $28.50

22. A senior stenographer spends about 40 hours a month taking dictation. Of that time, 44% is spent taking minutes of meetings, 38% is spent taking dictation of lengthy reports, and the rest of the time is spent taking dictation of letters and memoranda. 22.____
How much MORE time is spent taking minutes of meetings than in taking dictation of letters and memoranda?
10 hours _______minutes

A. 6 B. 16 C. 24 D. 40

23. In one week, a stenographer typed 65 letters. Forty letters had 4 copies on onion skin. The rest had 3 copies on onion skin. 23.____
If the stenographer had 500 sheets of onion skin on hand at the beginning of the week when she started typing the letters, how many sheets of onion skin did she have left at the end of the week?

A. 190 B. 235 C. 265 D. 305

24. An agency is planning to microfilm letters and other correspondence of the last five years. The number of letter size documents that can be photographed on a 100-foot roll of microfilm is 2,995. The agency estimates that it will need 240 feet of microfilm to do all the pages of all of the letters. 24.____
How many pages of letter size documents can be photographed on this microfilm?

A. 5,990 B. 6,786 C. 7,188 D. 7,985

25. In an agency, 2/3 of the total number of female stenographers and 1/2 of the total number of male stenographers attended a general staff meeting. 25.____
If there are a total of 56 stenographers in the agency and 25% of them are male, the number of female stenographers who attended the general staff meeting is

A. 14 B. 28 C. 36 D. 42

26. A worker is currently earning $42,850 a year and pays $875 a month for rent. He expects to get a raise that will enable him to move into an apartment where his rent will be 25% of his new yearly salary. 26.____
If this new apartment is going to cost him $975 a month, what is the TOTAL amount of raise that he expects to get?

A. $1,200 B. $2,450 C. $3,950 D. $4,600

27. The tops of five desks in an office are to be covered with a scratch-resistant material. Each desk top measures 60 inches by 36 inches. 27.____
How many square feet of material will be needed for the five desk tops?

A. 15 B. 75 C. 96 D. 180

Questions 28-33.

DIRECTIONS: Questions 28 through 33 test how well you understand what you read. It will be necessary for you to read carefully because your answers to these questions should be based ONLY on the information given in the following passage.

Years ago, senior stenographers needed to understand the basic operations of data processing. On punched cards, magnetic tape or on other media, data was recorded before being fed into the computer for processing. A machine such as the keypunch was used to convert the data written on the source document into the coded symbols on punched cards or tapes. After data was converted, it was verified to guarantee absolute accuracy of conversion. In this manner, data became a permanent record that can be read by electronic computers.

Today, senior stenographers enter similar data directly into computer systems using word-processing, spreadsheet, publishing and other types of software. Rather than concern themselves with symbols and conversions, stenographers can transcribe information in programs like Microsoft Word or Google Docs, and enter numerical information into Microsoft Excel, which can then create charts and formulas out of that basic data.

28. Of the following, the BEST title for the above passage is: 28.____

A. THE STENOGRAPHER AS DATA PROCESSOR
B. THE RELATION OF KEYPUNCHING TO STENOGRAPHY
C. THE EVOLUTION OF DATA PROCESSING
D. PERMANENT OFFICE RECORDS

29. According to the above passage, the role of the senior stenographer is different in the present day in that 29.____

A. data can be entered directly into computer programs
B. it requires knowledge of multiple methods of recording data
C. ultimately, all data winds up being recorded on a computer
D. stenographers must have an advanced understanding of software and programming

30. Based on the passage, which of the following is NOT an example of a task a senior stenographer would carry out today? 30.____

A. Entering text into a pamphlet using publishing software
B. Recording sales figures and sending them to a programmer for processing
C. Recording purchasing data in an Excel spreadsheet
D. Typing an orally dictated draft in a Word document

31. According to the above passage, computers are used MOST often to handle 31.____

A. management data
B. problems of higher education
C. the control of chemical processes
D. payroll operations

32. Computer programming is taught in many colleges and business schools. The above passage IMPLIES that programmers in industry 32.____

A. must have professional training
B. need professional training to advance
C. must have at least a college education to do adequate programming tasks
D. do not need college education to do programming work

33. According to the above passage, data to be processed by computer should be 33.____

A. recent B. complete C. basic D. verified

Questions 34-40.

DIRECTIONS: In each of the following groups of sentences, one of the four sentences is faulty in grammar, punctuation, or capitalization. Select the INCORRECT sentence in each case.

34. A. If you had stood at home and done your homework, you would not have failed in arithmetic. 34.____
B. Her affected manner annoyed every member of the audience.
C. How will the new law affect our income taxes?
D. The plants were not affected by the long, cold winter, but they succumbed to the drought of summer.

35. A. He is one of the most able men who have been in the Senate. 35.____
B. It is he who is to blame for the lamentable mistake.
C. Haven't you a helpful suggestion to make at this time?
D. The money was robbed from the blind man's cup.

36. A. The amount of children in this school is steadily increasing. 36.____
B. After taking an apple from the table, she went out to play.
C. He borrowed a dollar from me.
D. I had hoped my brother would arrive before me.

37. A. Whom do you think I hear from every week? 37.____
B. Who do you think is the right man for the job?
C. Who do you think I found in the room?
D. He is the man whom we considered a good candidate for the presidency.

38. A. Quietly the puppy laid down before the fireplace. 38.____
B. You have made your bed; now lie in it.
C. I was badly sunburned because I had lain too long in the sun.
D. I laid the doll on the bed and left the room.

39. A. Sailing down the bay was a thrilling experience for me. 39.____
B. He was not consulted about your joining the club.
C. This story is different than the one I told you yesterday.
D. There is no doubt about his being the best player.

40. A. He maintains there is but one road to world peace. 40.____
B. It is common knowledge that a child sees much he is not supposed to see.
C. Much of the bitterness might have been avoided if arbitration had been resorted to earlier in the meeting.
D. The man decided it would be advisable to marry a girl somewhat younger than him.

KEY (CORRECT ANSWERS)

1.	C	21.	D
2.	A	22.	C
3.	C	23.	C
4.	C	24.	C
5.	B	25.	B
6.	B	26.	C
7.	B	27.	B
8.	C	28.	C
9.	C	29.	A
10.	D	30.	B
11.	D	31.	A
12.	B	32.	D
13.	D	33.	D
14.	A	34.	A
15.	C	35.	D
16.	D	36.	A
17.	B	37.	C
18.	A	38.	A
19.	C	39.	C
20.	B	40.	D

WORD MEANING
EXAMINATION SECTION
TEST 1

DIRECTIONS: For the following questions, select the word or group of words lettered A, B, C, D, or E that means MOST NEARLY the same as the word in capital letters. *PRINT THE LETTER OF THE CORRECT ANSWER IN THE SPACE AT THE RIGHT.*

1. The lane was NARROW and led to a mountain lake. 1.____

   A. attractive
   B. not wide
   C. overgrown
   D. rough
   E. without trees

2. Blow the horn as you APPROACH the gate. 2.____

   A. discover
   B. leave
   C. draw near
   D. pass through
   E. unlock

3. It was part of our BARGAIN that you should wash dishes. 3.____

   A. agreement B. debt C. goal D. plan E. wish

4. I shall remember that little valley FOREVER. 4.____

   A. often B. yet C. always D. next E. no more

5. The boy was EAGER to go on the trip. 5.____

   A. able B. afraid C. anxious D. likely E. willing

6. The children were having a DISPUTE over the boy. 6.____

   A. conversation
   B. crying spell
   C. disagreement
   D. performance
   E. tantrum

7. The man was punished for his BRUTAL act. 7.____

   A. bloody
   B. cruel
   C. deadly
   D. defenseless
   E. ugly

8. We LAUNCHED our new business with great hope for the future. 8.____

   A. concluded B. started C. pursued D. steered E. watched

9. The two streets INTERSECT at the edge of town. 9.____

   A. run parallel
   B. change names
   C. end
   D. become thoroughfares
   E. cross

10. She suffered from an UNCOMMON disease. 10.____

   A. ordinary B. painful C. contagious D. rare E. new

11. The antique chair was very FRAGILE. 11.___

A. delicate B. worn C. beautiful D. well-made E. useless

12. They picked EDIBLE mushrooms. 12.___

A. poisonous B. well-formed C. unusual D. large E. eatable

13. He found the reception at the airport very GRATIFYING. 13.___

A. surprising
B. deafening
C. pleasant
D. disagreeable
E. impolite

14. DEFECTIVE brakes caused the mishap. 14.___

A. old-fashioned
B. uneven
C. squeaking
D. unused
E. faulty

15. After a little EXERTION the box was moved. 15.___

A. argument B. delay C. coaxing D. effort E. planning

KEY (CORRECT ANSWERS)

1. B
2. C
3. A
4. C
5. C
6. C
7. B
8. B
9. E
10. D
11. A
12. E
13. C
14. E
15. D

TEST 2

DIRECTIONS: For the following questions, select the word or group of words lettered A, B, C, D, or E that means MOST NEARLY the same as the word in capital letters. *PRINT THE LETTER OF THE CORRECT ANSWER IN THE SPACE AT THE RIGHT.*

1. The RAPIDITY of the attack surprised us. 1.____

   A. power B. effectiveness C. possibility
   D. strangeness E. swiftness

2. She enjoyed CONVERSING with her friends. 2.____

   A. meeting B. laughing C. talking D. dining E. traveling

3. There was a small VENT near the end of the tube. 3.____

   A. cap B. screw C. opening D. joint E. pump

4. With great CAUTION we opened the barn door. 4.____

   A. care B. fear C. distrust D. danger E. difficulty

5. The old man's coat was THREADBARE. 5.____

   A. spotted B. tight C. new D. ill-made E. shabby

6. I was sorry that I could not decide OTHERWISE. 6.____

   A. immediately B. differently C. favorably
   D. positively E. eagerly

7. The GIGANTIC switchboard controlled all the lights in the theatre. 7.____

   A. complicated B. up-to-date C. automatic
   D. huge E. stationary

8. The balls were made of SYNTHETIC rubber. 8.____

   A. artificial B. hard C. cheap D. imported E. crude

9. He was MERELY a servant in the house. 9.____

   A. occasionally B. in no way C. unhappily
   D. formerly E. no more than

10. The prisoner CONFERRED with his lawyer. 10.____

    A. argued B. interfered C. dined
    D. sympathized E. consulted

11. The soldier's GALLANTRY went unnoticed. 11.____

    A. strength B. fright
    C. disobedience D. injury
    E. bravery

12. The music was chosen for its SOOTHING effect. 12.___

A. tuneful B. calming C. magic D. exciting E. solemn

13. The owners were advised to REINFORCE the wall. 13.___

A. rebuild B. lengthen C. lower D. strengthen E. repaint

14. They performed their duties with UTMOST ease. 14.___

A. noticeable B. some C. surprising D. greatest E. increasing

15. We picnicked near a CASCADE. 15.___

A. pond B. camp C. waterfall D. trail E. slope

KEY (CORRECT ANSWERS)

1. E
2. C
3. C
4. A
5. E
6. B
7. D
8. A
9. E
10. E
11. E
12. B
13. D
14. D
15. C

TEST 3

DIRECTIONS: For the following questions, select the word or group of words lettered A, B, C, D, or E that means MOST NEARLY the same as the word in capital letters. *PRINT THE LETTER OF THE CORRECT ANSWER IN THE SPACE AT THE RIGHT.*

1. The chairman was anxious to ADJOURN the meeting. 1.____

   A. conduct B. attend C. start D. address E. close

2. The gown was made of a GLOSSY fabric. 2.____

   A. shiny B. embroidered C. many-colored
   D. transparent E. expensive

3. An ocean voyage in a small boat can be very HAZARDOUS. 3.____

   A. thrilling B. slow C. dangerous D. rough E. tiresome

4. The weatherman predicted VARIABLE winds. 4.____

   A. drying B. strong C. cool D. light E. changeable

5. Not long after the play began, the children began to FIDGET. 5.____

   A. clap B. move restlessly
   C. cry D. laugh aloud
   E. shriek

6. That person has a habit of MEDDLING. 6.____

   A. stumbling B. interfering C. play jokes
   D. cheating E. being late

7. Young children are frequently INQUISITIVE. 7.____

   A. curious B. saucy C. restless D. shy E. tearful

8. The FALSITY of the report was apparent at first glance. 8.____

   A. uselessness B. untidiness C. incompleteness
   D. incorrectness E. disagreeableness

9. Orders were given to LIBERATE the prisoners by noon. 9.____

   A. question B. transfer C. free D. sentence E. fingerprint

10. She is HABITUALLY late for her dental appointments. 10.____

    A. usually B. seldom C. extremely D. slightly E. never

11. The soldiers were given SPACIOUS living quarters. 11.____

    A. pleasant B. well-aired C. crowded
    D. well-furnished E. roomy

12. The witnesses gave STRAIGHTFORWARD answers. 12.___

A. hasty B. frank C. conflicting D. helpful E. serious

13. His income EXCEEDS that of his brother. 13.___

A. is less regular than
B. is greater than
C. is the same as
D. is less than
E. is spent sooner than

14. He SHUNNED all of his neighbors. 14.___

A. disapproved
B. welcomed
C. quarreled with
D. avoided
E. insulted

15. Many of the natives are ILLITERATE. 15.___

A. unable to read
B. unclean
C. unable to vote
D. unmanageable
E. sickly

KEY (CORRECT ANSWERS)

1. E
2. A
3. C
4. E
5. B
6. B
7. A
8. D
9. C
10. A
11. E
12. B
13. B
14. D
15. A

TEST 4

DIRECTIONS: For the following questions, select the word or group of words lettered A, B, C, D, or E that means MOST NEARLY the same as the word in capital letters. *PRINT THE LETTER OF THE CORRECT ANSWER IN THE SPACE AT THE RIGHT.*

1. We have always found this medicine to be RELIABLE. 1.____

   A. dependable B. easy to use C. pleasant-tasting
   D. bitter E. fast-acting

2. The cloth was left to BLEACH in the sun. 2.____

   A. dry B. soak C. whiten D. shrink E. rot

3. The work is ORDINARILY done on time. 3.____

   A. seldom B. without fail C. necessarily
   D. hardly ever E. usually

4. Jim is a very DISCOURTEOUS boy. 4.____

   A. impolite B. daring C. untruthful D. uneasy E. cautious

5. Paris is noted for its BOULEVARDS. 5.____

   A. crooked streets B. parks C. art galleries
   D. churches E. broad avenues

6. The group formed the SEMICIRCLE quickly. 6.____

   A. half-circle B. double circle C. complete circle
   D. uneven E. very small circle

7. The machine that he designed was PORTABLE. 7.____

   A. business-like B. practical C. of foreign manufacture
   D. easily transported E. difficult to use

8. The food supply DWINDLED during the winter. 8.____

   A. spoiled B. became less C. froze
   D. was wasted E. was rationed

9. The vase was one of the PERMANENT exhibits at the museum. 9.____

   A. historical B. lasting C. popular
   D. artistic E. well-planned

10. We could not understand why he left so ABRUPTLY. 10.____

    A. suddenly B. soon C. absent-mindedly
    D. mysteriously E. noisily

KEY (CORRECT ANSWERS)

1. A
2. C
3. E
4. A
5. E
6. A
7. D
8. B
9. B
10. A

EXAMINATION SECTION
TEST 1

DIRECTIONS: Each question or incomplete statement is followed by several suggested answers or completions. Select the one that BEST answers the question or completes the statement. *PRINT THE LETTER OF THE CORRECT ANSWER IN THE SPACE AT THE RIGHT.*

Questions 1-20.

DIRECTIONS: Column I below lists words used in medical practice. Column II lists phrases which describe the words in Column I. Opposite the number preceding each of the words in Column I, place the letter preceding the phrase in Column II which BEST describes the word in Column I.

COLUMN I

1. Abrasion 1.____
2. Aseptic 2.____
3. Cardiac 3.____
4. Catarrh 4.____
5. Contamination 5.____
6. Dermatology 6.____
7. Disinfectant 7.____
8. Dyspepsia 8.____
9. Epidemic 9.____
10. Epidermis 10.____
11. Incubation 11.____
12. Microscope 12.____
13. Pediatrics 13.____
14. Plasma 14.____
15. Prenatal 15.____
16. Retina 16.____
17. Syphilis 17.____
18. Syringe 18.____
19. Toxemia 19.____
20. Vaccine 20.____

COLUMN II

A. A disturbance of digestion
B. Destroying the germs of disease
C. A general poisoning of the blood
D. An instrument used for injecting fluids
E. A scraping off of the skin
F. Free from disease germs
G. An apparatus for viewing internal organs by means of x-rays
H. An instrument for assisting the eye in observing minute objects
I. An inoculable immunizing agent
J. The extensive prevalence in a community of a
K. Chemical product of an organ
L. Preceding birth
M. Fever
N. The branch of medical science that relates to the skin and its diseases
O. Fluid part of the blood
P. The science of the hygienic care of children
Q. Infection by contact
R. Relating to the heart
S. Inner structure of the eye
T. Outer portion of the skin
U. Pertaining to the ductless glands
V. An infectious venereal disease
W. The development of an infectious disease from the period of infection to that of the appearance of the first symptoms
X. Simple inflammation of a mucous membrane
Y. An instrument for measuring blood pressure

Questions 21-25.

DIRECTIONS: Each of Questions 21 through 25 consists of four words. Three of these words belong together. One word does NOT belong with the other three. For each group of words, you are to select the one word which does NOT belong with the other three words.

21. A. conclude B. terminate C. initiate D. end 21.___

22. A. deficient B. inadequate C. excessive D. insufficient 22.___

23. A. rare B. unique C. unusual D. frequent 23.___

24. A. unquestionable B. uncertain C. doubtful D. indefinite 24.___

25. A. stretch B. contract C. extend D. expand 25.___

KEY (CORRECT ANSWERS)

1.	E	11.	W
2.	F	12.	H
3.	R	13.	P
4.	X	14.	O
5.	Q	15.	L
6.	N	16.	S
7.	B	17.	V
8.	A	18.	D
9.	J	19.	C
10.	T	20.	I

21. C
22. C
23. D
24. A
25. B

TEST 2

DIRECTIONS: Each question or incomplete statement is followed by several suggested answers or completions. Select the one that BEST answers the question or completes the statement. *PRINT THE LETTER OF THE CORRECT ANSWER IN THE SPACE AT THE RIGHT.*

Questions 1-4.

DIRECTIONS: Questions 1 through 4 pertain to the meaning of terms which may be encountered in laboratory work. For each question, select the option whose meaning is MOST NEARLY the same as that of the numbered item.

1. Atrophied 1.____

   A. enlarged B. relaxed
   C. strengthened D. wasted

2. Leucocyte 2.____

   A. white cell B. red cell
   C. epithelial cell D. dermal cell

3. Permeable 3.____

   A. volatile B. variable
   C. flexible D. penetrable

4. Attenuate 4.____

   A. dilute B. infect
   C. oxidize D. strengthen

Questions 5-11.

DIRECTIONS: For Questions 5 through 11, select the letter preceding the word which means MOST NEARLY the same as the first word.

5. legible 5.____

   A. readable B. eligible C. learned D. lawful

6. observe 6.____

   A. assist B. watch C. correct D. oppose

7. habitual 7.____

   A. punctual B. occasional
   C. usual D. actual

8. chronological 8.____

   A. successive B. earlier
   C. later D. studious

9. arrest 9.____

A. punish B. run C. threaten D. stop

10. abstain 10.____

A. refrain B. indulge C. discolor D. spoil

11. toxic 11.____

A. poisonous
B. decaying
C. taxing
D. defective

12. The *initial* contact is of great importance in setting a pattern for future relations. 12.____
The word *initial,* as used in this sentence, means MOST NEARLY

A. first B. written C. direct D. hidden

13. The doctor prescribed a diet which was *adequate* for the patient's needs. 13.____
The word *adequate,* as used in this sentence, means MOST NEARLY

A. insufficient
B. unusual
C. required
D. enough

14. The child was reported to be suffering from a vitamin *deficiency.* 14.____
The word *deficiency,* as used in this sentence, means MOST NEARLY

A. surplus B. infection C. shortage D. injury

15. In obtaining medical case data, a medical record librarian should discourage the patient from giving *irrelevant* information. 15.____
The word *irrelevant,* as used in this sentence, means MOST NEARLY

A. too detailed
B. pertaining to relatives
C. insufficient
D. inappropriate

16. The doctor requested that a *tentative* appointment be made for the patient. 16.____
The word *tentative,* as used in this sentence, means MOST NEARLY

A. definite
B. subject to change
C. later
D. of short duration

17. The black plague resulted in an usually high *mortality rate* in the population of Europe. 17.____
The term *mortality rate,* as used in this sentence, means MOST NEARLY

A. future immunity of the people
B. death rate
C. general weakening of the health of the people
D. sickness rate

18. The public health assistant was asked to file a number of *identical* reports on the case. 18.____
The word *identical,* as used in this sentence, means MOST NEARLY

A. accurate B. detailed C. same D. different

19. The nurse assisted in *the biopsy* of the patient. 19.____
The word *biopsy,* as used in this sentence, means MOST NEARLY

A. autopsy
B. excision and diagnostic study of tissue
C. biography and health history
D. administering of anesthesia

20. The assistant noted that the swelling on the patient's face had *subsided.* 20.____
The word *subsided,* as used in this sentence, means MOST NEARLY

A. become aggravated
B. increased
C. vanished
D. abated

21. The patient was given food *intravenously.* 21.____
The word *intravenously,* as used in this sentence, means MOST NEARLY

A. orally
B. against his will
C. through the veins
D. without condiment

Questions 22-25.

DIRECTIONS: Each of Questions 22 through 25 consists of four words. Three of these words belong together. One word does NOT belong with the other three. For each group of words, you are to select the one word which does NOT belong with the other three words.

22. A. accelerate B. quicken C. accept D. hasten 22.____

23. A. sever B. rupture C. rectify D. tear 23.____

24. A. innocuous B. injurious C. dangerous D. harmful 24.____

25. A. adulterate B. contaminate C. taint D. disinfect 25.____

KEY (CORRECT ANSWERS)

1. D	11. A	21. C
2. A	12. A	22. C
3. D	13. D	23. C
4. A	14. C	24. A
5. A	15. D	25. D
6. B	16. B	
7. C	17. B	
8. A	18. C	
9. D	19. B	
10. A	20. D	

TEST 3

DIRECTIONS: Each question or incomplete statement is followed by several suggested answers or completions. Select the one that BEST answers the question or completes the statement. *PRINT THE LETTER OF THE CORRECT ANSWER IN THE SPACE AT THE RIGHT.*

Questions 1-25.

DIRECTIONS: Each of Questions 1 through 25 consists of a word, in capitals, followed by four suggested meanings of the word. For each question, indicate in the space at the right the letter preceding the word which means MOST NEARLY the same as the word in capitals.

1. TEMPORARY 1._____

A. permanently
B. for a limited time
C. at the same time
D. frequently

2. INQUIRE 2._____

A. order
B. agree
C. ask
D. discharge

3. SUFFICIENT 3._____

A. enough
B. inadequate
C. thorough
D. capable

4. AMBULATORY 4._____

A. bedridden
B. left-handed
C. walking
D. laboratory

5. DILATE 5._____

A. enlarge
B. contract
C. revise
D. restrict

6. NUTRITIOUS 6._____

A. protective
B. healthful
C. fattening
D. nourishing

7. CONGENITAL 7._____

A. with pleasure
B. defective
C. likeable
D. existing from birth

8. ISOLATION 8._____

A. sanitation
B. quarantine
C. rudeness
D. exposure

9. SPASM 9._____

A. splash
B. twitch
C. space
D. blow

10. HEMORRHAGE 10.____

A. bleeding
B. ulcer
C. hereditary disease
D. lack of blood

11. NOXIOUS 11.____

A. gaseous B. harmful C. soothing D. repulsive

12. PYOGENIC 12.____

A. disease producing
B. fever producing
C. pus forming
D. water forming

13. RENAL 13.____

A. brain B. heart C. kidney D. stomach

14. ENDEMIC 14.____

A. epidemic
B. endermic
C. endoblast
D. peculiar to a particular people or locality, as a disease

15. MACULATION 15.____

A. reticulation
B. inoculation
C. maturation
D. defilement

16. TOLERATE 16.____

A. fear B. forgive C. allow D. despise

17. VENTILATE 17.____

A. vacate B. air C. extricate D. heat

18. SUPERIOR 18.____

A. perfect
B. subordinate
C. lower
D. higher

19. EXTREMITY 19.____

A. extent B. limb C. illness D. execution

20. DIVULGED 20.____

A. unrefined B. secreted C. revealed D. divided

21. SIPHON 21.____

A. drain B. drink C. compute D. discard

22. EXPIRATION 22.____

A. trip
B. demonstration
C. examination
D. end

23. AEROSOL 23.____

A. a gas dispersed in a liquid
B. a liquid dispersed in a gas
C. a liquid dispersed in a solid
D. a solid dispersed in a liquid

24. ETIOLOGY 24.____

A. cause of a disease
B. method of cure
C. method of diagnosis
D. study of insects

25. IN VITRO 25.____

A. in alkali
B. in the body
C. in the test tube
D. in vacuum

KEY (CORRECT ANSWERS)

1. B
2. C
3. A
4. C
5. A
6. D
7. D
8. B
9. B
10. A
11. B
12. C
13. C
14. D
15. D
16. C
17. B
18. D
19. B
20. C
21. A
22. D
23. B
24. A
25. C

EXAMINATION SECTION
TEST 1

DIRECTIONS: Each question or incomplete statement is followed by several suggested answers or completions. Select the one that BEST answers the question or completes the statement. *PRINT THE LETTER OF THE CORRECT ANSWER IN THE SPACE AT THE RIGHT.*

Questions 1-50.

DIRECTIONS: Each of Questions 1 through 50 consists of a word in capital letters followed by four suggested meanings of the word. For each question, choose the word or phrase which means MOST NEARLY the same as the word in capital letters.

1. ABUT 1.___
   A. abandon B. assist C. border on D. renounce

2. ABSCOND 2.___
   A. draw in B. give up
   C. refrain from D. deal off

3. BEQUEATH 3.___
   A. deaden B. hand down C. make sad D. scold

4. BOGUS 4.___
   A. sad B. false C. shocking D. stolen

5. CALAMITY 5.___
   A. disaster B. female C. insanity D. patriot

6. COMPULSORY 6.___
   A. binding B. ordinary C. protected D. ruling

7. CONSIGN 7.___
   A. agree with B. benefit
   C. commit D. drive down

8. DEBILITY 8.___
   A. failure B. legality
   C. quality D. weakness

9. DEFRAUD 9.___
   A. cheat B. deny
   C. reveal D. tie

10. DEPOSITION 10.___
    A. absence B. publication
    C. removal D. testimony

11. DOMICILE 11.___
    A. anger B. dwelling
    C. tame D. willing

12. HEARSAY 12.____
A. selfish B. serious C. rumor D. unlikely

13. HOMOGENEOUS 13.____
A. human B. racial C. similar D. unwise

14. ILLICIT 14.____
A. understood B. uneven C. unkind D. unlawful

15. LEDGER 15.____
A. book of accounts
B. editor
C. periodical
D. shelf

16. NARRATIVE 16.____
A. gossip B. natural C. negative D. story

17. PLAUSIBLE 17.____
A. reasonable B. respectful C. responsible D. rightful

18. RECIPIENT 18.____
A. absentee B. receiver C. speaker D. substitute

19. SUBSTANTIATE 19.____
A. appear for
B. arrange
C. confirm
D. combine

20. SURMISE 20.____
A. aim B. break C. guess D. order

21. ALTER EGO 21.____
A. business partner
B. confidential friend
C. guide
D. subconscious conflict

22. FOURTH ESTATE 22.____
A. the aristocracy
B. the clergy
C. the judiciary
D. the newspapers

23. IMPEACH 23.____
A. accuse
B. find guilty
C. remove
D. try

24. PROPENSITY 24.____
A. dislike
B. helpfulness
C. inclination
D. supervision

25. SPLENETIC 25.____
A. charming B. peevish C. shining D. sluggish

26. SUBORN 26.____
A. bribe someone to commit perjury
B. demote someone several levels in rank
C. deride
D. substitute

27. TALISMAN 27.___
    A. charm
    B. juror
    C. prayer shawl
    D. native

28. VITREOUS 28.___
    A. corroding
    B. glassy
    C. nourishing
    D. sticky

29. WRY 29.___
    A. comic B. grained C. resilient D. twisted

30. SIGNATORY 30.___
    A. lawyer who draws up a legal document
    B. document that must be signed by a judge
    C. person who signs a document
    D. true copy of a signature

31. RETAINER 31.___
    A. fee paid to a lawyer for his services
    B. document held by a third party
    C. court decision to send a prisoner back to custody pending trial
    D. legal requirement to keep certain types of files

32. BEQUEATH 32.___
    A. to receive assistance from a charitable organization
    B. to give personal property by will to another
    C. to transfer real property from one person to another
    D. to receive an inheritance upon the death of a relative

33. RATIFY 33.___
    A. approve and sanction
    B. forego
    C. produce evidence
    D. summarize

34. CODICIL 34.___
    A. document introduced in evidence in a civil action
    B. subsection of a law
    C. type of legal action that can be brought by a plaintiff
    D. supplement or an addition to a will

35. ALIAS 35.___
    A. assumed name B. in favor of C. against D. a writ

36. PROXY 36.___
    A. a phony document in a real estate transaction
    B. an opinion by a judge of a civil court
    C. a document containing appointment of an agent
    D. a summons in a lawsuit

37. ALLEGED 37.___
    A. innocent B. asserted C. guilty D. called upon

38. EXECUTE 38.___
   A. to complete a legal document by signing it
   B. to set requirements
   C. to render services to a duly elected executive of a municipality
   D. to initiate legal action such as a lawsuit

39. NOTARY PUBLIC 39.___
   A. lawyer who is running for public office
   B. judge who hears minor cases
   C. public officer, one of whose functions is to administer oaths
   D. lawyer who gives free legal services to persons unable to pay

40. WAIVE 40.___
   A. to disturb a calm state of affairs
   B. to knowingly renounce a right or claim
   C. to pardon someone for a minor fault
   D. to purposely mislead a person during an investigation

41. ARRAIGN 41.___
   A. to prevent an escape
   B. to defend a prisoner
   C. to verify a document
   D. to accuse in a court of law

42. VOLUNTARY 42.___
   A. by free choice
   B. necessary
   C. important
   D. by design

43. INJUNCTION 43.___
   A. act of prohibiting
   B. process of inserting
   C. means of arbitrating
   D. freedom of action

44. AMICABLE 44.___
   A. compelled
   B. friendly
   C. unimportant
   D. insignificant

45. CLOSED SHOP 45.___
   A. one that employs only members of a union
   B. one that employs union members and unaffiliated employees
   C. one that employs only employees with previous experience
   D. one that employs skilled and unskilled workers

46. ABDUCT 46.___
   A. lead B. kidnap C. sudden D. worthless

47. BIAS 47.___
   A. ability B. envy C. prejudice D. privilege

48. COERCE 48.___
   A. cancel B. force C. rescind D. rugged

49. CONDONE 49.___
A. combine B. pardon C. revive D. spice

50. CONSISTENCY 50.___
A. bravery B. readiness
C. strain D. uniformity

KEY (CORRECT ANSWERS)

1.	C	11.	B	21.	B	31.	A	41.	D
2.	D	12.	C	22.	D	32.	B	42.	A
3.	B	13.	C	23.	A	33.	A	43.	A
4.	B	14.	D	24.	C	34.	D	44.	B
5.	A	15.	A	25.	B	35.	A	45.	A
6.	A	16.	D	26.	A	36.	C	46.	B
7.	C	17.	A	27.	A	37.	B	47.	C
8.	D	18.	B	28.	B	38.	A	48.	B
9.	A	19.	C	29.	D	39.	C	49.	B
10.	D	20.	C	30.	C	40.	B	50.	D

TEST 2

DIRECTIONS: Each question or incomplete statement is followed by several suggested answers or completions. Select the one that BEST answers the question or completes the statement. *PRINT THE LETTER OF THE CORRECT ANSWER IN THE SPACE AT THE RIGHT.*

1. In the sentence, *The prisoner was fractious when brought to the station house*, the word *fractious* means MOST NEARLY 1.___
   A. penitent B. talkative
   C. irascible D. broken-hearted

2. In the sentence, *The judge was implacable when the attorney pleaded for leniency*, the word *implacable* means MOST NEARLY 2.___
   A. inexorable B. disinterested
   C. inattentive D. indifferent

3. In the sentence, *The court ordered the mendacious statements stricken from the record*, the word *mendacious* means MOST NEARLY 3.___
   A. begging B. lying
   C. threatening D. lengthy

4. In the sentence, *The district attorney spoke in a strident voice*, the word *strident* means MOST NEARLY 4.___
   A. loud B. harsh-sounding
   C. sing-song D. low

5. In the sentence, *The speaker had a predilection for long sentences*, the word *predilection* means MOST NEARLY 5.___
   A. aversion B. talent
   C. propensity D. diffidence

6. A person who has an uncontrollable desire to steal without need is called a 6.___
   A. dipsomaniac B. kleptomaniac
   C. monomaniac D. pyromaniac

7. In the sentence, *Malice was immanent in all his remarks*, the word *immanent* means MOST NEARLY 7.___
   A. elevated B. inherent
   C. threatening D. foreign

8. In the sentence, *The extant copies of the document were found in the safe*, the word *extant* means MOST NEARLY 8.___
   A. existing B. original
   C. forged D. duplicate

9. In the sentence, *The recruit was more complaisant after the captain spoke to him*, the word *complaisant* means MOST NEARLY 9.___
   A. calm B. affable
   C. irritable D. confident

10. In the sentence, *The man was captured under highly creditable circumstances*, the word *creditable* means MOST NEARLY 10.___

A. doubtful B. believable
C. praiseworthy D. unexpected

11. In the sentence, *His superior officers were more sagacious than he*, the word *sagacious* means MOST NEARLY 11.___

A. shrewd B. obtuse
C. absurd D. verbose

12. In the sentence, *He spoke with impunity*, the word *impunity* means MOST NEARLY 12.___

A. rashness B. caution
C. without fear D. immunity

13. In the sentence, *The new officer displayed unusual temerity during the emergency*, the word *temerity* means MOST NEARLY 13.___

A. fear B. rashness
C. calmness D. anxiety

14. In the sentence, *The portions of food were parsimoniously served*, the word *parsimoniously* means MOST NEARLY 14.___

A. stingily B. piously
C. elaborately D. generously

15. In the sentence, *Generally the speaker's remarks were sententious*, the word *sententious* means MOST NEARLY 15.___

A. verbose B. witty
C. argumentative D. pithy

Questions 16-20.

DIRECTIONS: Next to the number which corresponds with the number of each item in Column I, place the letter preceding the adjective in Column II which BEST describes the persons in Column I.

COLUMN I	COLUMN II	
16. Talkative woman	A. abstemious	16.___
17. Person on a reducing diet	B. pompous	17.___
18. Scholarly professor	C. erudite	18.___
19. Man who seldom speaks	D. benevolent	19.___
20. Charitable person	E. docile	20.___
	F. loquacious	
	G. indefatigable	
	H. taciturn	

Questions 21-25.

DIRECTIONS: Next to the number which corresponds with the number preceding each profession in Column I, place the letter preceding the word in Column II which BEST explains the subject matter of that profession.

COLUMN I	COLUMN II	
21. Geologist	A. animals	21._
22. Oculist	B. eyes	22._
23. Podiatrist	C. feet	23._
24. Palmist	D. fortune-telling	24._
25. Zoologist	E. language	25._
	F. rocks	
	G. stamps	
	H. woman	

Questions 26-30.

DIRECTIONS: Next to the number corresponding to the number of each of the words in Column I, place the letter preceding the word in Column II that is MOST NEARLY OPPOSITE to it in meaning.

COLUMN I	COLUMN II	
26. comely	A. beautiful	26._
27. eminent	B. cowardly	27._
28. frugal	C. kind	28._
29. gullible	D. sedate	29._
30. valiant	E. shrewd	30._
	F. ugly	
	G. unknown	
	H. wasteful	

KEY (CORRECT ANSWERS)

1.	C	11.	A	21.	F
2.	A	12.	D	22.	B
3.	B	13.	B	23.	C
4.	B	14.	A	24.	D
5.	C	15.	D	25.	A
6.	B	16.	F	26.	F
7.	B	17.	A	27.	G
8.	A	18.	C	28.	H
9.	B	19.	H	29.	E
10.	C	20.	D	30.	B

EXAMINATION SECTION

TEST 1

DIRECTIONS: Each question or incomplete statement is followed by several suggested answers or completions. Select the one that BEST answers the question or completes the statement. *PRINT THE LETTER OF THE CORRECT ANSWER IN THE SPACE AT THE RIGHT.*

Questions 1-22.

DIRECTIONS: Read through each group of words. Indicate in the space at the right the letter of the misspelled word.

1. A. miniature B. recession C. accommodate D. supress 1.____

2. A. mortgage B. illogical C. fasinate D. pronounce 2.____

3. A. calendar B. heros C. ecstasy D. librarian 3.____

4. A. initiative B. extraordinary C. villian D. exaggerate 4.____

5. A. absence B. sense C. dosn't D. height 5.____

6. A. curiosity B. ninety C. truely D. grammar 6.____

7. A. amateur B. definate C. meant D. changeable 7.____

8. A. excellent B. studioes C. achievement D. weird 8.____

9. A. goverment B. description C. sergeant D. desirable 9.____

10. A. proceed B. anxious C. neice D. precede 10.____

11. A. environment B. omitted C. apparant D. misconstrue 11.____

12. A. comparative B. hindrance C. benefited D. unamimous 12.____

13. A. embarrass B. recommend 13.____
C. desciple D. argument

14. A. sophomore B. suprintendent 14.____
C. concievable D. disastrous

15. A. agressive B. questionnaire 15.____
C. occurred D. rhythm

16. A. peaceable B. conscientious 16.____
C. redicule D. deterrent

17. A. mischievious B. writing 17.____
C. competition D. athletics

18. A. auxiliary B. synonymous 18.____
C. maneuver D. repitition

19. A. existence B. optomistic 19.____
C. acquitted D. tragedy

20. A. hypocrisy B. parrallel 20.____
C. exhilaration D. prevalent

21. A. convalesence B. infallible 21.____
C. destitute D. grotesque

22. A. magnanimity B. asassination 22.____
C. incorrigible D. pestilence

Questions 23-40.

DIRECTIONS: In Questions 23 through 40, one sentence fragment contains an error in punctuation or capitalization. Indicate the letter of the INCORRECT sentence fragment and place it in the space at the right.

23. A. Despite a year's work 23.____
B. in a well-equipped laboratory
C. my Uncle failed to complete his research
D. now he will never graduate.

24. A. Gene, if you are going to sleep 24.____
B. all afternoon I will enter
C. that ladies' golf tournament
D. sponsored by the Chamber of Commerce.

25. A. Seeing the cat slink toward the barn, 25.____
B. the farmer's wife jumped off the
C. ladder picked up a broom, and began
D. shouting at the top of her voice.

26. A. Extending over southeast Idaho and 26.____
B. northwest Wyoming, the Tetons
C. are noted for their height; however the
D. highest peak is actually under 14,000 feet.

27. A. "Sarah, can you recall the name 27.____
B. of the English queen
C. who supposedly said, 'We are not
D. amused?"

28. A. My aunt's graduation present to me 28.____
B. cost, I imagine more than she could
C. actually afford. It's a
D. Swiss watch with numerous features.

29. A. On the left are examples of buildings 29.____
B. from the Classical Period; two temples
C. one of which was dedicated to Zeus; the
D. Agora, a marketplace; and a large arch.

30. A. Tired of sonic booms, the people who 30.____
B. live near Springfield's Municipal Airport
C. formed an anti noise organization
D. with the amusing name of Sound Off.

31. A. "Joe, Mrs. Sweeney said, "your family 31.____
B. arrives Sunday. Since you'll be in
C. the Labor Day parade, we could ask Mr.
D. Krohn, who has a big car, to meet them."

32. A. The plumber emerged from the basement and 32.____
B. said, "Mr. Cohen I found the trouble in
C. your water heater. Could you move those
D. Schwinn bikes out of my way?"

33. A. The President walked slowly to the 33.____
B. podium, bowed to Edward Everett Hale
C. the other speaker, and began his formal address:
D. "Fourscore and seven years ago...."

34. A. Mr. Fontana, I hope, will arrive before 34.____
B. the beginning of the ceremonies; however,
C. if his plane is delayed, I have a substitute
D. speaker who can be here at a moments' notice.

35. A. Gladys wedding dress, a satin creation, 35.____
B. lay crumpled on the floor; her veil,
C. torn and streaked, lay nearby. "Jilted!"
D. shrieked Gladys. She was clearly annoyed.

36. A. Although it is poor grammar, the word 36.____
B. hopefully has become television's newest
C. pet expression; I hope (to use the correct
D. form) that it will soon pass from favor.

37. A. Plaza Apartment Hotel 37.____
B. 103 Tower road
C. Hampstead, Iowa 52025
D. March 13, 2021

38. A. Circulation Department 38.____
B. British History Illustrated
C. 3000 Walnut Street
D. Boulder Colorado 80302

39. A. Dear Sirs: 39.____
B. Last spring I ordered a subscription to your
C. magazine. I had read and enjoyed the May
D. issue containing the article titled "kings."

40. A. I have not however, received a 40.____
B. single issue. Will you check this?
C. Sincerely,
D. Maria Herrera

Questions 41-70.

DIRECTIONS: Questions 41 through 70 represent common grammatical concerns: subject-verb agreement, appropriate use of pronouns, and appropriate use of verbs. Read each sentence and indicate the letter of the grammatically CORRECT answer in the space at the right.

41. THE REIVERS, one of William Faulkner's last works, _____ made into a movie starring Steve McQueen. 41.____
A. has been B. have been C. are being D. were

42. He _____ on the ground, his eyes fastened on an ant slowly pushing a morsel of food toward the ant hill. 42.____
A. layed B. laid C. had laid D. lay

43. Nobody in the tri-cities _____ to admit that a flood could be disastrous. 43.____
A. are willing B. have been willing
C. is willing D. were willing

44. "_____," the senator asked, "have you convinced to run against the incumbent?" 44.____
A. Who B. Whom C. Whomever D. Womsoever

45. Of all the psychology courses that I took, Statistics 101 _____ the most demanding. 45.____
A. was B. are C. is D. were

46. Neither the conductor nor the orchestra members _____ the music to be applauded so enthusiastically. 46.____
A. were expecting
B. was expecting
C. is expected
D. has been expecting

47. The requirements for admission to the Lettermen's Club _____ posted outside the athletic director's office for months. 47.____
A. was B. was being C. has been D. have been

48. Please give me a list of the people _____ to compete in the kayak race. 48.____
A. whom you think have planned
B. who you think has planned
C. who you think is planning
D. who you think are planning

49. I saw Eloise and Abelard earlier today; _____ were riding around in a fancy 1956 MG. 49.____
A. she and him B. her and him C. she and he D. her and he

50. If you _____ the trunk in the attic, I'll unpack it later today. 50.____
A. can sit
B. are able to sit
C. can set
D. have sat

51. _____ all of the flour been used, or may I borrow three cups? 51.____
A. Have B. Has C. Is D. Could

52. In exasperation, the cycle shop's owner suggested that _____ there too long. 52.____
A. us boys were
B. we boys were
C. us boys had been
D. we boys had been

53. Idleness as well as money _____ the root of all evil. 53.____
A. have been
B. were to have been
C. is
D. are

54. Only the string players from the quartet—Gregory, Isaac, _____—remained after the concert to answer questions. 54.____
A. him, and I
B. he, and I
C. him, and me
D. he, and me

55. Of all the antiques that _____ for sale, Gertrude chose to buy a stupid glass thimble. 55.____
A. was
B. is
C. would have
D. were

56. The detective snapped, "Don't confuse me with theories about _____ you believe committed the crime!" 56._____
A. who B. whom C. whomever D. which

57. _____ when we first called, we might have avoided our present predicament. 57._____
A. The plumber's coming
B. If the plumber would have come
C. If the plumber had come
D. If the plumber was to have come

58. We thought the sun _____ in the north until we discovered that our compass was defective. 58._____
A. had rose
B. had risen
C. had rised
D. had raised

59. Each play of Shakespeare's _____ more than _____ share of memorable characters. 59._____
A. contain its
B. contains; its
C. contains; it's
D. contain; their

60. Our English teacher suggested to _____ seniors that either Tolstoy or Dickens _____ the outstanding novelist of the nineteenth century. 60._____
A. we; was considered
B. we; were considered
C. us; was considered
D. us; were considered

61. Sherlock Holmes, together with his great friend and companion Dr. Watson, _____ to aid the woman _____ had stumbled into the room. 61._____
A. has agreed; who
B. have agreed; whom
C. has agreed; whom
D. have agreed; who

62. Several of the deer _____ when they spotted my backpack _____ open in the meadow. 62._____
A. was frightened; laying
B. were frightened; lying
C. were frightened; laying
D. was frightened; lying

63. After the Scholarship Committee announces _____ selection, hysterics often _____. 63._____
A. it's; occur
B. its; occur
C. their; occur
D. their; occurs

64. I _____ the key on the table last night so you and _____ could find it. 64._____
A. layed; her
B. lay; she
C. laid; she
D. laid; her

65. Some of the antelope _____ wandered away from the meadow where the rancher _____ the block of salt. 65._____
A. has; sat
B. has; set
C. have; had set
D. has; sets

66. Macaroni and cheese _____ best to us (that is, to Andy and _____) when Mother adds extra cheddar cheese. 66._____
  A. tastes; I
  B. tastes; me
  C. taste; me
  D. taste; I

67. Frank said, "It must have been _____ called the phone company." 67._____
  A. she who
  B. she whom
  C. her who
  D. her whom

68. The herd _____ moving restlessly at every bolt of lightning; it was either Ted or _____ who saw the beginning of the stampede. 68._____
  A. was; me
  B. were; I
  C. was; I
  D. have been; me

69. The foreman _____ his lateness by saying that his alarm clock _____ until six minutes before eight. 69._____
  A. explains; had not rang
  B. explained; has not rung
  C. has explained; rung
  D. explained; hadn't rung

70. Of all the coaches, Ms. Cox is the only one who _____ that Sherry dives more gracefully than _____. 70._____
  A. is always saying; I
  B. is always saying; me
  C. are always saying; I
  D. were always saying; me

Questions 71-90.

DIRECTIONS: Choose the word in Questions 71 through 90 that is MOST opposite in meaning to the italicized word.

71. *fact* 71._____
  A. statistic
  B. statement
  C. incredible
  D. conjecture

72. *stiff* 72._____
  A. fastidious
  B. babble
  C. supple
  D. apprehensive

73. *blunt* 73._____
  A. concise B. tactful C. artistic D. humble

74. *foreign* 74._____
  A. pertinent B. comely C. strange D. scrupulous

75. *anger* 75._____
  A. infer B. pacify C. taint D. revile

76. *frank* 76._____
  A. earnest B. reticent C. post D. expensive

77. *secure* 77.____
A. precarious B. acquire C. moderate D. frenzied

78. *petty* 78.____
A. harmonious B. careful
C. forthright D. momentous

79. *concede* 79.____
A. dispute B. reciprocate
C. subvert D. propagate

80. *benefit* 80.____
A. liquidation B. bazaar
C. detriment D. profit

81. *capricious* 81.____
A. preposterous B. constant
C. diabolical D. careless

82. *boisterous* 82.____
A. devious B. valiant C. girlish D. taciturn

83. *harmony* 83.____
A. congruence B. discord C. chagrin D. melody

84. *laudable* 84.____
A. auspicious B. despicable
C. acclaimed D. doubtful

85. *adherent* 85.____
A. partisan B. stoic C. renegade D. recluse

86. *exuberant* 86.____
A. frail B. corpulent C. austere D. bigot

87. *spurn* 87.____
A. accede B. flail C. efface D. annihilate

88. *spontaneous* 88.____
A. hapless B. corrosive
C. intentional D. willful

89. *disparage* 89.____
A. abolish B. exude C. incriminate D. extol

90. *timorous* 90.____
A. succinct B. chaste C. audacious D. insouciant

KEY (CORRECT ANSWERS)

1.	D	21.	A	41.	A	61.	A	81.	B
2.	C	22.	B	42.	D	62.		82.	D
3.	B	23.	C	43.	C	63.	B	83.	B
4.	C	24.	B	44.	B	64.	C	84.	B
5.	C	25.	C	45.	A	65.	C	85.	C
6.	C	26.	C	46.	A	66.	B	86.	C
7.	B	27.	D	47.	D	67.	A	87.	A
8.	B	28.	B	48.	A	68.	C	88.	C
9.	A	29.	B	49.	C	69.	D	89.	D
10.	C	30.	C	50.	C	70.	A	90.	C
11.	C	31.	A	51.	B	71.	D		
12.	D	32.	B	52.	D	72.	C		
13.	C	33.	B	53.	C	73.	B		
14.	C	34.	D	54.	B	74.	A		
15.	A	35.	A	55.	D	75.	B		
16.	C	36.	B	56.	B	76.	B		
17.	A	37.	B	57.	C	77.	A		
18.	D	38.	D	58.	B	78.	D		
19.	B	39.	D	59.	B	79.	A		
20.	B	40.	A	60.	C	80.	C		

EXAMINATION SECTION

TEST 1

DIRECTIONS: Each question or incomplete statement is followed by several suggested answers or completions. Select the one that BEST answers the question or completes the statement. *PRINT THE LETTER OF THE CORRECT ANSWER IN THE SPACE AT THE RIGHT.*

Questions 1-25.

DIRECTIONS: Select the word with the MOST appropriate meaning for the italicized word in each of Questions 1 through 25.

1. The directions were *explicit*. 1.____
   A. petulant B. satiric C. awkward
   D. unequivocal E. foreign

2. The teacher explained *mutability*. 2.____
   A. change B. harmony C. annihilation
   D. ethics E. candor

3. He was a *secular* man. 3.____
   A. holy B. evil C. worldly
   D. superior E. small

4. They submitted a list of their *progeny*. 4.____
   A. experiments B. books C. holdings
   D. theories E. offspring

5. She admired his *sententious* replies. 5.____
   A. simple B. pithy C. coherent
   D. lucid E. inane

6. He believed in the ancient *dogma*. 6.____
   A. priest B. prophet C. seer
   D. doctrine E. ruler

7. They studied a Grecian *archetype*. 7.____
   A. model B. urn C. epic D. ode E. play

8. The *insurrection* was described on the front page. 8.____
   A. surgery B. pageant C. ceremony
   D. game E. revolt

9. He was known for his *procrastination*. 9.____
   A. justification B. learning C. delay
   D. ambition E. background

10. The doctor analyzed the *toxic* ingredients. 10.____
    A. poisonous B. anemic C. trivial
    D. obscure E. distinct

11. It was a *portentous* occurrence. 11.____
    A. pleasant B. decisive C. ominous
    D. monetary E. hearty

12. His *espousal* of the plan was applauded. 12.____
    A. explanation B. rejection C. ridicule
    D. adoption E. revision

13. Her condition was *lachrymose*. 13.____
    A. improved B. tearful C. hopeful
    D. precocious E. tenuous

14. It was a *precarious* situation. 14.____
    A. uncomplicated B. peaceful C. precise
    D. uncertain E. precipitous

15. He was lost in a *reverie*. 15.____
    A. chancery B. dream C. forest
    D. cavern E. tarn

16. The hero was a young *gallant*. 16.____
    A. suitor B. fool C. gull
    D. lawyer E. executive

17. Their practices were *nefarious*. 17.____
    A. unprofitable B. ignorant C. multifarious
    D. wicked E. wishful

18. He insisted upon the *proviso*. 18.____
    A. stipulation B. pronunciation C. examination
    D. supply E. equipment

19. The spirit came from the *nether* regions. 19.____
    A. frozen B. lower C. lost
    D. bright E. mysterious

20. His actions were *malevolent*. 20.____
    A. unassuming B. silent C. evil
    D. peaceful E. constructive

21. He had a *florid* complexion. 21.____
    A. sanguine B. pallid C. fair
    D. sickly E. normal

22. The lawyer explained the legal *parlance*. 22.____
   A. action B. maneuver C. situation
   D. language E. procedure

23. They were present at the *interment*. 23.____
   A. concert B. trial C. embarkation
   D. burial E. performance

24. He made a *moot* point. 24.____
   A. definite B. sensible C. debatable
   D. strong E. correct

25. They carefully examined the *cryptic* message. 25.____
   A. occult B. legible C. valid
   D. familiar E. warning

Questions 26-40.

DIRECTIONS: Indicate the number of syllables in each of the following words.

26. vicissitude 26.____

27. blown 27.____

28. maintenance 28.____

29. symbolization 29.____

30. athletics 30.____

31. actually 31.____

32. friend 32.____

33. perseverance 33.____

34. physiology 34.____

35. pronunciation 35.____

36. vacuum 36.____

37. sophomore 37.____

38. opportunity 38.____

39. hungry 39.____

40. temperament 40.____

Questions 41-60.

DIRECTIONS: Indicate the one misspelled work in each of the following Questions 41 through 60 by indicating the letter of the misspelled word in the space at the right.

41. A. holiday B. noticeable C. fourty D. miniature E. yeast 41.____

42. A. grievance B. murmur C. occurance D. business E. captain 42.____

43. A. succeed B. vegatable C. pleasant D. picnicking E. shepherd 43.____

44. A. psychology B. plebian C. exercise D. fiery E. concise 44.____

45. A. ninety B. optimistic C. professor D. repitition E. siege 45.____

46. A. tarriff B. absence C. grammar D. license E. balloon 46.____

47. A. dissipation B. ecstasy C. prarie D. marriage E. consistent 47.____

48. A. supersede B. twelfth C. vacillate D. playright E. expense 48.____

49. A. fundamental B. government C. accomodate D. cafeteria E. surely 49.____

50. A. cemetary B. indispensable C. dormitory D. environment E. divine 50.____

51. A. irritible B. permissible C. irresistible D. rhythmical E. source 51.____

52. A. interprete B. opinion C. guard D. familiar E. possible 52.____

53. A. conscience B. existence C. loneliness D. leisure E. exhileration 53.____

54. A. villian B. weird C. seize D. tragedy E. crystal 54.____

55. A. develop B. bachelor C. dilemma D. operate E. synonym 55.____

56. A. university B. connoiseur C. aisle 56.____
D. transferred E. division

57. A. zoology B. conscious C. aptitude 57.____
D. restaurant E. sacriligious

58. A. tendency B. vital C. analyze 58.____
D. consistant E. proceed

59. A. proceedure B. surround C. disastrous 59.____
D. beginning E. arrival

60. A. encrease B. pursuing C. necessary 50.____
D. tyranny E. strength

Questions 61-80.

DIRECTIONS: Indicate the part of speech for each italicized word in the following sentences by selecting the letter of the part of speech from the key above each set of questions.

A. Noun
B. Pronoun
C. Verb
D. Adjective
E. Adverb

61. You are entirely *wrong*. 61.____

62. On *Sunday*, we will attend church. 62.____

63. *That* is the main problem. 63.____

64. He was invited to the party, *Saturday*. 64.____

65. I shall introduce a *technical* term. 65.____

66. It was a *novel* turn of events. 66.____

67. He wanted *that* gift for himself. 67.____

68. A few definitions will help *us* to understand. 68.____

69. He let them reach their own *conclusions*. 69.____

70. I must ask *you* to remain silent. 70.____

A. Preposition
B. Conjunction
C. Pronoun
D. Adverb
E. Adjective

71. *This* is a stupid answer. 71.____

72. He solved the mystery *without* the police. 72.____

73. She felt *secure* in his protection, 73.____

74. He believed in the *scientific* method. 74.____

75. Do not destroy their *traditional* beliefs. 75.____

76. They chartered the bus, *but* they did not go. 76.____

77. The young men are *quiet* with fear. 77.____

78. She talked *cheerfully* to the visitors. 78.____

79. The candidate was *certain* of victory. 79.____

80. I hope you will take *that* with you. 80.____

Questions 81-100.

DIRECTIONS: Indicate the use of each italicized word in the following sentences by choosing the letter of the CORRECT usage from the key above each set of questions.

A. Subject of Verb
B. Predicate Nominative or Subjective Complement
C. Predicate Adjective
D. Direct Object of Verb
E. Indirect Object of Verb

81. They made *him* president of the club. 81.____

82. There was nothing *odd* about the situation. 82.____

83. Give them *time* enough for thought. 83.____

84. He supervised the *work* himself. 84.____

85. Will you do *me* a favor? 85.____

86. The salad dressing tasted *good.* 86.____

87. In the crash, the *body* was thrown forward. 87._____

88. On a bench in the park was a single *man.* 88._____

89. There were two *men* who carried the trunk. 89._____

90. I am older than *you.* 90._____

A. Object of Preposition
B. Subject of Infinitive
C. Direct Object of Verb
D. Indirect Object of Verb
E. Predicate Nominative or Subjective Complement

91. Let *them* suffer the consequences. 91._____

92. Offer *them* the key to the apartment. 92._____

93. He heard the *bell* ring. 93._____

94. Let *us* try another solution. 94._____

95. No one except *John* had volunteered. 95._____

96. Show *us* one example of your style. 96._____

97. Will you send *her* the flowers? 97._____

98. I want *you* to take her home. 98._____

99. He told his *father* that he would obey. 99._____

100. Do not write on the second *page.* 100._____

Questions 101-115.

DIRECTIONS: Indicate the kind of verbal italicized in the following sentences by choosing the appropriate letter from the key below.

A. Gerund
B. Participle
C. Infinitive

101. The manuscript, *corrected* and typed, was on the desk. 101._____

102. He heard the bullet *ricochet.* 102._____

103. *Finding* the answer is a difficult task. 103._____

104. The animal, *hidden* from view, was trembling. 104.____

105. *Pretending* to be asleep, he listened attentively. 105.____

106. The professor, a *qualified* lecturer, entered the room. 106.____

107. They enjoyed *camping* at the lake. 107.____

108. Let them *come* to me. 108.____

109. He was annoyed by the *buzzing* sound. 109.____

110. It was a *stimulating* performance. 110.____

111. He had an accident while *returning* to the city. 111.____

112. *Encouraged* to study, the class opened the books. 112.____

113. He heard the gun *explode*. 113.____

114. They called him the *forgotten* man. 114.____

115. *Realizing* his mistake, he apologized. 115.____

Questions 116-130.

DIRECTIONS: Indicate the CORRECT punctuation for the following sentences by choosing the letter of the correct punctuation from the key below where brackets appear.

A. Comma
B. Semicolon
C. Colon
D. Dash
E. No punctuation

116. He explained [ ] that he could not attend. 116.____

117. The executive [ ] prepared for the interview and entered the room. 117.____

118. She admitted [ ] that the suggestion was wrong. 118.____

119. He did not object [ ] to dealing with him. 119.____

120. The chairman disagreed [ ] the members did not. 120.____

121. You must report to duty on November 10 [ ] 2022. 121.____

122. The father [ ] and two sons went fishing. 122.____

123. Act on the following problems [ ] administration, supervision, and policy. 123.____

124. This is excellent [ ] it has insight. 124.____

125. "I will take the car [ ]" he said. 125.____

126. I will do it [ ] however, you must help me. 126.____

127. When the show ended [ ] he returned home. 127.____

128. Stop [ ] making all of that noise. 128.____

129. Be firm [ ] exercise your authority. 129.____

130. The first example is poor [ ] the second is good. 130.____

Questions 131-150.

DIRECTIONS: Place a *C* in the space at the right if the sentence is correctly punctuated and a *W* in the space at the right if the sentence is incorrectly punctuated.

131. Its later than you think. 131.____

132. While I was eating the toast burned. 132.____

133. The fire started at ten o'clock in the morning. 133.____

134. She asked, "Did you say, 'I will go?" 134.____

135. Richards handling of the question warranted praise. 135.____

136. July 4 is a holiday. 136.____

137. Oh perhaps you are right. 137.____

138. Will you answer the door, John? 138.____

139. While he was bathing the dog came in. 139.____

140. He was a calm gentle person. 140.____

141. He wore a new bow tie. 141.____

142. The shout "Block that kick" echoed upon the field. 142.____

143. Ladies and gentlemen take your seats. 143.____

144. However you must do your work. 144.____

145. My brothers are: John, Bill, and Charles. 145.____

146. While I was painting the neighbor opened the door. 146.____

147. One should fight for honor: not fame. 147.____

148. "Will you sing" he asked? 148.____

149. He played tennis, and then bowled. 149.____

150. On Monday April 5, we leave for Europe. 150.____

11 (#1)

KEY (CORRECT ANSWERS)

1.	D	31.	4	61.	D	91.	C	121.	A
2.	A	32.	1	62.	A	92.	D	122.	E
3.	C	33.	4	63.	B	93.	C	123.	C
4.	E	34.	5	64.	A	94.	C	124.	D
5.	B	35.	5	65.	D	95.	A	125.	A
6.	D	36.	2	66.	D	96.	C	126.	B
7.	A	37.	3	67.	D	97.	C	127.	A
8.	E	38.	5	68.	B	98.	C	128.	E
9.	C	39.	2	69.	A	99.	C	129.	B
10.	A	40.	3	70.	B	100.	A	130.	B
11.	C	41.	C	71.	C	101.	B	131.	W
12.	D	42.	C	72.	A	102.	B	132.	W
13.	B	43.	B	73.	D	103.	A	133.	C
14.	D	44.	B	74.	E	104.	B	134.	W
15.	B	45.	D	75.	E	105.	A	135.	W
16.	A	46.	A	76.	B	106.	B	136.	C
17.	D	47.	C	77.	E	107.	A	137.	W
18.	A	48.	D	78.	D	108.	C	138.	C
19.	B	49.	C	79.	E	109.	B	139.	W
20.	C	50.	A	80.	C	110.	B	140.	W
21.	A	51.	A	81.	D	111.	A	141.	C
22.	D	52.	A	82.	C	112.	B	142.	W
23.	D	53.	E	83.	D	113.	C	143.	W
24.	C	54.	A	84.	D	114.	B	144.	W
25.	A	55.	C	85.	E	115.	A	145.	W
26.	3	56.	B	86.	C	116.	E	143.	W
27.	1	57.	E	87.	A	117.	E	147.	W
28.	3	58.	D	88.	B	118.	E	148.	W
29.	5	59.	A	89.	A	119.	E	149.	W
30.	3	60.	A	90.	C	120.	B	150.	W

EXAMINATION SECTION

TEST 1

DIRECTIONS: Each question or incomplete statement is followed by several suggested answers or completions. Select the one that BEST answers the question or completes the statement. *PRINT THE LETTER OF THE CORRECT ANSWER IN THE SPACE AT THE RIGHT.*

1. Which of the following sentences is punctuated INCORRECTLY? 1.____
   A. Johnson said, "One tiny virus, Blanche, can multiply so fast that it will become 200 viruses in 25 minutes."
   B. With economic pressures hitting them from all sides, American farmers have become the weak link in the food chain.
   C. The degree to which this is true, of course, depends on the personalities of the people involved, the subject matter, and the atmosphere in general.
   D. "What loneliness, asked George Eliot, is more lonely than distrust?"

2. Which of the following sentences is punctuated INCORRECTLY? 2.____
   A. Based on past experiences, do you expect the plumber to show up late, not have the right parts, and overcharge you.
   B. When polled, however, the participants were most concerned that it be convenient.
   C. No one mentioned the flavor of the coffee, and no one seemed to care that china was used instead of plastic.
   D. As we said before, sometimes people view others as things; they don't see them as living, breathing beings like themselves.

3. Convention members travelled here from Kingston New York Pittsfield Massachusetts Bennington Vermont and Hartford Connecticut. 3.____
   How many commas should there be in the above sentence?
   A. 3 B. 4 C. 5 D. 6

4. Of the two speakers the one who spoke about human rights is more famous and more humble. 4.____
   How many commas should there be in the above sentence?
   A. 1 B. 2 C. 3 D. 4

5. Which sentence is punctuated INCORRECTLY? 5.____
   A. Five people voted no; two voted yes; one person abstained.
   B. Well, consider what has been said here today, but we won't make any promises.
   C. Anthropologists divide history into three major periods: the Stone Age, the Bronze Age, and the Iron Age.
   D. Therefore, we may create a stereotype about people who are unsuccessful; we may see them as lazy, unintelligent, or afraid of success.

6. Which sentence is punctuated INCORRECTLY? 6.____
   A. Studies have found that the unpredictability of customer behavior can lead to a great deal of stress, particularly if the behavior is unpleasant or if the employee has little control over it.
   B. If this degree of emotion and variation can occur in spectator sports, imagine the role that perceptions can play when there are real stakes involved.
   C. At other times, however hidden expectations may sabotage or severely damage an encounter without anyone knowing what happened.
   D. There are usually four issues to look for in a conflict: differences in values, goals, methods, and facts.

Questions 7-10.

DIRECTIONS: Questions 7 through 10 test your ability to distinguish between words that sound alike but are spelled differently and have different meanings. In the following groups of sentences, one of the underlined words is used incorrectly.

7. 7.____
   A. By accepting responsibility for their actions, managers promote trust.
   B. Dropping hints or making illusions to things that you would like changed sometimes leads to resentment.
   C. The entire unit loses respect for the manager and resents the reprimand.
   D. Many people are averse to confronting problems directly; they would rather avoid them.

8. 8.____
   A. What does this say about the effect our expectations have on those we supervise?
   B. In an effort to save time between 9 A.M. and 1 P.M., the staff members devised their own interpretation of what was to be done on these forms.
   C. The taskmaster's principal concern is for getting the work done; he or she is not concerned about the need or interests of employees.
   D. The advisor's main objective was increasing Angela's ability to invest her capitol wisely.

9. 9.____
   A. A typical problem is that people have to cope with the internal censer of their feelings.
   B. Sometimes, in their attempt to sound more learned, people speak in ways that are barely comprehensible.
   C. The council will meet next Friday to decide whether Abrams should continue as representative.
   D. His descent from grace was assured by that final word.

10. 10.____
   A. The doctor said that John's leg had to remain stationary or it would not heal properly.
   B. There is a city ordinance against parking too close to fire hydrants.
   C. Meyer's problem is that he is never discrete when talking about office politics.
   D. Mrs. Thatcher probably worked harder than any other British Prime Minister had ever worked.

Questions 11-20.

DIRECTIONS: For each of the following groups of sentences in Questions 11 through 20, select the sentence which is the BEST example of English usage and grammar.

11. A. She is a woman who, at age sixty, is distinctly attractive and cares about how they look. 11.____
    B. It was a seemingly impossible search, and no one knew the problems better than she.
    C. On the surface, they are all sweetness and light, but his morbid character is under it.
    D. The minicopier, designed to appeal to those who do business on the run like architects in the field or business travelers, weigh about four pounds.

12. A. Neither the administrators nor the union representative regret the decision to settle the disagreement. 12.____
    B. The plans which are made earlier this year were no longer being considered.
    C. I would have rode with him if I had known he was leaving at five.
    D. I don't know who she said had it.

13. A. Writing at a desk, the memo was handed to her for immediate attention. 13.____
    B. Carla didn't water Carl's plants this week, which she never does.
    C. Not only are they good workers, with excellent writing and speaking skills, and they get to the crux of any problem we hand them.
    D. We've noticed that this enthusiasm for undertaking new projects sometimes interferes with his attention to detail.

14. A. It's obvious that Nick offends people by being unruly, inattentive, and having no patience. 14.____
    B. Marcia told Genie that she would have to leave soon.
    C. Here are the papers you need to complete your investigation.
    D. Julio was startled by you're comment.

15. A. The new manager has done good since receiving her promotion, but her secretary has helped her a great deal. 15.____
    B. One of the personnel managers approached John and tells him that the client arrived unexpectedly.
    C. If somebody can supply us with the correct figures, they should do so immediately.
    D. Like zealots, advocates seek power because they want to influence the policies and actions of an organization.

16. A. Between you and me, Chris probably won't finish this assignment in time. 16.___
B. Rounding the corner, the snack bar appeared before us.
C. Parker's radical reputation made to the Supreme Court his appointment impossible.
D. By the time we arrived, Marion finishes briefing James and returns to Hank's office.

17. A. As we pointed out earlier, the critical determinant of the success of middle managers is their ability to communicate well with others. 17.____
B. The lecturer stated there wasn't no reason for bad supervision.
C. We are well aware whose at fault in this instance.
D. When planning important changes, it's often wise to seek the participation of others because employees often have much valuable ideas to offer.

18. A. Joan had ought to throw out those old things that were damaged when the roof leaked. 18.____
B. I spose he'll let us know what he's decided when he finally comes to a decision.
C. Carmen was walking to work when she suddenly realized that she had left her lunch on the table as she passed the market.
D. Are these enough plants for your new office?

19. A. First move the lever forward, and then they should lift the ribbon casing before trying to take it out. 19.____
B. Michael finished quickest than any other person in the office.
C. There is a special meeting for we committee members today at 4 p.m.
D. My husband is worried about our having to work overtime next week.

20. A. Another source of conflicts are individuals who possess very poor interpersonal skills. 20.____
B. It is difficult for us to work with him on projects because these kinds of people are not interested in team building.
C. Each of the departments was represented at the meeting.
D. Poor boy, he never should of past that truck on the right.

Questions 21-28.

DIRECTIONS: In Questions 21 through 28, there may be a problem with English grammar or usage. If a problem does exist, select the letter that indicates the most effective change. If no problem exists, select Choice A.

21. He rushed her to the hospital and stayed with her, even though this took quite a bit of his time, he didn't charge her anything. 21.____
A. No changes are necessary.
B. Change <u>even though</u> to <u>although</u>
C. Change the first comma to a period and capitalize <u>even</u>
D. Change <u>rushed</u> to <u>had rushed</u>

22. Waiting that appears unfairly feels longer than waiting that seems justified. 22.____
    A. No changes are necessary.
    B. Change unfairly to unfair
    C. Change appears to seems
    D. Change longer to longest

23. May be you and the person who argued with you will be able to reach an agreement. 23.____
    A. No changes are necessary
    B. Change will be to were
    C. Change argued with to had an argument with
    D. Change May be to Maybe

24. Any one of them could of taken the file while you were having coffee. 24.____
    A. No changes are necessary
    B. Change any one to anyone
    C. Change of to have
    D. Change were having to were out having

25. While people get jobs or move from poverty level to better paying employment, they stop receiving benefits and start paying taxes. 25.____
    A. No changes are necessary
    B. Change While to As
    C. Change stop to will stop
    D. Change get to obtain

26. Maribeth's phone rang while talking to George about the possibility of their meeting Tom at three this afternoon. 26.____
    A. No changes are necessary
    B. Change their to her
    C. Move to George so that it follows Tom
    D. Change talking to she was talking

27. According to their father, Lisa is smarter than Chris, but Emily is the smartest of the three sisters. 27.____
    A. No changes are necessary
    B. Change their to her
    C. Change is to was
    D. Make two sentences, changing the second comma to a period and omitting but

28. Yesterday, Mark and he claim that Carl took Carol's ideas and used them inappropriately. 28.____
    A. No changes are necessary
    B. Change claim to claimed
    C. Change inappropriately to inappropriate
    D. Change Carol's to Carols'

Questions 29-34.

DIRECTIONS: For each group of sentences in Questions 29 through 34, select the choice that represents the BEST editing of the problem sentence.

29. The managers expected employees to be at their desks at all times, but they would always be late or leave unannounced. 29.____
   A. The managers wanted employees to always be at their desks, but they would always be late or leave unannounced.
   B. Although the managers expected employees to be at their desks no matter what came up, they would always be late and leave without telling anyone.
   C. Although the managers expected employees to be at their desks at all times, the managers would always be late or leave without telling anyone.
   D. The managers expected the employee to never leave their desks, but they would always be late or leave without telling anyone.

30. The one who is department manager he will call you to discuss the problem tomorrow morning at 10 A.M. 30.____
   A. The one who is department manager will call you tomorrow morning at ten to discuss the problem.
   B. The department manager will call you to discuss the problem tomorrow at 10 A.M.
   C. Tomorrow morning at 10 A.M., the department manager will call you to discuss the problem.
   D. Tomorrow morning the department manager will call you to discuss the problem.

31. A conference on child care in the workplace the $200 cost of which to attend may be prohibitive to childcare workers who earn less than that weekly. 31.____
   A. A conference on child care in the workplace that costs $200 may be too expensive for childcare workers who earn less than that each week.
   B. A conference on child care in the workplace, the cost of which to attend is $200, may be prohibitive to childcare workers who earn less than that weekly.
   C. A conference on child care in the workplace who costs $200 may be too expensive for childcare workers who earn less than that a week.
   D. A conference on child care in the workplace which costs $200 may be too expensive to childcare workers who earn less than that on a weekly basis.

32. In accordance with estimates recently made, there are 40,000 to 50,000 nuclear weapons in our world today. 32.____
   A. Because of estimates recently, there are 40,000 to 50,000 nuclear weapons in the world today.
   B. In accordance with estimates made recently, there are 40,000 to 50,000 nuclear weapons in the world today.

C. According to estimates made recently, there are 40,000 to 50,000 weapons in the world today.
D. According to recent estimates, there are 40,000 to 50,000 nuclear weapons in the world today.

33. Motivation is important in problem solving, but they say that excessive motivation can inhibit the creative process. 33.____
A. Motivation is important in problem solving, but, as they say, too much of it can inhibit the creative process.
B. Motivation is important in problem solving and excessive motivation will inhibit the creative process.
C. Motivation is important in problem solving, but excessive motivation can inhibit the creative process.
D. Motivation is important in problem solving because excessive motivation can inhibit the creative process.

34. In selecting the best option calls for consulting with all the people that are involved in it. 34.____
A. In selecting the best option consulting with all people concerned with it.
B. Calling for the best option, we consulted all the affected people.
C. We called all the people involved to select the best option.
D. To be sure of selecting the best option, one should consult all the people involved.

35. There are a number of problems with the following letter. From the options below, select the version that is MOST in accordance with standard business style, tone, and form. 35.____

Dear Sir:

We are so sorry that we have had to backorder your order for 15,000 widgets and 2,300 whatzits for such a long time. We have been having incredibly bad luck lately. When your order first came in no one could get to it because my secretary was out with the flu and her replacement didn't know what she was doing, then there was the dock strike in Cucamonga which held things up for awhile, and then it just somehow got lost. We think it may have fallen behind the radiator.

We are happy to say that all these problems have been taken care of, we are caught up on supplies, and we should have the stuff to you soon, in the near future—about two weeks. You may not believe us after everything you've been through with us, but it's true.

We'll let you know as soon as we have a secure date for delivery. Thank you so much for continuing to do business with us after all the problems this probably has caused you.

Yours very sincerely,
Rob Barker

8 (#1)

A. Dear Sir:

We are so sorry that we have had to backorder your order for 15,000 widgets and 2,300 whatzits. We have been having problems with staff lately and the dock strike hasn't helped anything.

We are happy to say that all these problems have been taken care of. I've told my secretary to get right on it, and we should have the stuff to you soon. Thank you so much for continuing to do business with us after all the problems this must have caused you.

We'll let you know as soon as we have a secure date for delivery.

Sincerely,
Rob Barker

B. Dear Sir:

We regret that we haven't been able to fill your order for 15,000 widgets and 2,300 whatzits in a timely fashion.

We'll let you know as soon as we have a secure date for delivery.

Sincerely,
Rob Barker

C. Dear Sir:

We are so very sorry that we haven't been able to fill your order for 15,000 widgets and 2,300 whatzits. We have been having incredibly bad luck lately, but things are much better now.

Thank you so much for bearing with us through all of this. We'll let you know as soon as we have a secure date for delivery.

Sincerely,
Rob Barker

D. Dear Sir:

We are very sorry that we haven't been able to fill your order for 15,000 widgets and 2,300 whatzits. Due to unforeseen difficulties, we have had to back-order your request. At this time, supplies have caught up to demand, and we foresee a delivery date within the next two weeks.

We'll let you know as soon as we have a secure date for delivery. Thank you for your patience.

Sincerely,
Rob Barker

KEY (CORRECT ANSWERS)

1.	D	11.	B	21.	C	31.	A
2.	A	12.	D	22.	B	32.	D
3.	B	13.	D	23.	D	33.	C
4.	A	14.	C	24.	C	34.	D
5.	B	15.	D	25.	B	35.	D
6.	C	16.	A	26.	D		
7.	B	17.	A	27.	A		
8.	D	18.	D	28.	B		
9.	A	19.	D	29.	C		
10.	C	20.	C	30.	B		

EXAMINATION SECTION

TEST 1

DIRECTIONS: In each of the following questions, only one of the four sentences conforms to standards of correct usage. The other three contain errors in grammar, diction, or punctuation. Select the choice in each question which BEST conforms to standards of correct usage. Consider a choice correct if it contains none of the errors mentioned above, even though there may be other ways of expressing the same thought. *PRINT THE LETTER OF THE CORRECT ANSWER IN THE SPACE AT THE RIGHT.*

1. A. Because he was ill was no excuse for his behavior 1.____
   B. I insist that he see a lawyer before he goes to trial.
   C. He said "that he had not intended to go."
   D. He wasn't out of the office only three days.

2. A. He came to the station and pays a porter to carry his bags into the train. 2.____
   B. I should have liked to live in medieval times.
   C. My father was born in Linville. A little country town where everybody knows everyone else.
   D. The car, which is parked across the street, is disabled.

3. A. He asked the desk clerk for a clean, quiet, room. 3.____
   B. I expected James to be lonesome and that he would want to go home.
   C. I have stopped worrying because I have heard nothing further on the subject.
   D. If the board of directors controls the company, they may take actions which are disapproved by the stockholders.

4. A. Each of the players knew their place. 4.____
   B. He whom you saw on the stage is the son of an actor.
   C. Susan is the smartest of the twin sisters.
   D. Who ever thought of him winning both prizes?

5. A. An outstanding trait of early man was their reliance on omens. 5.____
   B. Because I had never been there before.
   C. Neither Mr. Jones nor Mr. Smith has completed his work.
   D. While eating my dinner, a dog came to the window.

6. A. A copy of the lease, in addition to the Rules and Regulations, are to be given to each tenant. 6.____
   B. The Rules and Regulations and a copy of the lease is being given to each tenant.
   C. A copy of the lease, in addition to the Rules and Regulations, is to be given to each tenant.
   D. A copy of the lease, in addition to the Rules and Regulations, are being given to each tenant.

7. A. Although we understood that for him music was a passion, we were disturbed by the fact that he was addicted to sing along with the soloists. 7.____
   B. Do you believe that Steven is liable to win a scholarship?
   C. Give the picture to whomever is a connoisseur of art.
   D. Whom do you believe to be the most efficient worker in the office?

8. A. Each adult who is sure they know all the answers will some day realize their mistake. 8.____
   B. Even the most hardhearted villain would have to feel bad about so horrible a tragedy.
   C. Neither being licensed teachers, both aspirants had to pass rigorous tests before being appointed.
   D. The principal reason why he wanted to be designated was because he had never before been to a convention.

9. A. Being that the weather was so inclement, the party has been postponed for at least a month. 9.____
   B. He is in New York City only three weeks and he has already seen all the thrilling sights in Manhattan and in the other four boroughs.
   C. If you will look it up in the official directory, which can be consulted in the library during specified hours, you will discover that the chairman and director are Mr. T. Henry Long.
   D. Working hard at college during the day and at the post office during the night, he appeared to his family to be indefatigable.

10. A. I would have been happy to oblige you if you only asked me to do it. 10.____
    B. The cold weather, as well as the unceasing wind and rain, have made us decide to spend the winter in Florida.
    C. The politician would have been more successful in winning office if he would have been less dogmatic.
    D. These trousers are expensive; however, they will wear well.

11. A. All except him wore formal attire at the reception for the ambassador. 11.____
    B. If that chair were to be blown off of the balcony, it might injure someone below.
    C. Not a passenger, who was in the crash, survived the impact.
    D. To borrow money off friends is the best way to lose them.

12. A. Approaching Manhattan on the ferry boat from Staten Island, an unforgettable sight of the skyscrapers is seen. 12.____
    B. Did you see the exhibit of modernistic paintings as yet?
    C. Gesticulating wildly and ranting in stentorian tones, the speaker was the sinecure of all eyes.
    D. The airplane with crew and passengers was lost somewhere in the Pacific Ocean.

13. A. If one has consistently had that kind of training, it is certainly too late to change your entire method of swimming long distances. 13.____
    B. The captain would have been more impressed if you would have been more conscientious in evacuation drills.
    C. The passengers on the stricken ship were all ready to abandon it at the signal.
    D. The villainous shark lashed at the lifeboat with it's tail, trying to upset the rocking boat in order to partake of it's contents.

14. A. As one whose been certified as a professional engineer, I believe that the decision to build a bridge over that harbor is unsound. 14.____
    B. Between you and me, this project ought to be completed long before winter arrives.
    C. He fervently hoped that the men would be back at camp and to find them busy at their usual chores.
    D. Much to his surprise, he discovered that the climate of Korea was like his home town.

15. A. An industrious executive is aided, not impeded, by having a hobby which gives him a fresh point of view on life and its problems. 15.____
    B. Frequent absence during the calendar year will surely mitigate against the chances of promotion.
    C. He was unable to go to the committee meeting because he was very ill.
    D. Mr. Brown expressed his disapproval so emphatically that his associates were embarassed

16. A. At our next session, the office manager will have told you something about his duties and responsibilities. 16.____
    B. In general, the book is absorbing and original and have no hesitation about recommending it.
    C. The procedures followed by private industry in dealing with lateness and absence are different from ours.
    D We shall treat confidentially any information about Mr. Doe, to whom we understand you have sent reports to for many years.

17. A. I talked to one official, whom I knew was fully impartial. 17.____
    B. Everyone signed the petition but him.
    C. He proved not only to be a good student but also a good athlete.
    D. All are incorrect.

18. A. Every year a large amount of tenants are admitted to housing projects. 18.____
    B. Henry Ford owned around a billion dollars in industrial equipment.
    C. He was aggravated by the child's poor behavior.
    D. All are incorrect.

19. A. Before he was committed to the asylum he suffered from the illusion that he was Napoleon. 19.____
    B. Besides stocks, there were also bonds in the safe.
    C. We bet the other team easily.
    D. All are incorrect.

20. A. Bring this report to your supervisory. 20.____
    B. He set the chair down near the table.
    C. The capitol of New York is Albany.
    D. All are incorrect.

21. A. He was chosen to arbitrate the dispute because everyone knew he would be disinterested. 21.____
    B. It is advisable to obtain the best council before making an important decision.
    C. Less college students are interested in teaching than ever before.
    D. All are incorrect.

22. A. She, hearing a signal, the source lamp flashed. 22.____
    B. While hearing a signal, the source lamp flashed.
    C. In hearing a signal, the source lamp flashed.
    D. As she heard a signal, the source lamp flashed.

23. A. Every one of the time records have been initialed in the designated spaces. 23.____
    B. All of the time records has been initialed in the designated spaces.
    C. Each one of the time records was initialed in the designated spaces.
    D. The time records all been initialed in the designated spaces.

24. A. If there is no one else to answer the phone, you will have to answer it. 24.____
    B. You will have to answer it yourself if no one else answers the phone.
    C. If no one else is not around to pick up the phone, you will have to do it.
    D. You will have to answer the phone when nobodys here to do it.

25. A. Dr. Barnes not in his office. What could I do for you? 25.____
    B. Dr. Barnes is not in his office. Is there something I can do for you?
    C. Since Dr. Barnes is not in his office, might there be something I may do for you?
    D. Is there any ways I can assist you since Dr. Barnes is not in his office?

26. A. She do not understand how the new console works. 26.____
    B. The way the new console works, she doesn't understand.
    C. She doesn't understand how the new console works.
    D. The new console works, so that she doesn't understand.

27. A. Certain changes in my family income must be reported as they occur. 27.____
    B. When certain changes in family income occur, it must be reported.
    C. Certain family income change must be reported as they occur.
    D. Certain changes in family income must be reported as they have been occurring.

28. A. Each tenant has to complete the application themselves. 28.____
    B. Each of the tenants have to complete the application by himself.
    C. Each of the tenants has to complete the application himself.
    D. Each of the tenants has to complete the application by themselves.

29. A. Yours is the only building that the construction will effect. 29.____
    B. Your's is the only building affected by the construction.
    C. The construction will only effect your building.
    D. Yours is the only building that will be affected by the construction.

30. A. There is four tests left. 30.____
    B. The number of tests left are four.
    C. There are four tests left.
    D. Four of the tests remains.

31. A. Each of the applicants takes a test. 31.____
    B. Each of the applicant take a test.
    C. Each of the applicants take tests.
    D. Each of the applicants have taken tests.

32. A. The applicant, not the examiners, are ready. 32.____
    B. The applicants, not the examiners, is ready.
    C. The applicants, not the examiner, are ready.
    D. The applicant, not the examiner, are ready

33. A. You will not progress except you practice. 33.____
    B. You will not progress without you practicing.
    C. You will not progress unless you practice.
    D. You will not progress provided you do not practice.

34. A. Neither the director or the employees will be at the office tomorrow. 34.____
    B. Neither the director nor the employees will be at the office tomorrow.
    C. Neither the director, or the secretary nor the other employees will be at the office tomorrow.
    D. Neither the director, the secretary or the other employees will be at the office tomorrow.

35. A. In my absence, he and her will have to finish the assignment. 35.____
    B. In my absence he and she will have to finish the assignment.
    C. In my absence she and him, they will have to finish the assignment.
    D. In my absence he and her both will have to finish the assignment.

KEY (CORRECT ANSWERS)

1.	B	11.	A	21.	A	31.	A
2.	B	12.	D	22.	D	32.	C
3.	C	13.	C	23.	C	33.	C
4.	B	14.	B	24.	A	34.	B
5.	C	15.	A	25.	B	35.	B
6.	C	16.	C	26.	C		
7.	D	17.	B	27.	A		
8.	B	18.	D	28.	C		
9.	D	19.	B	29.	D		
10.	D	20.	B	30.	C		

TEST 2

DIRECTIONS: Each question or incomplete statement is followed by several suggested answers or completions. Select the one that BEST answers the question or completes the statement. *PRINT THE LETTER OF THE CORRECT ANSWER IN THE SPACE AT THE RIGHT.*

Questions 1-4.

DIRECTIONS: Questions 1 through 4 consist of three sentences each. For each question, select the sentence which contains NO error in grammar or usage.

1. A. Be sure that everybody brings his notes to the conference. 1.____
   B. He looked like he meant to hit the boy.
   C. Mr. Jones is one of the clients who was chosen to represent the district.
   D. All are incorrect.

2. A. He is taller than I. 2.____
   B. I'll have nothing to do with these kind of people.
   C. The reason why he will not buy the house is because it is too expensive.
   D. All are incorrect.

3. A. Aren't I eligible for this apartment. 3.____
   B. Have you seen him anywheres?
   C. He should of come earlier.
   D. All are incorrect.

4. A. He graduated college in 2022. 4.____
   B. He hadn't but one more line to write.
   C. Who do you think is the author of this report?
   D. All are incorrect.

Questions 5-35.

DIRECTIONS: In each of the following questions, only one of the four sentences conforms to standards of correct usage. The other three contain errors in grammar, diction, or punctuation. Select the choice in each question which BEST conforms to standards of correct usage. Consider a choice correct if it contains none of the errors mentioned above, even though there may be other ways of expressing the same thought.

5. A. It is obvious that no one wants to be a kill-joy if they can help it. 5.____
   B. It is not always possible, and perhaps it never ispossible, to judge a person's character by just looking at him.
   C. When Yogi Berra of the New York Yankees hit an immortal grandslam home run, everybody in the huge stadium including Pittsburgh fans, rose to his feet.
   D. Every one of us students must pay tuition today.

6. A. The physician told the young mother that if the baby is not able to digest its milk, it should be boiled. 6.____
   B. There is no doubt whatsoever that he felt deeply hurt because John Smith had betrayed the trust.
   C. Having partaken of a most delicious repast prepared by Tessie Breen, the hostess, the horses were driven home immediately thereafter.
   D. The attorney asked my wife and myself several questions.

7. A. Despite all denials, there is no doubt in my mind that 7.____
   B. At this time everyone must deprecate the demogogic attack made by one of our Senators on one of our most revered statesmen.
   C. In the first game of a crucial two-game series, Ted Williams, got two singles, both of them driving in a run.
   D. Our visitor brought good news to John and I.

8. A. If he would have told me, I should have been glad to help him in his dire financial emergency. 8.____
   B. Newspaper men have often asserted that diplomats or so-called official spokesmen sometimes employ equivocation in attempts to deceive.
   C. I think someones coming to collect money for the Red Cross.
   D. In a masterly summation, the young attorney expressed his belief that the facts clearly militate against this opinion.

9. A. We have seen most all the exhibits. 9.____
   B. Without in the least underestimating your advice, in my opinion the situation has grown immeasurably worse in the past few days.
   C. I wrote to the box office treasurer of the hit show that a pair of orchestra seats would be preferable.
   D. As the grim story of Pearl Harbor was broadcast on that fateful December 7, it was the general opinion that war was inevitable.

10. A. Without a moment's hesitation, Casey Stengel said that Larry Berra works harder than any player on the team. 10.____
    B. There is ample evidence to indicate that many animals can run faster than any human being.
    C. No one saw the accident but I.
    D. Example of courage is the heroic defense put up by the paratroopers against overwhelming odds.

11. A. If you prefer these kind, Mrs. Grey, we shall be more than willing to let you have them reasonably. 11.____
    B. If you like these here, Mrs. Grey, we shall be more than willing to let you have them reasonably.
    C. If you like these, Mrs. Grey, we shall be more than willing to let you have them.
    D. Who shall we appoint?

12. A. The number of errors are greater in speech than in writing. 12.____
    B. The doctor rather than the nurse was to blame for his being neglected.
    C. Because the demand for these books have been so great, we reduced the price.
    D. John Galsworthy, the English novelist, could not have survived a serious illness; had it not been for loving care.

13. A. Our activities this year have seldom ever been as interesting as they have been this month. 13.____
    B. Our activities this month have been more interesting, or at least as interesting as those of any month this year.
    C. Our activities this month has been more interesting than those of any other month this year.
    D. Neither Jean nor her sister was at home.

14. A. George B. Shaw's view of common morality, as well as his wit sparkling with a dash of perverse humor here and there, have led critics to term him "The Incurable Rebel." 14.____
    B. The President's program was not always received with the wholehearted endorsement of his own party, which is why the party faces difficulty in drawing up a platform for the coming election.
    C. The reason why they wanted to travel was because they had never been away from home.
    D. Facing a barrage of cameras, the visiting celebrity found it extremely difficult to express his opinions clearly.

15. A. When we calmed down, we all agreed that our anger had been kind of unnecessary and had not helped the situation. 15.____
    B. Without him going into all the details, he made us realize the horror of the accident.
    C. Like one girl, for example, who applied for two positions.
    D. Do not think that you have to be so talented as he is in order to play in the school orchestra.

16. A. He looked very peculiarly to me. 16.____
    B. He certainly looked at me peculiar.
    C. Due to the train's being late, we had to wait an hour.
    D. The reason for the poor attendance is that it is raining.

17. A. About one out of four own an automobile. 17.____
    B. The collapse of the old Mitchell Bridge was caused by defective construction in the central pier.
    C. Brooks Atkinson was well acquainted with the best literature, thus helping him to become an able critic.
    D. He has to stand still until the relief man comes up, thus giving him no chance to move about and keep warm.

18. A. He is sensitive to confusion and withdraws from people whom he feels are too noisy. 18.____
    B. Do you know whether the data is statistically correct?
    C. Neither the mayor or the aldermen are to blame.
    D. Of those who were graduated from high school, a goodly percentage went to college.

19. A. Acting on orders, the offices were searched by a designated committee. 19.____
    B. The answer probably is nothing.
    C. I thought it to be all right to excuse them from class.
    D. I think that he is as successful a singer, if not more successful, than Mary.

20. A. $360,000 is really very little to pay for such a wellbuilt house. 20.____
    B. The creatures looked like they had come from outer space.
    C. It was her, he knew!
    D. Nobody but me knows what to do.

21. A. Mrs. Smith looked good in her new suit. 21.____
    B. New York may be compared with Chicago.
    C. I will not go to the meeting except you go with me.
    D. I agree with this editorial.

22. A. My opinions are different from his. 22.____
    B. There will be less students in class now.
    C. Helen was real glad to find her watch.
    D. It had been pushed off of her dresser.

23. A. Almost everyone, who has been to California, returns with glowing reports. 23.____
    B. George Washington, John Adams, and Thomas Jefferson, were our first presidents.
    C. Mr. Walters, whom we met at the bank yesterday, is the man, who gave me my first job.
    D. One should study his lessons as carefully as he can.

24. A. We had such a good time yesterday. 24.____
    B. When the bell rang, the boys and girls went in the schoolhouse.
    C. John had the worst headache when he got up this morning.
    D. Today's assignment is somewhat longer than yesterday's.

25. A. Neither the mayor nor the city clerk are willing to talk. 25.____
    B. Neither the mayor nor the city clerk is willing to talk.
    C. Neither the mayor or the city clerk are willing to talk.
    D Neither the mayor or the city clerk is willing to talk.

26. A. Being that he is that kind of boy, cooperation cannot be expected. 26.____
    B. He interviewed people who he thought had something to say.
    C. Stop whomever enters the building regardless of rank or office held.
    D. Passing through the countryside, the scenery pleased us.

27. A. The childrens' shoes were in their closet. 27.____
    B. The children's shoes were in their closet.
    C. The childs' shoes were in their closet.
    D. The childs' shoes were in his closet.

28. A. An agreement was reached between the defendant, the plaintiff, the plaintiff's attorney and the insurance company as to the amount of the settlement. 28.____
    B. Everybody was asked to give their versions of the accident.
    C. The consensus of opinion was that the evidence was inconclusive.
    D. The witness stated that if he was rich, he wouldn't have had to loan the money.

29. A. Before beginning the investigation, all the materials related to the case were carefully assembled. 29.____
    B. The reason for his inability to keep the appointment is because of his injury in the accident.
    C. This here evidence tends to support the claim of the defendant.
    D. We interviewed all the witnesses who, according to the driver, were still in town.

30. A. Each claimant was allowed the full amount of their medical expenses. 30.____
    B. Either of the three witnesses is available.
    C. Every one of the witnesses was asked to tell his story.
    D. Neither of the witnesses are right.

31. A. The commissioner, as well as his deputy and various bureau heads, were present. 31.____
    B. A new organization of employers and employees have been formed.
    C. One or the other of these men have been selected.
    D. The number of pages in the book is enough to discourage a reader.

32. A. Between you and me, I think he is the better man. 32.____
    B. He was believed to be me.
    C. Is it us that you wish to see?
    D. The winners are him and her.

33. A. Beside the statement to the police, the witness spoke to no one. 33.____
    B. He made no statement other than to the police and I.
    C. He made no statement to any one else, aside from the police.
    D. The witness spoke to no one but me.

34. A. The claimant has no one to blame but himself. 34.____
    B. The boss sent us, he and I, to deliver the packages.
    C. The lights come from mine and not his car.
    D. There was room on the stairs for him and myself.

35. A. Admission to this clinic is limited to patients' inability to pay for medical care. 35.____
    B. Patients who can pay little or nothing for medical care are treated in this clinic.
    C. The patient's ability to pay for medical care is the determining factor in his admission to this clinic.
    D. This clinic is for the patient's that cannot afford to pay or that can pay a little for medical care.

KEY (CORRECT ANSWERS)

1.	A	11.	C	21.	A	31.	D
2.	A	12.	B	22.	A	32.	A
3.	D	13.	D	23.	D	33.	D
4.	C	14.	D	24.	D	34.	A
5.	D	15.	D	25.	B	35.	B
6.	D	16.	D	26.	B		
7.	B	17.	B	27.	B		
8.	B	18.	D	28.	C		
9.	D	19.	B	29.	D		
10.	B	20.	D	30.	C		

WRITTEN ENGLISH EXPRESSION
EXAMINATION SECTION
TEST 1

DIRECTIONS: The following questions are designed to test your knowledge of grammar, sentence structure, correct usage, and punctuation. In each group there is one sentence that contains no errors. Select the letter of the CORRECT sentence. *PRINT THE LETTER OF THE CORRECT ANSWER IN THE SPACE AT THE RIGHT.*

1. A. A low ceiling is when the atmospheric conditions make flying inadvisable. 1.____
   B. They couldn't tell who the card was from.
   C. No one but you and I are to help him.
   D. What kind of a teacher would you like to be?
   E. To him fall the duties of foster parent.

2. A. They couldn't tell whom the cable was from. 2.____
   B. We like these better than those kind.
   C. It is a test of you more than I.
   D. The person in charge being him, there can be no change in policy.
   E. Chicago is larger than any city in Illinois.

3. A. Do as we do for the celebration. 3.____
   B. Do either of you care to join us?
   C. A child's food requirements differ from the adult.
   D. A large family including two uncles and four grandparents live at the hotel.
   E. Due to bad weather, the game was postponed.

4. A. If they would have done that they might have succeeded. 4.____
   B. Neither the hot days or the humid nights annoy our Southern visitor.
   C. Some people do not gain favor because they are kind of tactless.
   D. No sooner had the turning point come than a new issue arose.
   E. I wish that I was in Florida now.

5. A. We haven't hardly enough tine. 5.____
   B. Immigration is when people come into a foreign country to live.
   C. After each side gave their version, the affair was over with.
   D. Every one of the cars were tagged by the police.
   E. He either will fail in his attempt or will seek other employment.

6. A. They can't seem to see it when I explain the theory. 6.____
   B. It is difficult to find the genuine signature between all those submitted.
   C. She can't understand why they don't remember who to give the letter to
   D. Every man and woman in America is interested in his tax bill.
   E. Honor as well as profit are to be gained by these studies.

7. A. He arrived safe. 7.____
   B. I do not have any faith in John running for office.
   C. The musicians began to play tunefully and keeping the proper tempo indicated for the selection.
   D. Mary's maid of honor bought the kind of an outfit suitable for an afternoon wedding.
   E. If you would have studied the problem carefully you would have found the solution more quickly.

8. A. The new plant is to be electric lighted. 8.____
   B. The reason the speaker was offended was that the audience was inattentive.
   C. There appears to be conditions that govern his behavior.
   D. Either of the men are influential enough to control the situation.
   E. The gallery with all its pictures were destroyed.

9. A. If you would have listened more carefully, you would have heard your name called. 9.____
   B. Did you inquire if your brother were returning soon?
   C. We are likely to have rain before nightfall.
   D. Let's you and I plan next summer's vacation together.
   E. The man whom I thought was my friend deceived me.

10. A. There's a man and his wife waiting for the doctor since early this morning. 10.____
    B. The owner of the market with his assistants is applying the most modern principles of merchandise display.
    C. Every one of the players on both of the competing teams were awarded a gold watch.
    D. The records of the trial indicated that, even before attaining manhood, the murderer's parents were both dead.
    E. We had no sooner entered the room when the bell rang.

11. A. Why don't you start the play like I told you? 11.____
    B. I didn't find the construction of the second house much different from that of the first one I saw.
    C. "When", inquired the child, "Will we begin celebrating my birthday?"
    D. There isn't nothing left to do but not to see him anymore.
    E. There goes the last piece of cake and the last spoonful of ice cream.

12. A. The child could find neither the shoe or the stocking. 12.____
    B. The musicians began to play tunefully and keeping the proper tempo indicated for the selection.
    C. The amount of curious people who turned out for Opening Night was beyond calculation.
    D. I fully expected that the children would be at their desks and to find them ready to begin work,
    E. "Indeed," mused the poll-taker, "the winning candidate is much happier than I."

13. A. Just as you said, I find myself gaining weight. 13.____
B. A teacher should leave the capable pupils engage in creative activities.
C. The teacher spoke continually during the entire lesson, which, of course, was poor procedure.
D. We saw him steal into the room, pick up the letter, and tear it's contents to shreds.
E. It is so dark that I can't hardly see.

14. A. The new schedule of working hours and rates was satis factory to both employees and employer. 14.____
B. Many common people feel keenly about the injustices of Power Politics.
C. Mr. and Mrs. Burns felt that their grandchild was awfully cute when he waved good-bye.
D. The tallest of the twins was also the most intelligent,
E. Please come here and try and help me finish this piece of work.

15. A. My younger brother insists that he is as tall as me. 15.____
B. Suffering from a severe headache all day, one dose of the prescribed medicine relieved me,
C. "Please let my brothers and I help you with your packages," said Frank to Mrs. Powers.
D. Every one of the rooms we visited had displays of pupils' work in them.
E. Do you intend bringing most of the refreshments yourself?

16. A. The telephone linesmen, working steadily at their task during the severe storm, the telephones soon began to ring again. 16.____
B. Meat, as well as fruits and vegetables, is considered essential to a proper diet.
C. He looked like a real good boxer that night in the ring.
D. The man has worked steadily for fifteen years before he decided to open his own business.
E. The winters were hard and dreary, nothing could live without shelter.

17. A. No one can foretell when I will have another opportunity like that one again. 17.____
B. The last group of paintings shown appear really to have captured the most modern techniques,
C. We searched high and low, both in the attic and cellar, but were unsuccessful in locating mementos.
D. None of the guests was able to give the rules of the game accurately.
E. When you go to the library tomorrow, please bring this book to the librarian in the reference room.

18. A. After the debate, every one of the speakers realized that, given another chance, he could have done better. 18.____
B. The reason given by the physician for the patient's trouble was because of his poor eating habits.
C. The fog was so thick that the driver couldn't hardly see more than ten feet ahead.
D. I suggest that you present the medal to who you think best.
E. I don't approve of him going along.

19. A. A decision made by a man without much deliberation is sometimes no different than a slow one. 19.____
B. By the time Mr. Brown's son will graduate Dental School, he will be twenty-six years of age.
C. Who did you predict would win the election?
D. The auctioneer had less stamps to sell this year than last year.
E. Being that he is occupied, I shall not disturb him.

20. A. Having pranced into the arena with little grace and unsteady hoof for the jumps ahead, the driver reined his horse. 20.____
B. Once the dog wagged it's tail, you knew it was a friendly animal.
C. Like a great many artists, his life was a tragedy.
D. When asked to choose corn, cabbage, or potatoes, the diner selected the latter.
E. The record of the winning team was among the most noteworthy of the season.

21. A. The maid wasn't so small that she couldn't reach the top window for cleaning. 21.____
B. Many people feel that powdered coffee produces a really good flavor.
C. Would you mind me trying that coat on for size?
D. This chair looks much different than the chair we selected in the store.
E. I wish that he would have talked to me about the lesson before he presented it.

22. A. After trying unsuccessfully to land a job in the city, Will located in the country on a farm. 22.____
B. On the last attempt, the pole-vaulter came nearly to getting hurt.
C. The observance of Armistice Day throughout the world offers an opportunity to reflect on the horrors of war.
D. Outside of the mistakes in spelling, the child's letter was a very good one.
E. The annual income of New York is far greater than Florida.

23. A. Scissors is always dangerous for a child to handle. 23.____
B. I assure you that I will not yield to pressure to sell my interest.
C. Ask him if he has recall of the incident which took place at our first meeting.
D. The manager felt like as not to order his usher-captain to surrender his uniform,
E. Everyone on the boat said their prayers when the storm grew worse.

24. A. The mother of the bride climaxed the occasion by exclaiming, "I want my children should be happy forever." 24.____
B. We read in the papers where the prospects for peace are improving.
C. "Can I share the cab with you?" was frequently heard during the period of gas rationing.
D. The man was enamored with his friend"s sister.
E. Had the police suspected the ruse, they would have taken proper precautions.

25. A. The teacher admonished the other students neither to speak to John, nor should they annoy him. 25.____
B. Fortunately we had been told that there was but one service station in that area.
C. An usher seldom rises above a theatre manager.
D. The epic, "Gone With the Wind," is supposed to have taken place during the Civil War Era.
E. Now that she has been graduated she should be encouraged to make her own choice as to the career she is to follow.

KEY (CORRECT ANSWERS)

1. E
2. A
3. A
4. D
5. E
6. D
7. A
8. B
9. C
10. B
11. B
12. E
13. A
14. A
15. E
16. B
17. D
18. A
19. C
20. E
21. B
22. C
23. B
24. E
25. B

TEST 2

DIRECTIONS: The following questions are designed to test your knowledge of grammar, sentence structure, correct usage, and punctuation. In each group, there is one sentence that contains no errors. Select the letter of the CORRECT sentence. *PRINT THE LETTER OF THE CORRECT ANSWER IN THE SPACE AT THE RIGHT.*

1. A. Shall you be at home, let us say, on Sunday at two o'clock? 1.____
   B. We see Mr. Lewis take his car out of the garage daily, newly polished always.
   C. We have no place to keep our rubbers, only in the hall closet.
   D. Isn't it true what you told me about the best way to prepare for an examination?
   E. Mathematics is among my favorite subjects.

2. A. The host thought the guests were of the hungry kinds so he prepared much food. 2.____
   B. The museum is often visited by students who are fond of early inventions, and especially patent attorneys.
   C. I rose to nominate the man who most of us felt was the most diligent worker in the group.
   D. The child was sent to the store to purchase a bottle of milk, and brought home fresh rolls, too.
   E. Hidden away in the closet, I found the long-lost purse.

3. A. The garden tool was sent to be sharpened, and a new handle to be put on. 3.____
   B. At the end of her vacation, Joan came home with little money, but which systematic thrift soon overcame.
   C. We people have opportunities to show the rest of the world how real democracy functions.
   D. The guide paddled along, then fell in a reverie which he related the history of the region.
   E. No sooner had the curtain dropped when the audience shouted its approval in chorus.

4. A. The data you need is to be made available shortly. 4.____
   B. The first few strokes of the brush were enough to convince me that Tom could paint much better than me.
   C. We inquired if we could see the owner of the store, after we waited for one hour.
   D. The highly-strung parent was aggravated by the slightest noise that the baby made.
   E. We should have investigated the cause of the noise by bringing the car to a halt.

5. A. The police, investigating the crime, were successful in discovering only one possibly valuable clue. 5.____
   B. Due to an unexpected change in plans, the violin soloist did not perform.
   C. Besides being awarded a Bachelor's degree at college, the scientist has since received many honorary degrees.
   D. The data offered in advance of the recent Presidential election seems to have possessed elements of inaccuracy.
   E. I don't believe your the only one who has been asked to come here.

6. A. I don't quite see that I will be able to completely finish the job in time. 6.____
   B. By my statement, I infer that you are guilty of the offense as charged.
   C. Wasn't it strange that they wouldn't let no one see the body?
   D. I hope that this is the kind of rolls you requested me to buy.
   E. The storekeeper distributed cigars as bonuses between his many customers.

7. A. He said he preferred the climate of Florida to California. 7.____
   B. Because of the excessive heat, a great amount of fruit juice was drunk by the guests.
   C. This week's dramatic presentation was neither as lively nor as entertaining as last week.
   D. The fashion expert believed that no one could develop new creations more successfully than him.
   E. A collection of Dicken's works is a "must" for every library.

8. A. There was such a large amount of books on the floor that I couldn't find a place for my rocking chair. 8.____
   B. Walking up the rickety stairs, the bottle slipped from his hands and smashed.
   C. The reason they granted his request was because he had a good record.
   D. Little Tommy was proud that the teacher always asked him to bring messages to the office.
   E. That kind of orange is grown only in Florida.

9. A. The new mayor is a resident of this city for thirty years. 9.____
   B. Do you mean to imply that had he not missed that shot he would have won?
   C. Next term I shall be studying French and history.
   D. I read in last night's paper where the sales tax is going to be abolished.
   E. In order to prevent breakage, she placed a sheet of paper between each of the plates when she packed them.

10. A. To have children vie against one another is psychologically unsound. 10.____
    B. Would anyone else care to discuss his baby?
    C. He was interested and aware of the problem.
    D. I sure would like to discover if he is motivating the lesson properly.
    E. The cloth was first lain on a flat surface; then it was pressed with a hot iron.

11. A. She graduated Barnard College twenty-five years ago. 11.____
    B. He studied the violin since he was seven.
    C. She is not so diligent a researcher as her classmate.
    D. He discovered that the new data corresponds with the facts disclosed by Werner.
    E. How could he enjoy the television program; the dog was barking and the baby was crying.

12. A. You have three alternatives: law, dentistry, or teaching. 12.____
    B. If I would have worked harder, I would have accomplished my purpose.
    C. He affected a rapid change of pace and his opponents were outdistanced.
    D. He looked prosperous, although he had been unemployed for a year.
    E. The engine not only furnishes power but light and heat as well.

13. A. The children shared one anothers toys and seemed quite happy. 13.___
B. They lay in the sun for many hours, getting tanned.
C. The reproduction arrived, and had been hung in the living room.
D. First begin by calling the roll.
E. Tell me where you hid it; no one shall ever find it.

14. A. Deliver these things to whomever arrives first. 14.___
B. Everybody but she and me is going to the conference.
C. If the number of patrons is small, we can serve them.
D. When each of the contestants find their book, the debate may begin.
E. Some people, farmers in particular, lament the substitution of butter by margarine.

15. A. After his illness, he stood in the country three weeks. 15.___
B. If you wish to effect a change, submit your suggestions.
C. It is silly to leave children play with knives.
D. Play a trick on her by spilling water down her neck.
E. There was such a crowd of people at the crossing we couldn't hardly get on the bus.

16. A. This is a time when all of us must show our faith and devotion to our country. 16.___
B. Either you or I are certain to be elected president of the new club.
C. The interpellation of the Minister of Finance forced him to explain his policies.
D. After hoisting the anchor and removing the binnacle, the ship was ready to set sail.
E. Please bring me a drink of cold water from the refrigerator.

17. A. Mistakes in English, when due to carelessness or haste, can easily be rectified. 17.___
B. Mr. Jones is one of those persons who will try to keep a promise and usually does.
C. Being very disturbed by what he had heard, Fred decided to postpone his decision.
D. There is a telephone at the other end of the corridor which is constantly in use.
E. In his teaching, he always kept the childrens' interests and needs in mind.

18. A. The lazy pupil, of course, will tend to write the minimum amount of words acceptable. 18.___
B. His success as a political leader consisted mainly of his ability to utter platitudes in a firm and convincing manner.
C. To be cognizant of current affairs, a person must not only read newspapers and magazines but also recent books by recognized authorities.
D. Although we intended to have gone fishing, the sudden outbreak of a storm caused us to change our plans.
E. It is the colleges that must take the responsibility for encouraging greater flexibility in the high-school curriculum.

19. A. "I am sorry," he said, "but John's answer was 'No'." 19.____
B. A spirited argument followed between those who favored and opposed Marie's expulsion from the club.
C. Whether a forward child should be humored or punished often depends upon the circumstances.
D. Excessive alcoholism is certainly not conducive with efficient performance of one's work.
E. Stroking his beard thoughtfully, an idea suddenly came to him.

20. A. "Take care, my children," he said sadly, "lest you not be deceived." 20.____
B. Those continuous telephone calls are preventing Betty from completing her homework.
C. They dug deep into the earth at the spot indicated on the map, but they found nothing.
D. We petted and cozened the little girl until she finally stopped weeping.
E. There was, in the mail, an inquiry for a house by a young couple with two or three bedrooms.

21. A. Please fill in the required information on the application form and return same by April 15. 21.____
B. Tom was sitting there idly, watching the clouds scud across the sky.
C. We started for home so that our parents would not suspect that anything out of the ordinary took place.
D. The sudden abatement from the storm enabled the ladies to resume their journey.
E. Each of the twelve members were agreed that the accused man was innocent.

22. A. The number of gifted students not continuing their education beyond secondary school present a nationwide problem. 22.____
B. A man's animadversions against those he considers his enemies are usually reflections of his own inadequacies.
C. The alembic of his fevered imagination produced some of the greatest romantic poetry of his era.
D. The first case of smallpox dates back more than 3000 years and has gone unchecked until recently.
E. He promised to go irregardless of the rain or snow.

23. A. The child picked up several of the coracles, which he had seen glittering in the sand, and brought them to his mother. 23.____
B. He muttered in dejected tones – and no one contradicted him – "We have failed."
C. A girl whom I believed to be she waved cheerily to me from a passing automobile.
D. We discovered that she was a former resident of our own neighborhood who eloped some years ago with a milkman.
E. It looks now like he will not be promoted after all.

24. A. Mary is the kind of a person on whom you can depend in any emergency. 24.____
B. I am sure that either applicant can fill the job you offer competently and efficiently.
C. Although we searched the entire room, the scissors was not to be found.
D. Being that you are here, we can proceed with the discussion.
E. In spite of our warning whistle, the huge ship continued to sail athwart our course.

25. A. The salaries earned by college graduates vary as much if not more than those earned by high school graduates. 25.____
B. The apothegms that he felt to be so witty were all too often either trite or platitudinous.
C. She read the letter carefully, took out one of the pages, and tore it into small pieces.
D. A young man, who hopes to succeed, must be diligent in his work and alert to his opportunities.
E. No one should plan a long journey for pleasure in these days.

KEY (CORRECT ANSWERS)

1. A
2. C
3. C
4. E
5. A

6. D
7. B
8. E
9. B
10. B

11. C
12. D
13. E
14. C
15. B

16. C
17. A
18. E
19. C
20. C

21. B
22. C
23. B
24. E
25. B

SPELLING
EXAMINATION SECTION

TEST 1

DIRECTIONS: In answering these questions, select the letter of the one MISSPELLED word in each of the following groups of words. *PRINT THE LETTER OF THE CORRECT ANSWER IN THE SPACE AT THE RIGHT.*

1.	A. aggrieve	B. conceive	C. beseige	D. relieve	1.____
2.	A. liege	B. weird	C. feign	D. sieze	2.____
3.	A. concede	B. intercede	C. precede	D. supercede	3.____
4.	A. chagrinned	B. preferred	C. changeable	D. chargeable	4.____
5.	A. therefor	B. pastime	C. oftimes	D. allspice	5.____
6.	A. forfeit	B. glacier	C. heifer	D. feindish	6.____
7.	A. filiament	B. inferable	C. soliloquy	D. codeine	7.____
8.	A. formidable	B. impassible	C. susceptible	D. lamentible	8.____
9.	A. strategem C. mountainous		B. reconnaissance D. consensus		9.____
10.	A. attendent	B. attorneys	C. iridescence	D. subterfuge	10.____
11.	A. unparalleled	B. sovereign	C. indite	D. heiroglyphic	11.____
12.	A. pinnacle	B. hypocrisy	C. meridien	D. palatable	12.____
13.	A. maintainence	B. ninety	C. inoculate	D. connoisseur	13.____
14.	A. haranguing	B. distilation	C. unwieldy	D. chandelier	14.____
15.	A. glazier	B. unrivalled	C. triennial	D. quintescence	15.____
16.	A. stenciled	B. similiar	C. councilor	D. gazetteer	16.____
17.	A. receptable	B. calsimine	C. hideous	D. mimicking	17.____
18.	A. infringment	B. abridgment	C. symmetrical	D. forgettable	18.____
19.	A. naptha	B. vaccinate	C. chiffonier	D. annulling	19.____
20.	A. guise	B. guerilla	C. guage	D. guinea	20.____

KEY (CORRECT ANSWERS)

1.	C	besiege	11.	D	hieroglyphic
2.	D	seize	12.	C	meridian
3.	D	supersede	13.	A	maintenance
4.	A	chagrined	14.	B	distillation
5.	C	offtimes	15.	D	quintessence
6.	D	fiendish	16.	B	similar
7.	A	filament	17.	B	calcimine
8.	D	lamentable	18.	A	infringement
9.	A	stratagem	19.	A	naphtha
10.	A	attendant	20.	C	gauge

TEST 2

DIRECTIONS: In answering these questions, select the letter of the one MISSPELLED word in each of the following groups of words. *PRINT THE LETTER OF THE CORRECT ANSWER IN THE SPACE AT THE RIGHT.*

1. A. zigzagged B. excelsior C. maneuverable D. effervesence 1.____
2. A. reminiscence B. stupify C. embargoes D. mosquitoes 2.____
3. A. mistatement B. occurrence C. vanilla D. allotted 3.____
4. A. someone B. requital C. ecstasy D. excize 4.____
5. A. picayunish B. colossal C. interelatedness D. rarefy 5.____
6. A. dyeing B. oscillatory C. bouillion D. lavalliere 6.____
7. A. hieing B. disasterous C. ninetieth D. cinnamon 7.____
8. A. leisure B. reconciliable C. singeing D. fetish 8.____
9. A. Chatanooga B. Pittsburgh C. Bismarck D. Raleigh 9.____
10. A. supercilious B. puntilious C. sacrilegious D. deleterious 10.____
11. A. irreparably B. comparitively C. lovable D. audible 11.____
12. A. nullify B. siderial C. salability D. irrelevant 12.____
13. A. asinine B. dissonent C. opossum D. indispensable 13.____
14. A. discomfit B. sapient C. exascerbate D. sarsaparilla 14.____
15. A. valleys B. maintainance C. abridgment D. reticence 15.____
16. A. transmittance B. undoubtly C. indubitably D. sustenance 16.____
17. A. appraisor B. creditor C. auditor D. consignor 17.____
18. A. mottoes B. pianos C. soloes D. mementoes 18.____
19. A. sisters-in-law B. alumini C. cross-purposes D. 1960's 19.____
20. A. idiocyncracy B. kimono C. propeller D. buoyancy 20.____

KEY (CORRECT ANSWERS)

1.	D	effervescence	11.	B	comparatively
2.	B	stupefy	12.	B	sidereal
3.	A	misstatement	13.	B	dissonant
4.	D	excise	14.	C	exacerbate
5.	C	interrelatedness	15.	B	maintenance
6.	D	lavaliere	16.	B	undoubtedly
7.	B	disastrous	17.	A	appraiser
8.	B	reconcilable	18.	C	solos
9.	A	Chattanooga	19.	B	alumni
10.	B	punctilious	20.	A	idiosyncracy

TEST 3

DIRECTIONS: In answering these questions, select the letter of the one MISSPELLED word in each of the following groups of words. *PRINT THE LETTER OF THE CORRECT ANSWER IN THE SPACE AT THE RIGHT.*

1.	A. inditement	B. hierarchy	C. hawser	D. monogomous	1.____
2.	A. timbre	B. tremulo	C. nicknack	D. cybernetics	2.____
3.	A. zuchinni	B. familiar	C. similar	D. frontispiece	3.____
4.	A. homolagous	B. homogenous	C. homunculous	D. pabulum	4.____
5.	A. withheld	B. gutteral	C. dumbbell	D. glutinous	5.____
6.	A. pusillanimity	B. repetition	C. scythe	D. spermacetti	6.____
7.	A. variegated	B. coolly	C. corrolary	D. commissariat	7.____
8.	A. doggerel	B. evenness	C. gossamer	D. gossippy	8.____
9.	A. hemorrhage	B. japanned	C. bachanal	D. supersede	9.____
10.	A. ballbriggan	B. barrette	C. annihilate	D. ammeter	10.____
11.	A. cinnabar	B. epiglotis	C. cachinnate	D. chaparral	11.____
12.	A. philipic	B. flagellate	C. medallion	D. obligate	12.____
13.	A. questionnaire	B. whipoorwill	C. ukulele	D. jinrikisha	13.____
14.	A. dishabille	B. naphtha	C. placque	D. diapason	14.____
15.	A. rhinoceros C. dinossaur		B. hippopotamus D. giraffe		15.____
16.	A. threshold	B. withold	C. newsstand	D. peccadillo	16.____
17.	A. prejudicial	B. inoculate	C. procedures	D. inocuous	17.____
18.	A. practitioner	B. oriel	C. ormolu	D. resusitate	18.____
19.	A. ricochet	B. raillery	C. garulous	D. complaisant	19.____
20.	A. predeliction	B. sacrilegious	C. antedate	D. tourniquet	20.____

KEY (CORRECT ANSWERS)

1.	D	monogamous	11.	B	epiglottis
2.	B	tremolo	12.	A	philippic
3.	A	zucchini	13.	B	whippoorwill
4.	A	homologous	14.	C	plaque
	B	guttural	15.	C	dinosaur
6.	D	spermaceti	16.	B	withhold
7.	C	corollary	17.	D	innocuous
8.	D	gossipy	18.	D	resuscitate
9.	C	bacchanal	19.	C	garrulous
10.	A	balbriggan	20.	A	predilection

TEST 4

DIRECTIONS: In answering these questions, select the letter of the one MISSPELLED word in each of the following groups of words. *PRINT THE LETTER OF THE CORRECT ANSWER IN THE SPACE AT THE RIGHT.*

1. A. abhorrent B. aquittal C. accessible D. ammeter 1.____

2. A. amanuensis B. annihalate C. battalion D. beneficent 2.____

3. A. cateclysm B. catechism C. beneficiary D. catarrh 3.____

4. A. avoirdupois B. catercornered C. cemetary D. caterpillar 4.____

5. A. cerement B. chalcedony C. effervesence D. collectible 5.____

6. A. chiffonier B. coalesce C. exorcise D. friccasee 6.____

7. A. consencus B. corollary C. denouement D. desuetude 7.____

8. A. dysentery B. emissary C. gazzetteer D. fuchsia 8.____

9. A. ecquinoctial B. evanescent C. excrescence D. exudation 9.____

10. A. Fahrenheit B. in as much as C. frontispiece D. imbroglio 10.____

11. A. gunwhale B. intercede C. irascible D. kaleidoscope 11.____

12. A. indefatigable B. supercede C. iridescence D. malleable 12.____

13. A. medallion B. moiety C. obsequies D. mayonaise 13.____

14. A. omniscience B. pavilion C. penitentiary D. pantomime 14.____

15. A. proscenium B. putrify C. ramify D. liquefy 15.____

16. A. predecessor B. plenipotentiary C. salutery D. solder 16.____

17. A. sasparilla B. stertorous C. supererogate D. vilify 17.____

18. A. soliloquy B. vicissitude C. somnambulance D. labyrinth 18.____

19. A. chrysalis B. corroborative C. Czechoslovakia D. Cincinati 19.____

20. A. idiocyncrasy B. crystallize C. deficiency D. deceive 20.____

KEY (CORRECT ANSWERS)

1.	B	acquittal	11.	A	gunwale
2.	B	annihilate	12.	B	supersede
3.	A	cataclysm	13.	D	mayonnaise
4.	C	cemetery	14.	D	pantomime
5.	C	effervescence	15.	B	putrefy
6.	D	fricassee	16.	C	salutatory
7.	A	consensus	17.	A	sarsaparilla
8.	C	gazetteer	18.	B	vicissitude
9.	A	equinoctial	19.	D	Cincinnati
10.	B	inasmuch as	20.	A	idiosyncrasy

TEST 5

DIRECTIONS: In answering these questions, select the letter of the one MISSPELLED word in each of the following groups of words. *PRINT THE LETTER OF THE CORRECT ANSWER IN THE SPACE AT THE RIGHT.*

1. A. ceremoniously B. desireability C. hazards D. heritage 1.____
2. A. proceeds B. preceding C. supercede D. procedure 2.____
3. A. interoffice B. intrammural C. intestate D. intercede 3.____
4. A. prevaricated B. prefabricate C. chrysantenums D. juxtaposition 4.____
5. A. adjustable B. tangible C. noticeable D. formidable 5.____
6. A. assiduous B. enlightening C. cancellation D. colateral 6.____
7. A. questionnaire B. sacriligious C. mendacious D. fallacious 7.____
8. A. embezzlement B. impanel C. casuality D. subpoena 8.____
9. A. pecuniary B. commissary C. comptroller D. resevoir 9.____
10. A. pramatism B. emphasize C. hyphenizes D. hypercritical 10.____
11. A. paragon B. metamorphesis C. collaboration D. colleague 11.____
12. A. aphorism B. benediction C. benignent D. seizure 12.____
13. A. bankrupcy B. coherency C. ascendancy D. truancy 13.____
14. A. withdrawal B. withal C. wearisome D. withold 14.____
15. A. ecrue B. edification C. ecclesiastic D. effluence 15.____
16. A. accidentally B. remembrance C. grievous D. sufferage 16.____
17. A. forfeit B. mischief C. antidote D. antidate 17.____
18. A. benefited B. regretable C. disastrous D. mountainous 18.____
19. A. perseverance B. insistence C. preponderence D. recurrence 19.____
20. A. facetious B. factitious C. fictitious D. fractous 20.____

KEY (CORRECT ANSWERS)

1.	B	desirability	11.	B	metamorphosis
2.	C	supersede	12.	C	benignant
3.	B	intramural	13.	A	bankruptcy
4.	C	chrysanthemums	14.	D	withhold
5.	A	adjustable	15.	A	ecru
6.	D	collateral	16.	D	suffrage
7.	B	sacrilegious	17.	D	antedate
8.	C	casualty	18.	B	regrettable
9.	D	reservoir	19.	C	preponderance
10.	A	pragmatism	20.	D	fractious

TEST 6

DIRECTIONS: In answering these questions, select the letter of the one MISSPELLED word in each of the following groups of words. *PRINT THE LETTER OF THE CORRECT ANSWER IN THE SPACE AT THE RIGHT.*

1.	A. proscenium	B. resillient	C. biennial	D. connoisseur	1.____
2.	A. queue	B. equable	C. ecstacy	D. obsequious	2.____
3.	A. quizes	B. frolicking	C. maelstrom	D. homonym	3.____
4.	A. pseudonym	B. annihilate	C. questionaire	D. irascible	4.____
5.	A. diptheria	B. annular	C. acolyte	D. descendant	5.____
6.	A. truculant	B. rescind	C. dilettante	D. innuendo	6.____
7.	A. prevalence	B. discrete	C. efrontery	D. admissiblde	7.____
8.	A. igneous	B. annullment	C. dissipate	D. abattoir	8.____
9.	A. quiescent	B. apologue	C. myrrh	D. inocuous	9.____
10.	A. propoganda	B. gaseous	C. iridescent	D. similar	10.____
11.	A. supercede	B. tyranny	C. beauteous	D. victuals	11.____
12.	A. geneology	B. tragedy	C. soliloquy	D. prejudice	12.____
13.	A. remittance	B. shoeing	C. category	D. gutteral	13.____
14.	A. catarrh	B. parlamentary	C. villain	D. omitted	14.____
15.	A. vengeance	B. parallel	C. nineth	D. mayoralty	15.____
16.	A. changeable	B. therefor	C. incidently	D. dissatisfy	16.____
17.	A. orifice	B. deferrment	C. harass	D. accommodate	17.____
18.	A. picnicking	B. proceedure	C. hypocrisy	D. seize	18.____
19.	A. vilify	B. efflorescence	C. sarcophagus	D. sacreligious	19.____
20.	A. paraphenalia	B. apothecaries	C. occurrence	D. plagiarize	20.____

KEY (CORRECT ANSWERS)

1.	B	resilient	11.	A	supersede
2.	C	ecstasy	12.	A	genealogy
3.	A	quizzes	13.	D	gutteral
4.	C	questionnaire	14.	B	parliamentary
5.	A	diphtheria	15.	C	ninth
6.	A	truculent	16.	C	incidentally
7.	C	effrontery	17.	B	deferment
8.	B	annulment	18.	B	procedure
9.	D	innocuous	19.	D	sacrilegious
10.	A	propaganda	20.	A	paraphernalia

TEST 7

DIRECTIONS: In answering these questions, select the letter of the one MISSPELLED word in each of the following groups of words. *PRINT THE LETTER OF THE CORRECT ANSWER IN THE SPACE AT THE RIGHT.*

1. A. absence B. accummulate C. acknowledgment D. audible 1.____

2. A. benificiary B. disbursement C. exorbitant D. incidentally 2.____

3. A. inoculate B. liaison C. acquire D. noticable 3.____

4. A. peddler B. permissible C. persuade D. pertenant 4.____

5. A. reconciliation B. responsable C. sizable D. substantial 5.____

6. A. minion B. lineage C. hypothicate D. frugal 6.____

7. A. lethargy B. mercenary C. inuendo D. frolicky 7.____

8. A. martial B. pettiness C. innumerable D. habitible 8.____

9. A. toboggan B. inquisitor C. galleon D. fourty 9.____

10. A. giraffe B. picayunish C. indellible D. intermittent 10.____

11. A. collateral B. possesion C. relevant D. superficial 11.____

12. A. fluorescent B. maintenance C. occurrence D. tecnical 12.____

13. A. hindrance B. interval C. liquidate D. preceeding 13.____

14. A. questionnaire B. superintendant C. temporarily D. vaccination 14.____

15. A. resipient B. significant C. unanimous D. variable 15.____

16. A. monocrome B. deceit C. parsimonious D. excrete 16.____

17. A. fecund B. syllable C. supine D. saytrap 17.____

18. A. salacious B. judgement C. systolic D. allegory 18.____

19. A. glimpse B. overun C. protuberance D. threshold 19.____

20. A. falacious B. forfeit C. calamity D. lamasery 20.____

KEY (CORRECT ANSWERS)

1.	B	accumulate	11.	B	possession
2.	A	beneficiary	12.	D	technical
3.	D	noticeable	13.	D	preceding
4.	D	pertinent	14.	B	superintendent
5.	B	responsible	15.	A	recipient
6.	C	hypothecate	16.	A	monochrome
7.	C	innuendo	17.	D	satrap
8.	D	habitable	18.	B	judgment
9.	D	forty	19.	B	overrun
10.	C	indelible	20.	A	fallacious

TEST 8

DIRECTIONS: In answering these questions, select the letter of the one MISSPELLED word in each of the following groups of words. *PRINT THE LETTER OF THE CORRECT ANSWER IN THE SPACE AT THE RIGHT.*

1. A. reconnaissance B. mayonnaise C. perfectability D. fuselage 1.____

2. A. publicly B. leige C. tragically D. sieve 2.____

3. A. pavillion B. inoculate C. surveillance D. abstemious 3.____

4. A. dungeon B. cinnamon C. abhorrance D. catarrh 4.____

5. A. chlorophyll B. diptheria C. icicle D. periphery 5.____

6. A. queue B. deterent C. idiosyncrasy D. connoisseur 6.____

7. A. revocable B. changeable C. irreducible D. permissable 7.____

8. A. embarrass B. recommend C. emolient D. concomitant 8.____

9. A. sherbet B. losenge C. revelatory D. privilege 9.____

10. A. stupefy B. indispensable C. mocassin D. forcibly 10.____

11. A. miscellaneous B. rebuttal C. scintillate D. tempermentally 11.____

12. A. carnage B. martial C. extravagent D. nuptial 12.____

13. A. analogy B. calender C. cant D. cantaloupe 13.____

14. A. sterotype B. abstinence C. leisurely D. rarefy 14.____

15. A. clothier B. desirability C. dificiency D. grandeur 15.____

16. A. gauge B. knowledgeable C. prairie D. sufficent 16.____

17. A. abridgment B. inexhaustable C. enlightenment D. endeavor 17.____

18. A. vengence B. reddened C. stupefying D. obstacle 18.____

19. A. harassed B. imperative C. nuisance D. tumultous 19.____

20. A. collision B. extremely C. grievious D. rehearsal 20.____

KEY (CORRECT ANSWERS)

1.	C	perfectibility	11.	D	temperamentally
2.	B	liege	12.	C	extravagant
3.	A	pavilion	13.	B	calendar
4.	C	abhorrence	14.	A	stereotype
5.	B	diphtheria	15.	C	deficiency
6.	B	deterrent	16.	D	sufficient
7.	D	permissible	17.	B	inexhaustible
8.	C	emollient	18.	A	vengeance
9.	B	lozenge	19.	D	tumultuous
10.	C	moccasin	20.	C	grievous

TEST 9

DIRECTIONS: In answering these questions, select the letter of the one MISSPELLED word in each of the following groups of words. *PRINT THE LETTER OF THE CORRECT ANSWER IN THE SPACE AT THE RIGHT.*

1. A. siege B. seize C. neice D. weird 1.____
2. A. resemblance B. occurrance C. independence D. correspondence 2.____
3. A. accommodate B. athletics C. accidently D. benefited 3.____
4. A. hindrance B. harassment C. embarrassing D. comparitive 4.____
5. A. judgment B. prejudice C. acknowledgment D. priviledge 5.____
6. A. preceding B. proceedure C. supersede D. exceeding 6.____
7. A. crysanthemum B. picknicking C. mimicked D. misspelled 7.____
8. A. catarrh B. crocheted C. daguerreotype D. bragadocio 8.____
9. A. antedeluvian B. dilettante C. vermilion D. pusillanimous 9.____
10. A. arpeggio B. allegretto C. appelation D. bouillon 10.____
11. A. compatible B. luxuriance C. psychiatry D. sacreligious 11.____
12. A. irresistible B. permissable C. feint D. peaceable 12.____
13. A. aggressor B. archetype C. concensus D. tariff 13.____
14. A. kaleidoscope B. anesthesia C. vermilion D. tafetta 14.____
15. A. congruent B. barrenness C. plebescite D. vigilance 15.____
16. A. weird B. gauge C. license D. resucitation 16.____
17. A. pantomine B. bacchanalian C. chlorophyll D. dipthong 17.____
18. A. picknicking B. promissory C. resevoir D. omission 18.____
19. A. supercede B. banister C. wholly D. seize 19.____
20. A. alyssum B. boutonniere C. abhorrence D. phyrric 20.____

KEY (CORRECT ANSWERS)

1.	C	niece	11.	D	sacrilegious
2.	B	occurrence	12.	B	permissible
3.	C	accidentally	13.	C	consensus
4.	D	comparative	14.	D	taffeta
5.	D	privilege	15.	C	plebiscite
6.	B	procedure	16.	D	resuscitation
7.	A	chrysanthemum	17.	D	diphthong
8.	D	braggadocio	18.	C	reservoir
9.	A	antediluvian	19.	A	supersede
10.	C	appellation	20.	D	pyrrhic

TEST 10

DIRECTIONS: In answering these questions, select the letter of the one MISSPELLED word in each of the following groups of words. *PRINT THE LETTER OF THE CORRECT ANSWER IN THE SPACE AT THE RIGHT.*

1.	A. cancelled	B. regrettable	C. unforgettable	D. gutteral	1.____
2.	A. caffeine	B. inviegle	C. heinous	D. sieve	2.____
3.	A. fusible	B. dispensable	C. conductable	D. salable	3.____
4.	A. parallelism	B. annihilate	C. crystalize	D. comptroller	4.____
5.	A. irremediable	B. exhilarate	C. conoisseur	D. serviceable	5.____
6.	A. prophecied	B. emigrate	C. ukulele	D. trafficking	6.____
7.	A. stupefy	B. rarefy	C. liquefy	D. vilefy	7.____
8.	A. cantaloupe	B. broccoli	C. rhubarb	D. rotisserie	8.____
9.	A. dahlia C. camellia		B. rhododendron D. crysanthemum		9.____
10.	A. bachelor	B. archeology	C. geneology	D. coercion	10.____
11.	A. moustache	B. sovereignty	C. drunkeness	D. staccato	11.____
12.	A. mocassin	B. assassin	C. battalion	D. despicable	12.____
13.	entymology	B. echoing	C. subtly	D. stupefy	13.____
14.	A. calcimine	B. seive	C. procedure	D. poinsettia	14.____
15.	A. coercion	B. rescission	C. license	D. prophecied	15.____
16.	A. dispensable	B. compatable	C. recommend	D. feasible	16.____
17.	A. frolicking	B. caramel	C. germaine	D. kohlrabi	17.____
18.	A. diphtheria	B. collander	C. seize	D. sleight	18.____
19.	A. emminent	B. imminent	C. blatant	D. privilege	19.____
20.	A. queue	B. gladioluses	C. kindergarden	D. tonnage	20.____

KEY (CORRECT ANSWERS)

1.	D	guttural	11.	C	drunkenness
2.	B	inveigle	12.	A	moccasin
3.	C	conductible	13.	A	entomology
4.	C	crystallize	14.	B	sieve
5.	C	connoisseur	15.	D	prophesied
6.	A	prophesied	16.	B	compatible
7.	D	vilify	17.	C	germane
8.	A	cantaloupe	18.	B	colander
9.	D	chrysanthemum	19.	A	eminent
10.	C	genealogy	20.	C	kindergarten

TEST 11

DIRECTIONS: In answering these questions, select the letter of the one MISSPELLED word in each of the following groups of words. *PRINT THE LETTER OF THE CORRECT ANSWER IN THE SPACE AT THE RIGHT.*

1. A. shreik B. siege C. sheik D. sieve 1.____
2. A. chrystal B. chrysanthemum C. chrysalis D. chrome 2.____
3. A. censer B. queue C. obbligato D. antartic 3.____
4. A. courtsey B. buoyancy C. fiery D. shepherd 4.____
5. A. Phillipines B. currant C. dietitian D. coercion 5.____
6. A. diphthong B. rhododendron C. inviegle D. shellacked 6.____
7. A. holocaust B. irascible C. bucanneer D. mischievous 7.____
8. A. maintenance B. mountainous C. sustenance D. gluttinous 8.____
9. A. guerrilla B. carousal C. maneuver D. staide 9.____
10. A. passable B. dispensable C. deductable D. irreducible 10.____
11. A. reconnaissance B. mayonnaise C. perfectability D. fuselage 11.____
12. A. publicly B. leige C. tragically D. sieve 12.____
13. A. pavillion B. inoculate C. surveillance D. abstemious 13.___
14. A. dungeon B. cinnamon C. abhorrance D. catarrh 14.____
15. A. chlorophyll B. diptheria C. icicle D. periphery 15.____
16. A. queue B. deterent C. idiosyncrasy D. connoisseur 16.____
17. A. revocable B. changeable C. irreducible D. permissable 17.____
18. A. embarrass B. recommend C. emolient D. concomitant 18.____
19. A. sherbet B. losenge C. revelatory D. privilege 19.____
20. A. stupefy B. indispensable C. mocassin D. forcibly 20.____

KEY (CORRECT ANSWERS)

1.	A	shriek	11.	C	perfectibility
2.	A	crystal	12.	B	liege
3.	D	antarctic	13.	A	pavilion
4.	A	curtsey	14.	C	abhorrence
5.	A	Philippines	15.	B	diphtheria
6.	C	inveigle	16.	B	deterrent
7.	C	buccaneer	17.	D	permissible
8.	D	glutinous	18.	C	emollient
9.	A	guerilla	19.	B	lozenge
10.	C	deductible	20.	C	moccasin

TEST 12

DIRECTIONS: In answering these questions, select the letter of the one MISSPELLED word in each of the following groups of words. *PRINT THE LETTER OF THE CORRECT ANSWER IN THE SPACE AT THE RIGHT.*

1.	A. colossal	B. renascent	C. parallel	D. omniverous	1.____
2.	A. prophesied	B. soliliquy	C. hemorrhage	D. supersede	2.____
3.	A. sestet	B. denouement	C. liason	D. tatooing	3.____
4.	A. embarrassing	B. playright	C. symmetrical	D. unmanageable	4.____
5.	A. grievious	B. dilettante	C. gibberish	D. upbraid	5.____
6.	A. naphtha	B. mediocrity	C. rododendron	D. parliamentary	6.____
7.	A. bilious	B. pedagogue	C. appendectomy	D. exhilerating	7.____
8.	A. irridescent	B. synonymous	C. mimicking	D. irrelevant	8.____
9.	A. mnemonic	B. connoisseur	C. millenium	D. assassinate	9.____
10.	A. cantaloup	B. occurrence	C. tyrannical	D. pneumatic	10.____
11.	A. innoculate	B. recommend	C. deterrent	D. innocuous	11.____
12.	A. moccasin	B. questionaire	C. millionaire	D. emigrate	12.____
13.	A. kaleidoscope	B. anesthesia	C. vermilion	D. tafetta`	13.____
14.	A. innuendo	B. align	C. sacreligious	D. violoncello	14.____
15.	A. indispensable	B. predjudice	C. idiosyncrasy	D. hypotheses	15.____
16.	A. consignee C. apologize		B. perseverance D. biennial		16.____
17.	A. excede	B. curriculum	C. depreciation	D. promissory	17.____
18.	A. accessible	B. remittance	C. plaintif	D. guttural	18.____
19.	A. analysis	B. amateur	C. phosphorous	D. apropriation	19.____
20.	A. oscillate	B. absorbant	C. ecstasy	D. panicky	20.____

KEY (CORRECT ANSWERS)

1.	D	omnivorous	11.	A	inoculate
2.	B	soliloquy	12.	B	questionnaire
3.	C	liaison	13.	D	taffeta
4.	B	playwright	14.	C	sacrilegious
5.	A	grievous	15.	B	prejudice
6.	C	rhododendron	16.	B	perseverance
7.	D	exhilarating	17.	A	exceed
8.	A	iridescent	18.	C	plaintiff
9.	C	millennium	19.	D	appropriation
10.	A	cantaloupe	20.	B	absorbent

TEST 13

DIRECTIONS: In answering these questions, select the letter of the one MISSPELLED word in each of the following groups of words. *PRINT THE LETTER OF THE CORRECT ANSWER IN THE SPACE AT THE RIGHT.*

1.	A. artificial	B. completely	C. rarefy	D. stubborness	1.____
2.	A. calendar	B. cirriculum	C. consensus	D. liquefy	2.____
3.	A. captaincy	B. harrass	C. naphtha	D. ordnance	3.____
4.	A. challange	B. embargoes	C. separation	D. surprised	4.____
5.	A. definate	B. dextrous	C. environment	D. knowledgeable	5.____
6.	A. fission	B. icicle	C. larceny	D. prevelent	6.____
7.	A. fulfiled	B. ghettos	C. prejudiced	D. repentance	7.____
8.	A. government	B. luminous	C. sufficent	D. transparent	8.____
9.	A. mischievious	B. ominous	C. severely	D. withheld	9.____
10.	A. posessions	B. potable	C. procedure	D. procurator	10.____
11.	A. orifice	B. deferrment	C. harass	D. accommodate	11.____
12.	A. picknicking	B. proceedure	C. hypocrisy	D. seize	12.____
13.	A. vilify C. sarcophagus		B. efflorescence D. sacreligious		13.____
14.	A. paraphenalia	B. apothecaries	C. occurrence	D. plagiarize	14.____
15.	A. irreparably	B. comparitively	C. amateur	D. audible	15.____
16.	A. nullify	B. siderial	C. salability	D. irrelevant	16.____
17.	A. asinine	B. dissonent	C. opossum	D. indispensable	17.____
18.	A. changeable	B. therefor	C. incidently	D. dissatisfy	18.____
19.	A. discomfit	B. sapient	C. exascerbate	D. sarsaparilla	19.____
20.	A. categorize	B. maintainance	C. abridgment	D. reticence	20.____

KEY (CORRECT ANSWERS)

1.	D	stubbornness	11.	B	deferment
2.	B	curriculum	12.	B	procedure
3.	B	harass	13.	D	sacrilegious
4.	A	challenge	14.	A	paraphernalia
5.	A	definite	15.	B	comparatively
6.	D	prevalent	16.	B	sidereal
7.	A	fulfilled	17.	B	dissonant
8.	C	sufficient	18.	C	incidentally
9.	A	mischievous	19.	C	exacerbate
10.	A	possessions	20.	B	maintenance

TEST 14

DIRECTIONS: In answering these questions, select the letter of the one MISSPELLED word in each of the following groups of words. *PRINT THE LETTER OF THE CORRECT ANSWER IN THE SPACE AT THE RIGHT.*

1. A. ambivalant B. occurrence C. procedure D. rectify 1.____
2. A. foibles B. indomitable C. quiescant D. ricochet 2.____
3. A. feasible B. persistence C. tubuler D. victuals 3.____
4. A. declination B. frenetic C. grandiose D. serverance 4.____
5. A. cynosure B. flacid C. ilk D. malaise 5.____
6. A. abeyance B. grievious C. nuance D. numismatics 6.____
7. A. iridescent B. generosity C. existence D. sacriligious 7.____
8. A. languor B. environment C. mayorality D. pharaoh 8.____
9. A. privileged B. correspondence C. parallel D. recalcitrant 9.____
10. A. asterik B. Antarctic C. receivership D. alienation 10.____
11. A. mileage B. subpoena C. prolapse D. sacrilegous 11.____
12. A. pharaoh B. vengence C. quandary D. lien 12.____
13. A. biennial B. empathy C. personnell D. bankruptcy 13.____
14. A. maintainance B. exorcise C. canvass D. remembrance 14.____
15. A. deductable B. necessarily C. specious D. therefor 15.____
16. A. councilor B. venturous C. disastrous D. facsimilie 16.____
17. A. scrupulous B. presumptuous C. complementary D. medieval 17.____
18. A. managable B. tangible C. ptomaine D. weird 18.____
19. A. mediocre B. enforceable C. liaision D. murmur 19.____
20. A. stupendous B. recommend C. parentheses D. labled 20.____

KEY (CORRECT ANSWERS)

1.	A	ambivalent	11.	D	sacrilegious
2.	C	quiescent	12.	B	vengeance
3.	C	tubular	13.	C	personnel
4.	D	severance	14.	A	maintenance
5.	B	flaccid	15.	A	deductible
6.	B	grievous	16.	D	facsimile
7.	D	sacrilegious	17.	B	presumptuous
8.	C	mayoralty	18.	A	manageable
9.	B	correspondence	19.	C	liaison
10.	A	asterisk	20.	D	labeled

TEST 15

DIRECTIONS: In answering these questions, select the letter of the one MISSPELLED word in each of the following groups of words. *PRINT THE LETTER OF THE CORRECT ANSWER IN THE SPACE AT THE RIGHT.*

1.	A. perennial	B. liscence	C. deterrent	D. obloquy	1.____
2.	A. cacophonous	B. heterodox	C. analogous	D. feasable	2.____
3.	A. antarctic	B. plebian	C. irreverent	D. emersion	3.____
4.	A. idiosyncrasy	B. acquatic	C. fiduciary	D. liaison	4.____
5.	A. accoustical	B. forfeit	C. ichthyologist	D. diphthong	5.____
6.	A. pretense	B. unforgettable	C. perseverance	D. maintenance	6.____
7.	A. dissipate	B. minature	C. soliloquy	D. rescind	7.____
8.	A. kumquat	B. musilage	C. reminisce	D. peremptory	8.____
9.	A. permissible	B. illegible	C. indispensible	D. irresistible	9.____
10.	A. harass	B. spontaneity	C. carrouse	D. Pharisaical	10.____
11.	A. moustache	B. sovereignty	C. drunkeness	D. staccato	11.____
12.	A. mocassin	B. assassin	C. battalion	D. despicable	12.____
13.	A. entymology	B. echoing	C. subtly	D. stupefy	13.____
14.	A. calcimine	B. seive	C. procedure	D. poinsettia	14.____
15.	A. coercion	B. rescission	C. license	D. prophecied	15.____
16.	A. dispensable	B. compatable	C. recommend	D. feasible	16.____
17.	A. frolicking	B. caramel	C. germaine	D. kohlrabi	17.____
18.	A. diphtheria	B. collander	C. seize	D. sleight	18.____
19.	A. emminent	B. imminent	C. blatant	D. privilege	19.____
20.	A. queue	B. gladioluses	C. kindergarden	D. tonnage	20.____

KEY (CORRECT ANSWERS)

1.	B	license	11.	C	drunkenness
2.	D	feasible	12.	A	moccasin
3.	B	plebeian	13.	A	entomology
4.	B	aquatic	14.	B	sieve
5.	A	acoustical	15.	D	prophesied
6.	C	perseverance	16.	B	compatible
7.	B	miniature	17.	C	germane
8.	B	mucilage	18.	B	colander
9.	C	indispensable	19.	A	eminent
10.	C	carouse	20.	C	kindergarten

TEST 16

DIRECTIONS: In answering these questions, select the letter of the one MISSPELLED word in each of the following groups of words. *PRINT THE LETTER OF THE CORRECT ANSWER IN THE SPACE AT THE RIGHT.*

1.	A. preceeding	B. administer	C. vaccination	D. conscientious	1.____
2.	A. inferred	B. elegibility	C. hypocrisy	D. vacuum	2.____
3.	A. calendar	B. disipate	C. assessment	D. itinerary	3.____
4.	A. chaufeur	B. occasionally	C. trousseau	D. conciliation	4.____
5.	A. eighth	B. accelerated	C. centenial	D. endorsement	5.____
6.	A. separate	B. possessive	C. facsimile	D. bookeeper	6.____
7.	A. appelant	B. discipline	C. restaurant	D. acknowledge	7.____
8.	A. apparatus	B. deceitful	C. occulist	D. treasurer	8.____
9.	A. permissible	B. parliament	C. fiduciary	D. preliminery	9.____
10.	A. gazetteer	B. dissatisfied	C. advantageous	D. intestate	10.____
11.	A. affidavit	B. indicia	C. belligerent	D. ommission	11.____
12.	A. transmittal	B. inaugurate	C. grievious	D. irresistible	12.____
13.	A. irrelevent	B. duplicator	C. periodical	D. phenomena	13.____
14.	A. exhibition	B. recievable	C. irreparable	D. architecture	14.____
15.	A. mileage	B. annually	C. amendment	D. pronounciation	15.____
16.	A. sergeant	B. pantomine	C. dependable	D. sovereignty	16.____
17.	A. temperance C. cemetary		B. superintendent D. thermometer		17.____
18.	A. bacalaureate	B. believing	C. simultaneous	D. notoriety	18.____
19.	A. catalogue	B. collateral	C. bankruptcy	D. deductable	19.____
20.	A. exonerate	B. sacharine	C. intercede	D. attendant	20.____

KEY (CORRECT ANSWERS)

1.	A	preceding	11.	D	omission
2.	B	eligibility	12.	C	grievous
3.	B	dissipate	13.	A	irrelevant
4.	A	chauffeur	14.	B	receivable
5.	C	centennial	15.	D	pronunciation
6.	D	bookkeeper	16.	B	pantomime
7.	A	appellant	17.	C	cemetery
8.	C	oculist	18.	A	baccalaureate
9.	D	preliminary	19.	D	deductible
10.	B	dissatisfied	20.	B	saccharine

TEST 17

DIRECTIONS: In answering these questions, select the letter of the one MISSPELLED word in each of the following groups of words. *PRINT THE LETTER OF THE CORRECT ANSWER IN THE SPACE AT THE RIGHT.*

1. A. surveillance B. trousseau C. suzeranity D. trekked 1.____
2. A. sexagenarian B. soliloquy C. versimilitude D. laity 2.____
3. A. semophore B. ubiquitous C. insouciant D. homiletic 3.____
4. A. tatterdemalion B. terrestrial C. gladiolus D. infinitestimal 4.____
5. A. tranquility B. enrolment C. eleemosynary D. plebescite 5.____
6. A. battalion B. vilify C. fusilage D. inoculate 6.____
7. A. boundries B. fuchsia C. plaguy D. cotillion 7.____
8. A. hinderance B. obbligato C. dumbfound D. picnicking 8.____
9. A. sacrilegious B. sibylline C. sergeant D. temperment 9.____
10. A. vermilion B. paraffin C. floculent D. violoncello 10.____
11. A. pimentoes B. desperadoes C. innuendoes D. mementoes 11.____
12. A. miscellaneous B. vignette C. arhythmic D. vicessitude 12.____
13. A. exorcise B. plagiarize C. macadamise D. mortise 13.____
14. A. spiritural B. capriccio C. beriberi D. doggerel 14.____
15. A. acreage B. annoint C. counterfeit D. eighths 15.____
16. A. cameos B. sopranos C. mottoes D. dynamoes 16.____
17. A. aquarium B. acqueduct C. balustrade D. bivouacked 17.____
18. A. chrysanthemum B. frolicsome C. guage D. idiosyncrasy 18.____
19. A. isosceles B. inundate C. mimicked D. minerology 19.____
20. A. beneficent B. pastime C. phthisis D. pavillion 20.____

KEY (CORRECT ANSWERS)

1.	C	suzerainty	11.	A	pimentos
2.	C	verisimilitude	12.	D	vicissitude
3.	A	semaphore	13.	C	macadamize
4.	D	infinitesimal	14.	A	spiritual
5.	D	plebiscite	15.	B	anoint
6.	C	fuselage	16.	D	dynamos
7.	A	boundaries	17.	B	aqueduct
8.	A	hindrance	18.	C	gauge
9.	D	temperament	19.	D	mineralogy
10.	C	flocculant	20.	D	pavilion

TEST 18

DIRECTIONS: In answering these questions, select the letter of the one MISSPELLED word in each of the following groups of words. *PRINT THE LETTER OF THE CORRECT ANSWER IN THE SPACE AT THE RIGHT.*

1. A. innundate B. oracle C. ghoul D. gingham 1.____
2. A. lapidery B. neophyte C. abstemious D. sjupersede 2.____
3. A. tetanus B. mayhem C. utterence D. jocular 3.____
4. A. largesse B. gherkin C. therapist D. inhalent 4.____
5. A. nuisance B. invincible C. knicknack D. optometry 5.____
6. A. hepatitis B. forfeit C. negotiater D. echelon 6.____
7. A. mnemonic B. drunkeness C. notable D. liaison 7.____
8. A. ingenious B. eleemosynery C. orchid D. salable 8.____
9. A. acquitted B. oriole C. jambore D. systemize 9.____
10. A. hippodrome B. sapphire C. sedentery D. pariah 10.____
11. A. orchesteral B. effete C. canard D. hierarchy 11.____
12. A. diagramatic B. soulless C. ocelot D. secede 12.____
13. A. thesaurus B. sophamore C. telepathy D. ukulele 13.____
14. A. inheritance B. plebian C. herbaceous D. xylophone 14.____
15. A. occult B. lightning C. p;arenthesize D. erantry 15.____
16. A. nonchalant B. vengence C. porosity D. testament 16.____
17. A. gyratory B. tumultous C. jauntily D. malice 17.____
18. A. versatility B. wierd C. pitiless D. forgivable 18.____
19. A. zigzag B. hemorhage C. yodeler D. hippopotamus 19.____
20. A. triumvirate B. elegibility C. inseparable D. gypsy 20.____

KEY (CORRECT ANSWERS)

1.	A	inundate	11.	A	orchestral
2.	A	lapidary	12.	A	diagrammatic
3.	C	utterance	13.	B	sophomore
4.	D	inhalant	14.	B	plebeian
5.	C	knickknack	15.	D	errantry
6.	C	negotiator	16.	B	vengeance
7.	B	drunkenness	17.	B	tumultuous
8.	B	eleemosynary	18.	B	weird
9.	C	jamboree	19.	B	hemorrhage
10.	C	sedentary	20.	B	eligibility

TEST 19

DIRECTIONS: In answering these questions, select the letter of the one MISSPELLED word in each of the following groups of words. *PRINT THE LETTER OF THE CORRECT ANSWER IN THE SPACE AT THE RIGHT.*

1. A. accession B. abhorence C. dilemma D. octagonal 1.____
2. A. sovreign B. abridgment C. deductible D. vacillate 2.____
3. A. invalidate B. rhythmic C. supercede D. sapphires 3.____
4. A. benefitial B. insolvable C. picayune D. parentheses 4.____
5. A. familiar B. dissimilar C. pyorrhea D. asterik 5.____
6. A. usage B. desicate C. grievous D. metallic 6.____
7. A. annoint B. miscellaneous 7.____
   C. saturnine D. aperture
8. A. secretarial B. bookkeeping C. procede D. biennial 8.____
9. A. conciliation B. alienated C. garrolous D. auxiliary 9.____
10. A. appropriation B. counterfeit C. simultaneous D. exhuberance 10.____
11. A. chauffeur B. insiduous C. heroine D. extortionary 11.____
12. A. equivocal B. credulity C. inveterate D. guage 12.____
13. A. plebeian B. heresy C. plaintiff D. heliocopter 13.____
14. A. sonorous B. syncronize C. investitute D. assessment 14.____
15. A. legionaire B. commodious C. psaltery D. inhalant 15.____
16. A. compendium B. nautical C. lisence D. putrefy 16.____
17. A. systemetize B. holocaust C. omission D. meteoric 17.____
18. A. repertoir B. ebullient C. irrelevant D. rhinoceros 18.____
19. A. impresario B. hindrance C. conspicuous D. lithsome 19.____
20. A. sibeling B. antogonistic C. remembrance D. pantomime 20.____

KEY (CORRECT ANSWERS)

1.	B	abhorrence	11.	B	insidious
2.	A	sovereign	12.	D	gauge
3.	C	supersede	13.	D	helicopter
4.	A	beneficial	14.	B	synchronize
5.	D	asterisk	15.	A	legionnaire
6.	B	dessicate	16.	C	license
7.	A	anoint	17.	A	systematize
8.	C	proceed	18.	A	repertoire
9.	C	garrulous	19.	D	lithesome
10.	D	exuberance	20.	A	sibling

TEST 20

DIRECTIONS: In answering these questions, select the letter of the one MISSPELLED word in each of the following groups of words. *PRINT THE LETTER OF THE CORRECT ANSWER IN THE SPACE AT THE RIGHT.*

1.	A. annotation	B. percent	C. inoculate	D. indispensible	1.____
2.	A. flammable	B. impressario	C. accredited	D. guerrilla	2.____
3.	A. desiccate	B. boundry	C. anoint	D. mattress	3.____
4.	A. acquitted	B. adolescence	C. heavyness	D. irascible	4.____
5.	A. ukulele	B. presumptious	C. isosceles	D. Pittsburgh	5.____
6.	A. innate	B. cannoneer	C. passtime	D. auditorium	6.____
7.	A. hinderance	B. benefited	C. embarrass	D. syllabus	7.____
8.	A. Cincinnati	B. pavilion	C. ebulient	D. questionnaire	8.____
9.	A. dilletante	B. liquefy	C. physiology	D. proscribe	9.____
10.	A. harass	B. vilify	C. similar	D. supercede	10.____
11.	A. connoisseur	B. ancilary	C. coliseum	D. buccaneer	11.____
12.	A. auxiliary	B. plebescite	C. millionaire	D. Philippines	12.____
13.	A. educable	B. beneficent	C. medalion	D. corollary	13.____
14.	A. miscellaneous	B. vicissitude	C. imbroglio	D. temperment	14.____
15.	A. familiar	B. milleniuim	C. privilege	D. notable	15.____
16.	A. chagrined	B. demurred	C. holacoust	D. underrate	16.____
17.	A. occured	B. accede	C. annulling	D. parallel	17.____
18.	A. cotillion	B. Albuquerque	C. iredescent	D. rememberance	18.____

19. A. prerogative B. extracurricular 19.____
C. iredescent D. rarefy

20. A. chrysanthemum B. sexogenarian 20.____
C. drily D. enameled

KEY (CORRECT ANSWERS)

1.	D	indispensable	11.	B	ancillary
2.	B	impresario	12.	B	plebiscite
3.	B	boundary	13.	C	medallion
4.	C	heaviness	14.	D	temperament
5.	B	presumptuous	15.	B	millennium
6.	C	pastime	16.	C	holocaust
7.	A	hindrance	17.	A	occurred
8.	C	ebullient	18.	D	remembrance
9.	A	dilettante	19.	C	iridescent
10.	D	supersede	20.	B	sexagenarian

PRACTICE AND DRILL IN SHORTHAND OUTLINES
FOR
LEGAL(HEARING/REPORTING) STENOGRAPHERS
(SIMPLIFIED & ANNIVERSARY)

CONTENTS

PRACTICE AND DRILL IN SHORTHAND OUTLINES
FOR
LEGAL STENOGRAPHERS
(SIMPLIFIED & ANNIVERSARY)

A

SIMPLIFIED | ANNIVERSARY

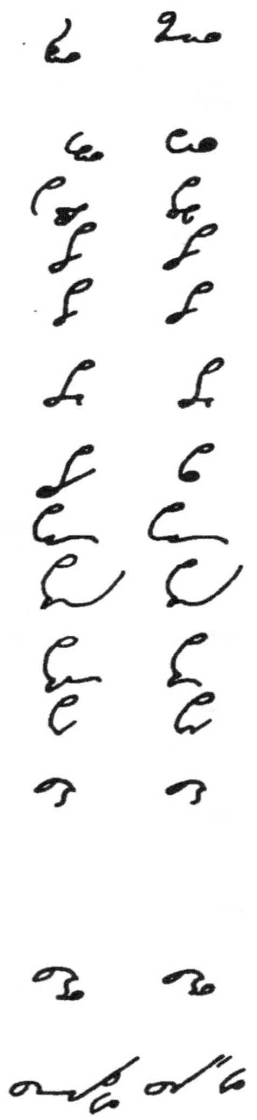

a fortiori	A term meaning you can reason one thing from the existence of certain facts.
a priori	From what goes before.
ab initio	From the beginning.
abate	To diminish or put an end to.
abet	To encourage the commission of a crime.
abeyance	Suspension, temporary suppression.
abide	To accept the consequences of.
abrogate	To annul, repeal, or destroy.
abscond	To hide or absent oneself to avoid legal action.
abstract	A summary.
abut	To border on, to touch.
access	Approach; in real property law it means the right of the owner of property to the use of the highway or road next to his land, without obstruction by intervening property owners.
accessory	In criminal law, it means the person who contributes or aids in the commission of a crime.
accommodated party	One to whom credit is extended on the strength of another person signing a commercial paper.

SIMPLIFIED | ANNIVERSARY

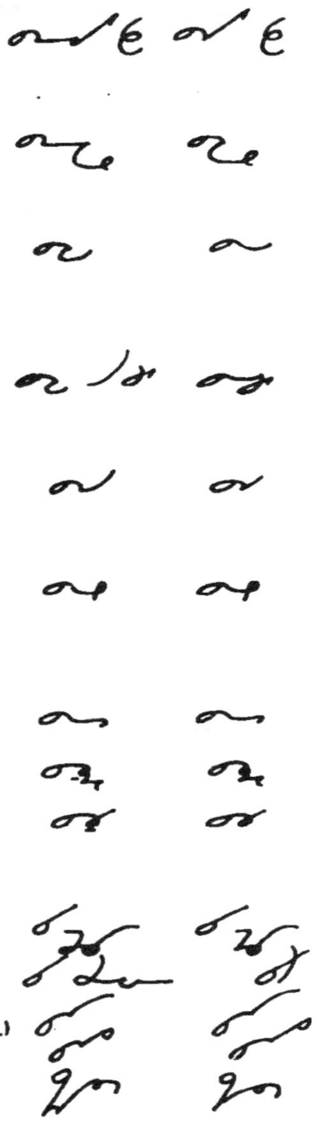

accommodation paper	A commercial paper to which the accommodating party has put his name.
accomplice	In criminal law, it means a person who together with the principal offender commits a crime.
accord	An agreement to accept something different or less than that to which one is entitled, which extinguishes the entire obligation.
accord and satisfaction	When the agreement (accord) is executed and performed according to its terms.
account	A statement of mutual demands in the nature of debt and credit between parties.
accretion	The act of adding to a thing; in real property law, it means gradual accumulation of land by natural causes.
accrue	To grow to; to be added to.
acquiescence	A silent appearance of consent.
acquit	To legally determine the innocence of one charged with a crime.
ad infinitum	Indefinitely.
ad valorem	According to value.
addendum (sing.) addenda (pl.)	An addition; a supplement to a book.
adjudication	The judgment given in a case.

A

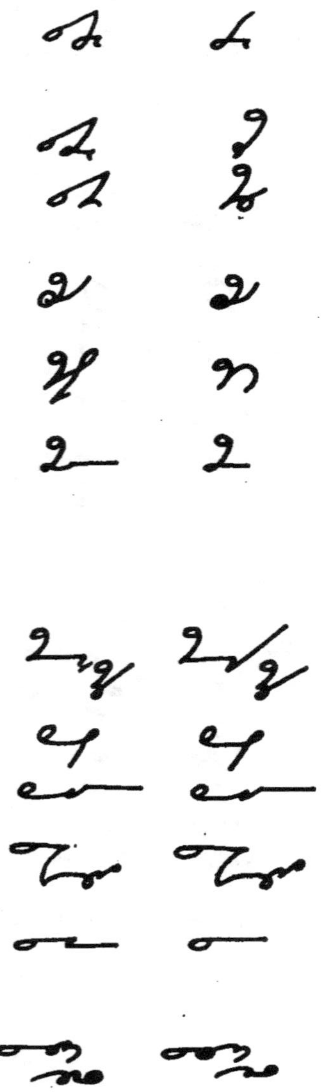

Term	SIMPLIFIED	ANNIVERSARY	Definition
advance			In commercial law, it means to pay money or render other value before it is due.
adverse			Opposed; contrary.
advocate			(v.) To speak in favor of; (n.) one who assists, defends, or pleads for another.
affiant			A person who makes and signs an affidavit.
affidavit			A written and sworn to declaration of facts, voluntarily made.
affirm			To ratify; also when an appellate court affirms a judgment, decree, or order, it means that it is valid and right and must stand as rendered in the lower court.
aforementioned aforesaid			Before or already said.
allege			To assert.
allotment			A share or portion.
ambiguity			Uncertainty; capable of being understood in more than one way.
amendment			Any language made or proposed as a change in some principal writing.
amicus curiae			A friend of the court; one who has an interest in a case, although not a party in the case, who volunteers advice upon matters of law to the judge. For example, a brief amicus curiae.

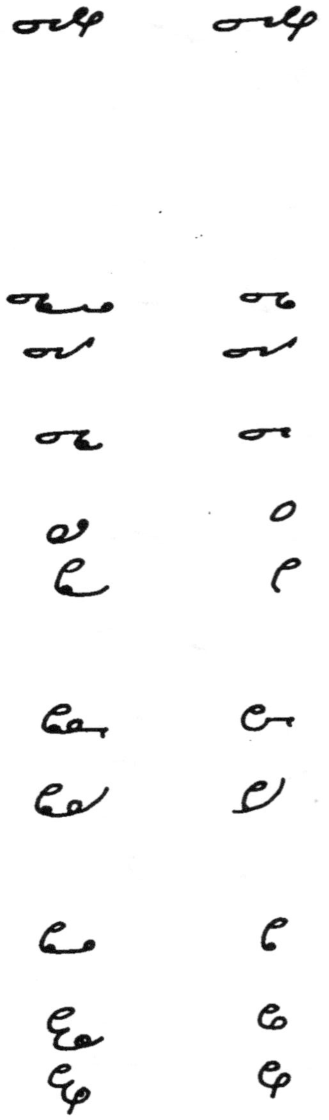

Term	SIMPLIFIED	ANNIVERSARY	Definition
amortization			To provide for a gradual extinction of (a future obligation) in advance of maturity, especially, by periodical contributions to a sinking fund which will be adequate to discharge a debt or make a replacement when it becomes necessary.
ancillary			Aiding, auxiliary.
annotation			A note added by way of comment or explanation.
answer			A written statement made by a defendant setting forth the grounds of his defense.
ante			Before.
appeal			The removal of a case from a lower court to one of superior jurisdiction for the purposes of obtaining a review.
appearance			Coming into court as a party to a suit.
appellant			The party who takes an appeal from one court or jurisdiction to another (appellate) court for review.
appellee			The party against whom an appeal is taken.
appropriate			To make a thing one's own.
appropriation			Prescribing the destination of a thing; the act of the legislature designating a particular fund, to be applied to some object of government expenditure.

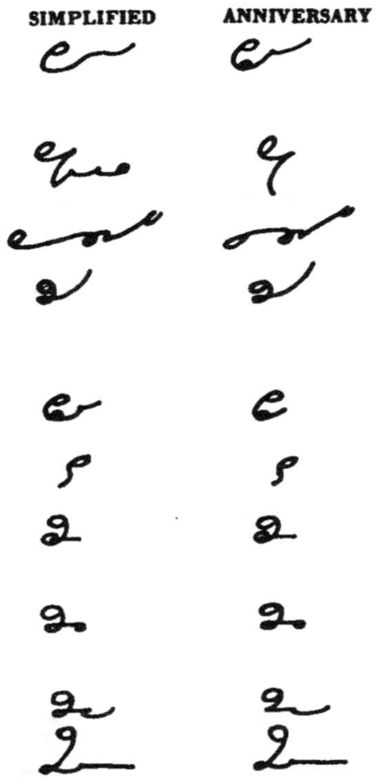

Term	Definition
appurtenant	Belonging to; accessory or incident to.
arbitrary	Unreasoned; not governed by any fixed rules or standard.
arguendo	By way of argument.
assent	A declaration of willingness to do something in compliance with a request.
assert	Declare.
assess	To fix the rate or amount.
assign	To transfer; to appoint; to select for a particular purpose.
assignee	One who receives an assignment.
assignor	One who makes an assignment.
averment	A positive statement of facts.

B

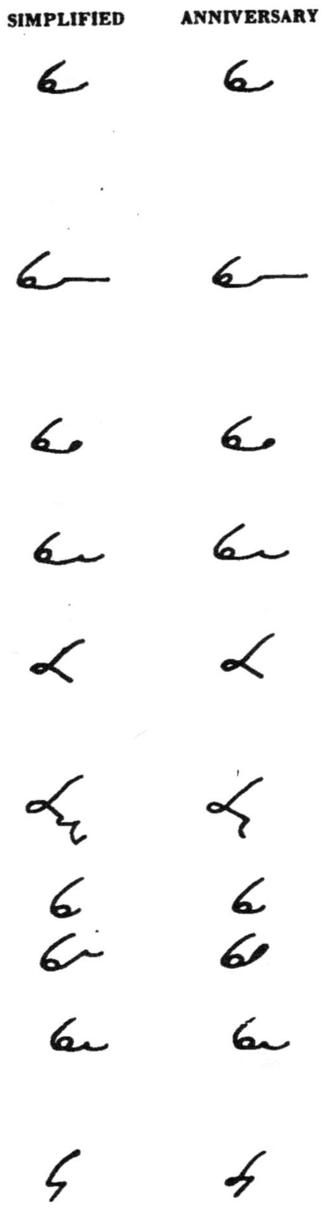

Term	Definition
bail	To obtain the release of a person from legal custody by giving security and promising that he shall appear in court; to deliver (goods, etc.) in trust to a person for a special purpose.
bailment	Delivery of personal property to another to be held for a certain purpose and to be returned when the purpose is accomplished.
bailee	One to whom personal property is delivered under a contract of bailment.
bailor	The party who delivers goods to another, under a contract of bailment.
banc (or bank)	Bench; the place where a court sits permanently or regularly; also the assembly of all the judges of a court.
bankrupt	An insolvent person, technically, one declared to be bankrupt after a bankruptcy proceeding.
bar	The legal profession.
barter	A contract by which parties exchange goods for other goods.
bearer	In commercial law, it means the person in possession of a commercial paper which is payable to the bearer.
bench	The court itself; or the judge.

B

	SIMPLIFIED / ANNIVERSARY	
beneficiary		A person benefiting under a will, trust, or agreement.
bequest		A gift of personal property under a will.
bill		A formal written statement of complaint to a court of justice; also, a draft of an act of the legislature before it becomes a law; also, accounts for goods sold, services rendered, or work done.
bona fide		In or with good faith; honestly.
bond		An instrument by which the maker promises to pay a sum of money to another, usually providing that upon performance of a certain condition the obligation shall be void.
breach		The breaking or violating of a law, or the failure to carry out a duty.
brief		A written document, prepared by a lawyer to serve as the basis of an argument upon a case in court, usually an appellate court.
by-laws		Regulations, ordinances, or rules enacted by a corporation, association, etc., for its own government.

C

	SIMPLIFIED / ANNIVERSARY	
canon		A doctrine; also, a law or rule, of a church or association in particular.
caption		In a pleading, deposition or other paper connected with a case in court, it is the heading or introductory clause which shows the names of the parties, name of the court, number of the case on the docket or calendar, etc.
carrier		A person or corporation undertaking to transport persons or property.
case		A general term for an action; cause, suit, or controversy before a judicial body.
cause		A suit, litigation or action before a court.
caveat emptor		Let the buyer beware. This term expresses the rule that the purchaser of an article must examine, judge, and test it for himself, being bound to discover any obvious defects or imperfections.
certificate		A written representation that some legal formality has been complied with.
certiorari		To be informed of; the name of a writ issued by a superior court directing the lower court to send up to the former the record and proceedings of a case.

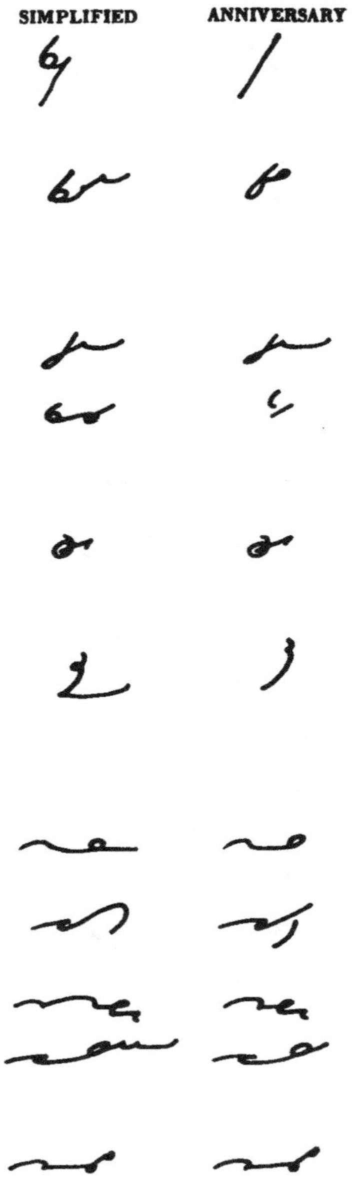

charge — An obligation or duty; a formal complaint; an instruction of the court to the jury upon a case.

charter — (n.) The authority by virtue of which an organized body acts; (v.) in mercantile law, it means to hire or lease a vehicle or vessel for transportation.

chattel — An article of personal property.

circuit — A division of the country, for the administration of justice; a geographical area served by a court.

citation — The act of the court by which a person is summoned or cited; also, a reference to legal authority.

civil (actions) — It indicates the private rights and remedies of individuals in contrast to the word "criminal" (actions) which relates to prosecution for violation of laws.

claim — (n.) Any demand held or asserted as of right.

codify — To arrange the laws of a country into a code.

cognizance — Notice or knowledge.

collateral — By the side; accompanying; an article or thing given to secure performance of a promise.

comity — Courtesy; the practice by which one court follows the decision of another court on the same question.

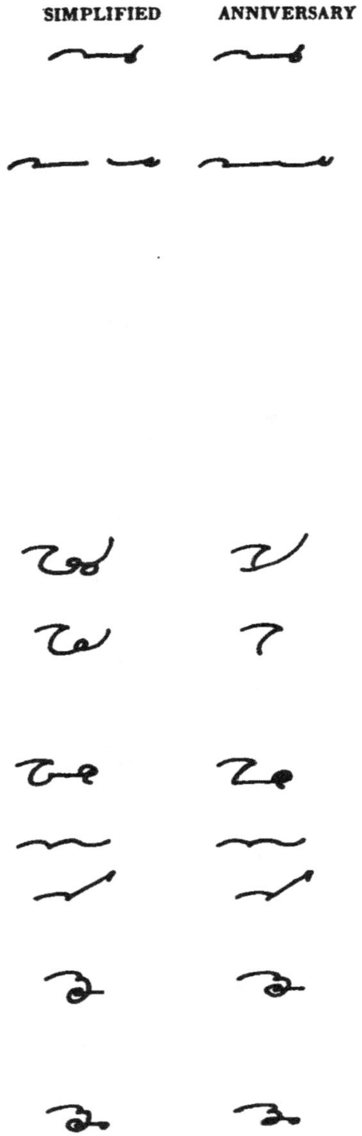

commit — To perform, as an act; to perpetrate, as a crime; to send a person to prison.

common law — As distinguished from law created by the enactment of legislature (called statutory law), it relates to those principles and rules of action which derive their authority solely from usages and customs of immemorial antiquity, particularly with reference to the ancient unwritten law of England. The written pronouncements of the common law are found in court decisions.

complainant — One who applies to the court for legal redress.

complaint — The pleading of a plaintiff in a civil action; or a charge that a person has committed a specified offense.

compromise — An arrangement for settling a dispute by agreement.

concur — To agree, consent.

condition — Mode or state of being; a qualification or restriction.

consign — To give in charge; commit; entrust; to send or transmit goods to a merchant, factor, or agent for sale.

consignee — One to whom a consignment is made.

C

	SIMPLIFIED / ANNIVERSARY	
consignor		One who sends or makes a consignment.
conspiracy		In criminal law, it means an agreement between two or more persons to commit an unlawful act.
conspirators		Persons involved in a conspiracy.
constitution		The fundamental law of a nation or state.
constructive		An act or condition assumed from other acts or conditions.
construe		To ascertain the meaning of language.
consummate		To complete.
contiguous		Adjoining; touching; bounded by.
contingent		Possible, but not assured; dependent upon some condition.
continuance		The adjournment or postponement of an action pending in a court.
contra		Against, opposed to; contrary.
contract		An agreement between two or more persons to do or not to do a particular thing.
conversion		Dealing with the personal property of another as if it were one's own, without right.
conveyance		An instrument transferring title to land.

	SIMPLIFIED / ANNIVERSARY	
conviction		Generally, the result of a criminal trial which ends in a judgment or sentence that the defendant is guilty as charged.
co-operative (also cooperative)		A cooperative is a voluntary organization of persons with a common interest, formed and operated along democratic lines for the purpose of supplying services at cost to its members and other patrons, who contribute both capital and business.
corroborate		To strengthen; to add weight by additional evidence.
counterclaim		A claim presented by a defendant in opposition to or deduction from the claim of the plaintiff.
county		Political subdivision of a state.
covenant		Agreement.
credible		Worthy of belief.
creditor		A person to whom a debt is owing by another person, called the "debtor".
criterion (sing.) **criteria (pl.)**		A means or tests for judging; a standard or standards.

D

Term	Definition
damages	A monetary compensation, which may be recovered in the courts by any person who has suffered loss, or injury, whether to his person, property or rights through the unlawful act or omission or negligence of another.
de facto	In fact; actually but without legal authority.
de jure	Of right; legitimate; lawful.
de minimis	Very small or trifling.
de novo	Anew; afresh; a second time.
debt	A specified sum of money owing to one person from another, including not only the obligation of the debtor to pay, but the right of the creditor to receive and enforce payment.
decedent	A dead person.
decision	A judgment or decree pronounced by a court in determination of a case.
decree	An order of the court, determining the rights of all parties to a suit.
deed	A writing containing a contract sealed and delivered; particularly to convey real property.
default	The failure to fulfill a duty, observe a promise, discharge an obligation, or perform an agreement.

SIMPLIFIED / ANNIVERSARY (shorthand outlines above, in order of the entries)

Term	Definition
defendant	The person defending or denying; the party against whom relief or recovery is sought in an action or suit.
defraud	To practice fraud; to cheat or trick.
delegate	(v.) To entrust to the care or management of another.
demur (v.) **demurrer (n.)**	(v.) To dispute the sufficiency in law of the pleading of the other side.
demurrage	In maritime law, it means, the sum fixed or allowed as remuneration to the owners of a ship for the detention of their vessel beyond the number of days allowed for loading and unloading or for sailing; also used in railroad terminology.
denial	A form of pleading; refusing to admit the truth of a statement, charge, etc.
deposition	Testimony given under oath outside of court for use in court or for the purpose of obtaining information in preparation for trial of a case.
deponent	One who gives under oath testimony which is reduced to writing.
deterioration	A degeneration such as from decay, corrosion or disintegration.

SIMPLIFIED / ANNIVERSARY (shorthand outlines above, in order of the entries)

D

SIMPLIFIED

ANNIVERSARY

detriment	Any loss or harm to person or property.
deviation	A turning aside.
devise	A gift of real property by the last will and testament of the donor.
dictum (sing.) dicta (pl.)	Any statements made by the court in an opinion concerning some rule of law not necessarily involved nor essential to the determination of the case.
disaffirm	To repudiate.
dismiss	In an action or suit, it means to dispose of the case without any further consideration or hearing.
dissent	To denote disagreement of one or more judges of a court with the decision passed by the majority upon a case before them.
docket	(n.) A formal record, entered in brief, of the proceedings in a court.
doctrine	A rule, principle, theory of law.
domicile	That place where a man has his true, fixed and permanent home to which whenever he is absent he has the intention of returning.
draft	(n.) A commercial paper ordering payment of money drawn by one person on another.
drawee	The person who is requested to pay the money.

SIMPLIFIED

ANNIVERSARY

drawer	The person who draws the commercial paper and addresses it to the drawee.
duress	Use of force to compel performance or non-performance of an act.

8

E

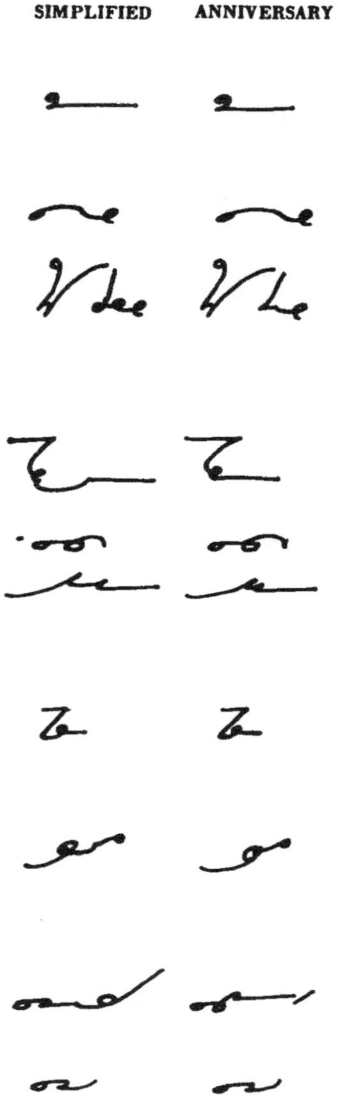

Term	Definition
easement	A liberty, privilege, or advantage without profit, in the lands of another.
egress	Act or right of going out or leaving; emergence.
<u>ejusdem</u> <u>generis</u>	Of the same kind, class or nature. A rule used in the construction of language in a legal document.
embezzlement	To steal; to appropriate fraudulently to one's own use property entrusted to one's care.
enact	To make into a law.
endorsement	Act of writing one's name on the back of a note, bill or similar written instrument.
enjoin	To require a person, by writ of injunction from a court of equity, to perform or to abstain or desist from some act.
entirety	The whole; that which the law considers as one whole, and not capable of being divided into parts.
enumerated	Mentioned specifically; designated.
enure	To operate or take effect.

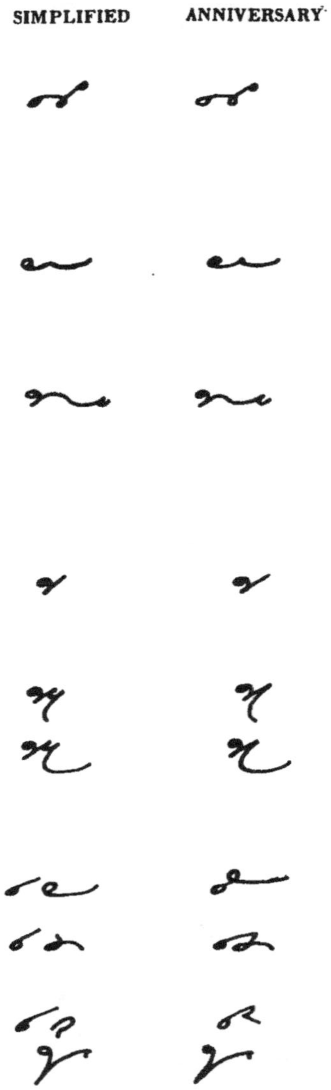

Term	Definition
equity	In its broadest sense, this term denotes the spirit and the habit of fairness, justness, and right dealing which regulate the conduct of men.
error	A mistake of law, or the false or irregular application of law as will nullify the judicial proceedings.
escrow	A deed, bond or other written engagement, delivered to a third person, to be delivered by him only upon the performance or fulfillment of some condition.
estate	The interest which any one has in lands, or in any other subject of property.
estop	To stop, bar, or impede.
estoppel	A rule of law which prevents a man from alleging or denying a fact, because of his own previous act.
<u>et</u> <u>al.</u> (alii)	And others.
<u>et</u> <u>seq.</u> (sequentia)	And the following.
<u>et</u> <u>ux.</u> (uxor)	And wife.
evidence	Documents or testimony of witnesses which tend to prove or disprove any matter in question, usually submitted to a jury to enable them to decide.

E

599894 O-61-2

	SIMPLIFIED	ANNIVERSARY	
ex contractu / **ex delicto**	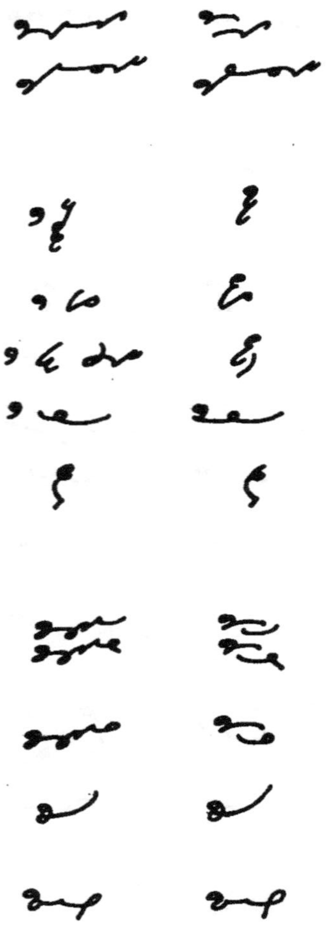		In law, rights and causes of action are divided into two classes, those arising *ex contractu* (from a contract) and those arising *ex delicto* (from a delict or tort).
ex officio			From office; by virtue of the office.
ex parte			On one side only; by or for one.
ex post facto			After the fact.
ex rel. (relations)			Upon relation or information.
exception			An objection upon a matter of law to a decision made, either before or after judgment by a court.
executor (male) / **executrix** (female)			A person who has been appointed by will to execute the will.
executory			That which is yet to be executed or performed.
exempt			To release from some liability to which others are subject.
exoneration			The removal of a burden, charge or duty.

F

	SIMPLIFIED	ANNIVERSARY	
f.a.s.	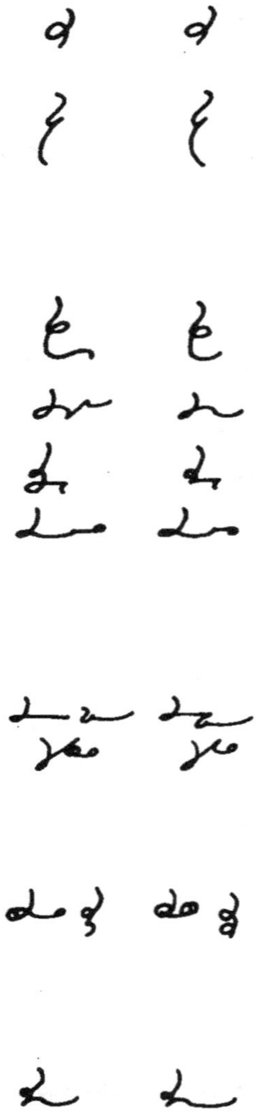		"Free alongside ship"; delivery at dock for ship named.
f.o.b.			"Free on board"; seller will deliver to car, truck, vessel, or other conveyance by which goods are to be transported, without expense or risk of loss to the buyer or consignee.
fabricate			To construct; to invent a false story.
factor			A commercial agent.
feasance			The doing of an act.
felony			Generally, a criminal offense that may be punished by death or imprisonment for more than one year as differentiated from a misdemeanor.
feme sole			A single woman.
fiduciary			A person who is invested with rights and powers to be exercised for the benefit of another person.
fieri facias			A writ of execution commanding the sheriff to levy and collect the amount of a judgment from the goods and chattels of the judgment debtor.
fiscal			Relating to accounts or the management of revenue.

10

F

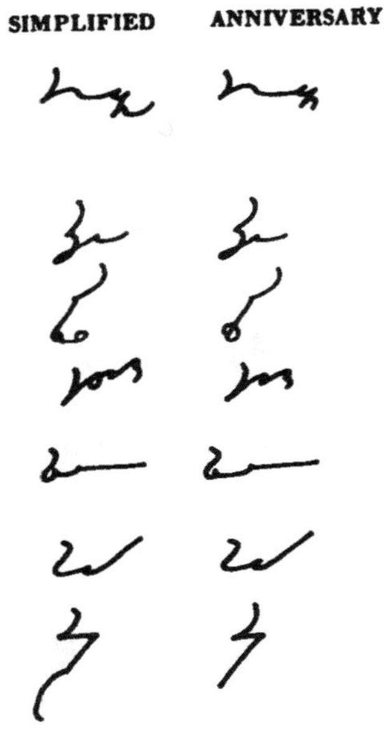

Term	Definition
foreclosure (sale)	A sale of mortgaged property to obtain satisfaction of the mortgage out of the sale proceeds.
forfeiture	A penalty, a fine.
forgery	Fabricating or producing falsely, counterfeited.
fortuitous	Accidental.
forum	A court of justice; a place of jurisdiction.
fraud	Deception; trickery.
fungible	Of such kind or nature that one specimen or part may be used in the place of another.

G

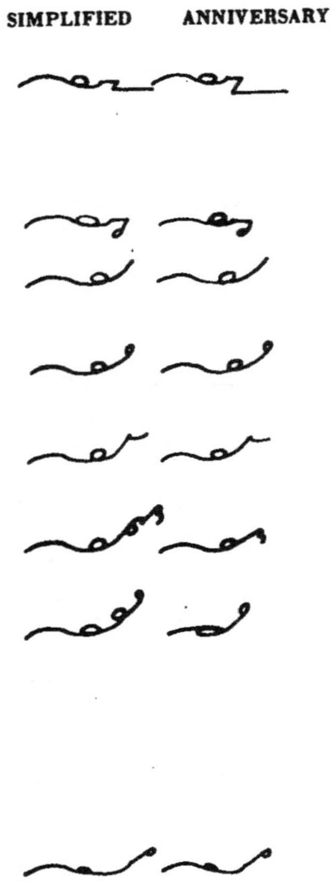

Term	Definition
garnishment	A legal process to reach the money or effects of a defendant, in the possession or control of a third person.
garnishee	Person garnished.
grant	To agree to; convey, especially real property.
grantee	The person to whom a grant is made.
grantor	The person by whom a grant is made.
gratuitous	Given without a return, compensation or consideration.
guaranty	(n.) A promise to answer for the payment of some debt, or the performance of some duty, in case of the failure of another person, who, in the first instance, is liable for such payment or performance.
guilty	Establishment of the fact that one has committed a breach of conduct; especially a violation of law.

H

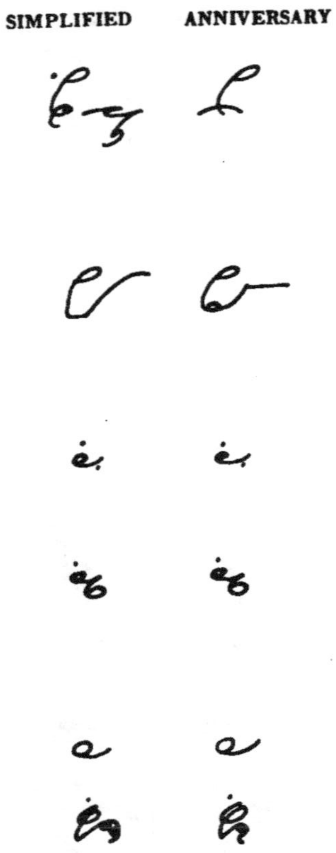

Term	Definition
habeas corpus	You have the body; the name given to a variety of writs, having for their object to bring a party before a court or judge for decision as to whether such person is being lawfully held prisoner.
<u>habendum</u>	In conveyancing; it is the clause in a deed conveying land which defines the extent of ownership to be held by the grantee.
hearing	A proceeding whereby the arguments of the interested parties are heard.
hearsay	A type of testimony given by a witness who relates, not what he knows personally, but what others have told him, or what he has heard said by others.
heir	Generally, one who inherits property, real or personal.
hypothesis	A supposition, assumption, or theory.

I

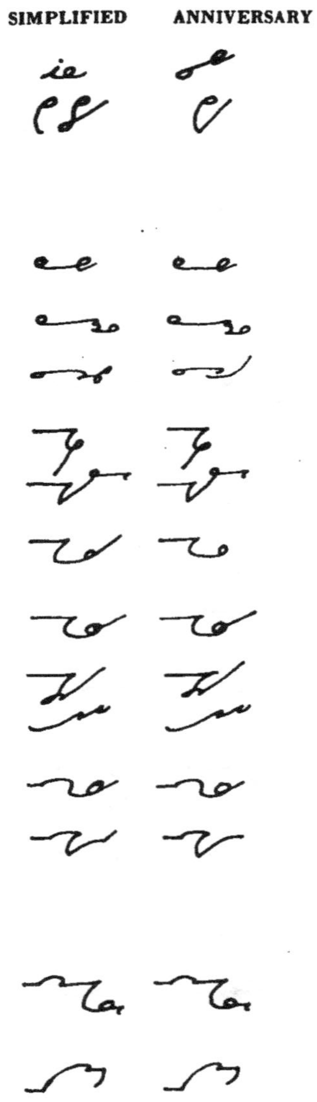

Term	Definition
<u>i.e.</u> (id est)	That is.
<u>ib.</u>, or <u>ibid.</u> (ibidem)	In the same place; used to refer to a legal reference previously cited to avoid repeating the entire citation.
illicit	Prohibited; unlawful.
illusory	Deceiving by false appearance.
immunity	Exemption.
impeach	To accuse, to dispute.
impediments	Disabilities, or hindrances.
implead	To sue or prosecute by due course of law.
implied	Not expressly stated; inferential.
imputed	Attributed or charged to.
in toto	In the whole; completely.
inchoate	Imperfect; unfinished.
incompetent	One who is incapable of caring for his own affairs because he is mentally deficient or undeveloped.
incumbrance	Generally a claim, lien, charge or liability attached to and binding real property.
indemnify	To secure against loss or damage; also, to make reimbursement to one for a loss already incurred by him.

H

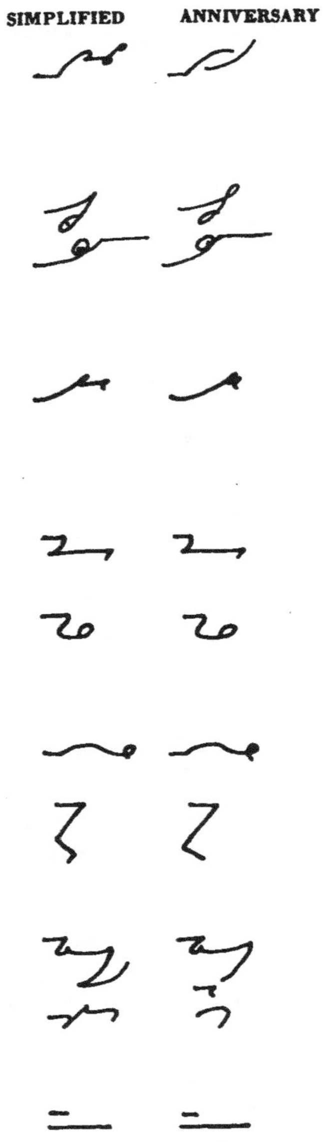

Term	SIMPLIFIED / ANNIVERSARY	Definition
indemnity		An agreement to reimburse another person in case of an anticipated loss falling upon him.
indicia		Signs; indications.
indictment		An accusation in writing found and presented by a grand jury charging that a person has committed a crime.
indorse		To write a name on the back of a legal paper or document generally, a negotiable instrument.
information		A formal accusation of crime made by a prosecuting attorney.
infra		Below, under; this word occurring by itself in a publication refers the reader to a future part of the publication.
ingress		The act of going into.
injunction		A writ or order by the court requiring a person generally, to do or to refrain from doing an act.
insolvent		The condition of a person who is unable to pay his debts.
instruction		A direction given by the judge to the jury concerning the law of the case.
interim		In the meantime; time intervening.

Term	SIMPLIFIED / ANNIVERSARY	Definition
interlocutory		Temporary, not final; something intervening between the commencement and the end of a suit which decides some point or matter, but is not a final decision of the whole controversy.
interrogatories		A series of formal written questions used in the examination of a party or a witness usually prior to a trial.
intestate		A person who dies without a will.
inure		To result, to take effect.
ipso facto		By the fact itself; by the mere fact.
issue		(n.) The disputed point or question in a case.

I

J

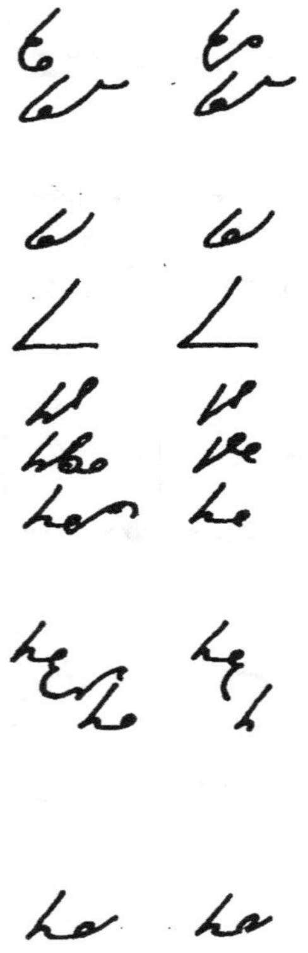

	SIMPLIFIED	ANNIVERSARY	
jeopardy			Danger, hazard, peril.
joinder			Joining; uniting with another person in some legal steps or proceeding.
joint			United; combined.
judgment			The official decision of a court of justice.
judicial or judiciary			Relating to or connected with the administration of justice.
jurisdiction			The authority to hear and determine controversies between parties.
jurisprudence			The philosophy of law.
jury			A body of persons legally selected to inquire into any matter of fact, and to render their verdict according to the evidence.
jurat			The clause written at the foot of an affidavit, stating when, where and before whom such affidavit was sworn.

L

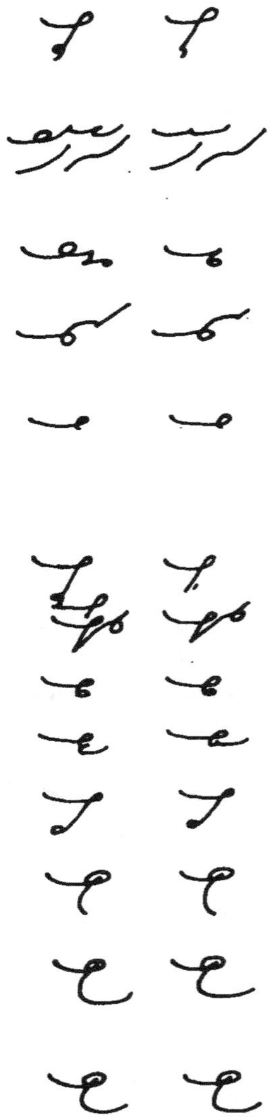

	SIMPLIFIED	ANNIVERSARY	
laches			The failure to diligently assert a right, which results in a refusal to allow relief.
landlord and tenant			A phrase used to denote the legal relation existing between the owner and occupant of real estate.
larceny			Stealing personal property belonging to another.
latent			Hidden; that which does not appear on the face of a thing.
lease			A contract by which one conveys real estate for a limited time usually for a specified rent; personal property also may be leased.
legislation			The act of enacting laws.
legitimate			Lawful.
lessee			One to whom a lease is given.
lessor			One who grants a lease.
levy			A collecting or exacting by authority.
liable			Responsible; bound or obligated in law or equity.
libel			(v.) To defame or injure a person's reputation by a published writing.
libel			(n.) The initial pleading on the part of the plaintiff in an admiralty proceeding.

J

	SIMPLIFIED / ANNIVERSARY	
lien		A hold or claim which one person has upon the property of another as a security for some debt or charge.
liquidated		Fixed; settled.
lis pendens		A pending suit.
literal		According to the language.
litigant		A party to a lawsuit.
litigation		A judicial controversy.
locus		A place.

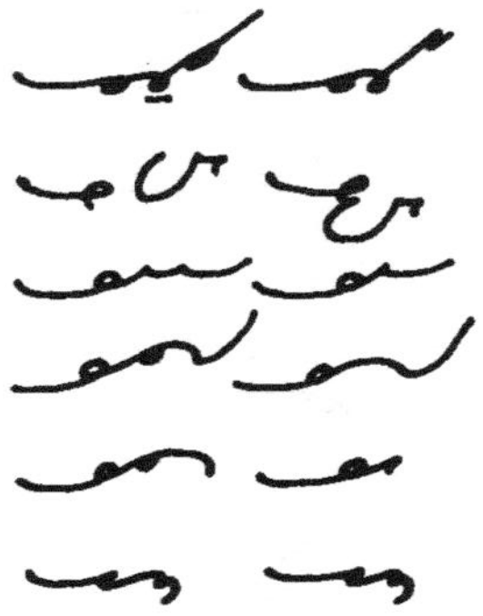

L

M

	SIMPLIFIED / ANNIVERSARY	
malice		The doing of a wrongful act intentionally without just cause or excuse.
mandamus		The name of a writ issued by a court to enforce the performance of some public duty.
mandatory		(adj.) Containing a command.
marshaling		Arranging or disposing of in order.
maxim		An established principle or proposition.
ministerial		That which involves obedience to instruction, but demands no special discretion, judgment or skill.
misappropriate		Dealing fraudulently with property entrusted to one.
misdemeanor		A crime less than a felony and punishable by a fine or imprisonment for less than one year.
misrepresentation		An untrue representation of facts.
mitigate		To make or become less severe, harsh.
moot		(adj.) Unsettled, undecided, not necessary to be decided.
mortgage		A conveyance of property upon condition, as security for the payment of a debt or the performance of a duty, and to become void upon payment or performance according to the stipulated terms.

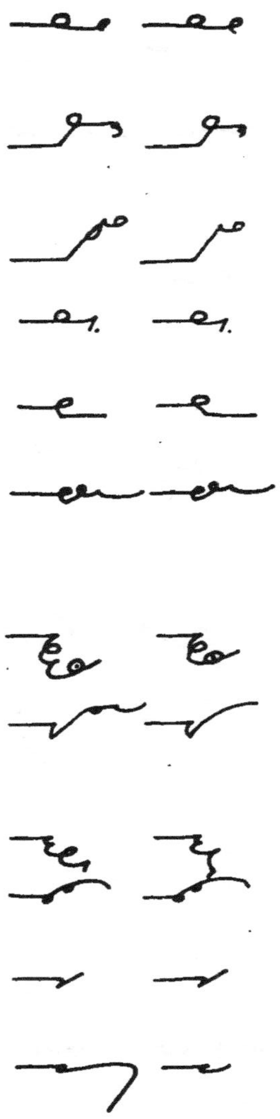

M

	SIMPLIFIED / ANNIVERSARY	
mortgagee		A person to whom property is mortgaged.
mortgagor	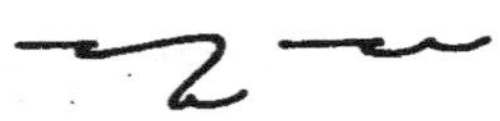	One who gives a mortgage.
motion		In legal proceedings, a "motion" is an application, either written or oral, addressed to the court by a party to an action or a suit requesting the ruling of the court on a matter of law.
mutuality		Reciprocation.

N

	SIMPLIFIED / ANNIVERSARY	
negligence	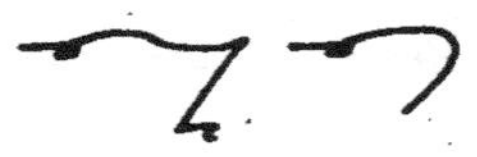	The failure to exercise that degree of care which an ordinarily prudent person would exercise under like circumstances.
negotiable (instrument)		Any instrument obligating the payment of money which is transferable from one person to another by endorsement and delivery or by delivery only.
negotiate	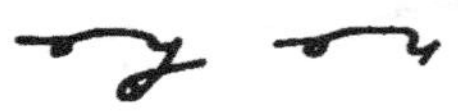	To transact business; to transfer a negotiable instrument; to seek agreement for the amicable disposition of a controversy or case.
nolle prosequi	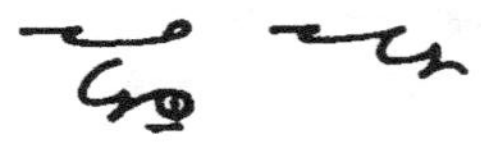	A formal entry upon the record, by the plaintiff in a civil suit or the prosecuting officer in a criminal action, by which he declares that he "will no further prosecute" the case.
nolo contendere		The name of a plea in a criminal action, having the same effect as a plea of guilty; but not constituting a direct admission of guilt.
nominal		Not real or substantial.
novation		The substitution of a new debt or obligation for an existing one.
nunc pro tunc	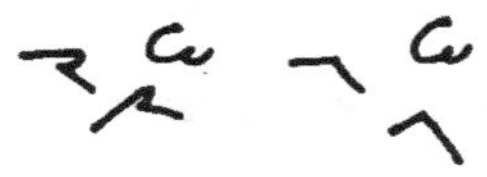	A phrase applied to acts allowed to be done after the time when they should be done, with a retroactive effect.

O

	SIMPLIFIED / ANNIVERSARY	
object		(v.) To oppose as improper or illegal and referring the question of its propriety or legality to the court.
obligation		A legal duty, by which a person is bound to do or not to do a certain thing.
obligee		The person to whom an obligation is owed.
obligor		The person who is to perform the obligation.
offer		(v.) To present for acceptance or rejection.
offer		(n.) A proposal to do a thing, usually a proposal to make a contract.
offset		A deduction.
opinion		The statement by a judge of the decision reached in a case, giving the law as applied to the case and giving reasons for the judgment; also, a belief or view.
option		The exercise of the power of choice; also a privilege existing in one person, for which he has paid money, which gives him the right to buy or sell real or personal property at a given price within a specified time.
order		A rule or regulation; every direction of a court or judge made or entered in writing but not including a judgment.
ordinance		Generally, a rule established by authority; also commonly used to designate the legislative acts of a municipal corporation.

O

599894 O-61-3

P

SIMPLIFIED ANNIVERSARY

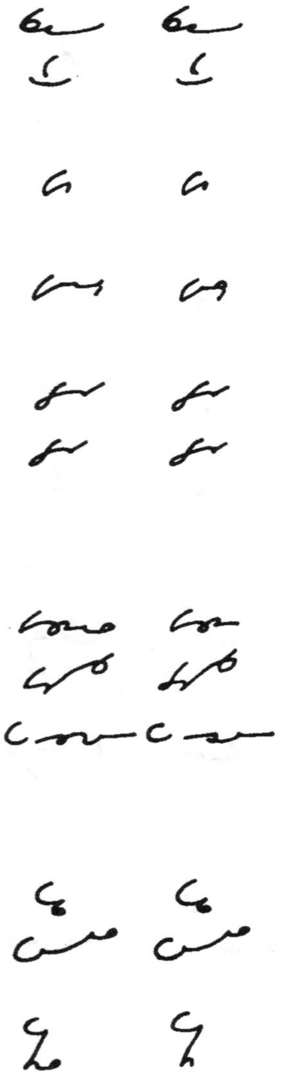

parol	Oral or verbal.
parity	Equality in purchasing power between the farmer and other segments of the economy.
partition	A legal division of real or personal property between one or more owners.
partnership	An association of two or more persons to carry on as co-owners a business for profit.
patent	(adj.) Evident.
patent	(n.) A grant of some privilege, property, or authority, made by the government or sovereign of a country to one or more individuals.
pecuniary	Monetary.
penultimate	Next to the last.
per curiam	A phrase used in the report of a decision to distinguish an opinion of the whole court from an opinion written by any one judge.
per se	In itself; taken alone.
peremptory	Imperative; absolute.
perjury	To lie or state falsely under oath.

SIMPLIFIED ANNIVERSARY

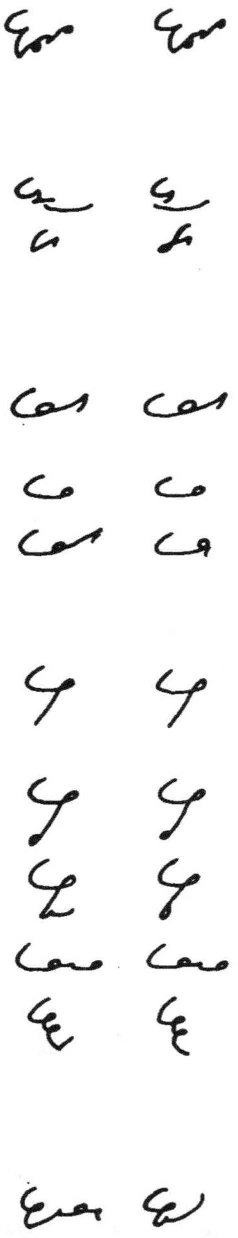

perpetuity	Perpetual existence; also the quality or condition of an estate limited so that it will not take effect or vest within the period fixed by law.
personalty	Short term for personal property.
petition	An application in writing for an order of the court, stating the circumstances upon which it is founded and requesting any order or other relief from a court.
plaintiff	A person who brings a court action.
plea	A pleading in a suit or action.
pleadings	Formal allegations made by the parties of their respective claims and defenses, for the judgment of the court.
pledge	A deposit of personal property as a security for the performance of an act.
pledgee	The party to whom goods are delivered in pledge.
pledgor	The party delivering goods in pledge.
plenary	Full; complete.
precept	An order, warrant, or writ issued to an officer or body of officers, commanding him or them to do some act within the scope of his or their powers.
preponderance	Outweighing.

P

	SIMPLIFIED	ANNIVERSARY	
prima facie			At first sight.
principal			The source of authority or rights; a person primarily liable as differentiated from "principle" as a primary or basic doctrine.
pro rata			Proportionally.
probate			Relating to proof, especially to the proof of wills.
procedure			In law, this term generally denotes rules which are established by the Federal, State or local Governments regarding the types of pleading and courtroom practice which must be followed by the parties involved in a criminal or civil case.
proclamation			A public notice by an official of some order, intended action, or state of facts.
promissory (note)			A promise in writing to pay a specified sum at an expressed time, or on demand, or at sight, to a named person, or to his order, or bearer.
proprietary			(adj.) Relating or pertaining to ownership; usually a single owner.
prosecute			To carry on an action or other judicial proceeding; to proceed against a person criminally.
proviso			A limitation or condition in a legal instrument.
proximate			Immediate; nearest.
punitive			Relating to punishment.

Q

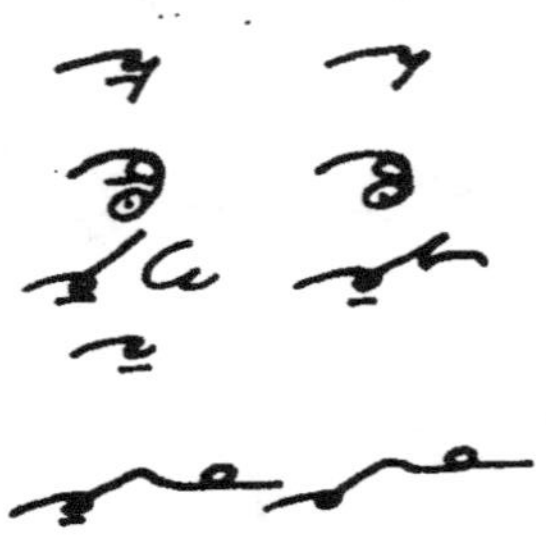

	SIMPLIFIED / ANNIVERSARY	
quash		To make void.
quasi		As if; as it were.
quid pro quo		Something for something; the giving of one valuable thing for another.
quitclaim		(v.) To release or relinquish claim or title to, especially in deeds to realty.

R

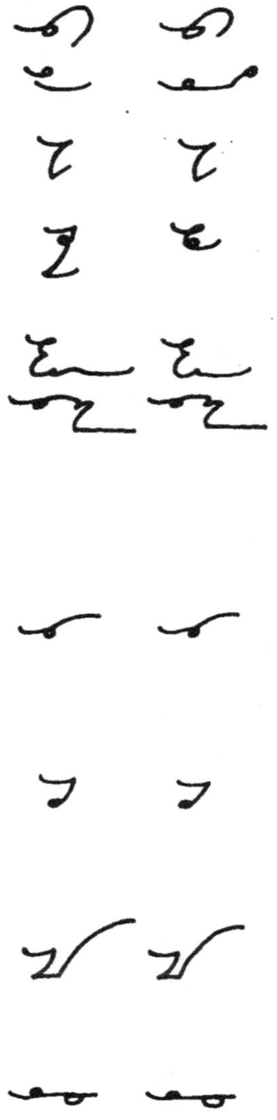

	SIMPLIFIED / ANNIVERSARY	
ratify		To approve and sanction.
realty		A brief term for real property.
rebut		To contradict; to refute, especially by evidence and arguments.
receiver		A person who is appointed by the court to receive, and hold in trust, property in litigation.
reciprocal		Mutual.
recoupment		To keep back or get something which is due; also, it is the right of a defendant to have a deduction from the amount of the plaintiff's damages because the plaintiff has not fulfilled his part of the same contract.
redeem		To release an estate or article from mortgage or pledge by paying the debt for which it stood as security.
referee		A person to whom a cause pending in a court is referred by the court, to take testimony, hear the parties, and report thereon to the court.
referendum		A method of submitting an important legislative or administrative matter to a direct vote of the people.
remand		To send a case back to the lower court from which it came, for further proceedings.

Q

R

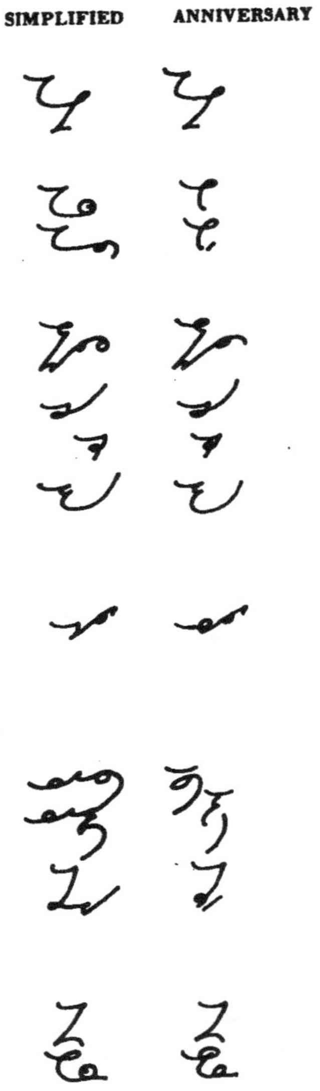

Term	Definition
replevin	An action to recover goods or chattels wrongfully taken or detained.
reply (replication)	Generally, a reply is what the plaintiff or other person who has instituted proceedings says in answer to the defendant's case.
res judicata	A thing judicially acted upon or decided.
rescind (rescission)	To avoid or cancel a contract.
respondent	A defendant in a proceeding in chancery or admiralty; also, the person who contends against the appeal in a case.
restitution	In equity, it is the restoration of both parties to their original condition (when practicable), upon the rescission of a contract for fraud or similar cause.
retroactive (retrospective)	Looking back; effective as of a prior time.
reversed	A term used by appellate courts to indicate that the decision of the lower court in the case before it has been set aside.
revoke	To recall or cancel.
riparian (rights)	The rights of a person owning land containing or bordering on a water course or other body of water, such as lakes and rivers.

S

Term	Definition
sale	A contract whereby the ownership of property is transferred from one person to another for a sum of money or for any consideration.
sanction	A penalty or punishment provided as a means of enforcing obedience to a law; also, an authorization.
satisfaction	The discharge of an obligation by paying a party what is due to him; or what is awarded to him, by the judgment of a court or otherwise.
scienter	Knowingly; also, it is used in pleading to denote the defendant's guilty knowledge.
scintilla	A spark; also the least particle.
security	Indemnification; the term is applied to an obligation, such as a mortgage or deed of trust, given by a debtor to insure the payment or performance of his debt, by furnishing the creditor with a resource to be used in case of the debtor's failure to fulfill the principal obligation.
sentence	The judgment formally pronounced by the court or judge upon the defendant after his conviction in a criminal prosecution.
set-off	A claim or demand which one party in an action credits against the claim of the opposing party.
situs	Location.

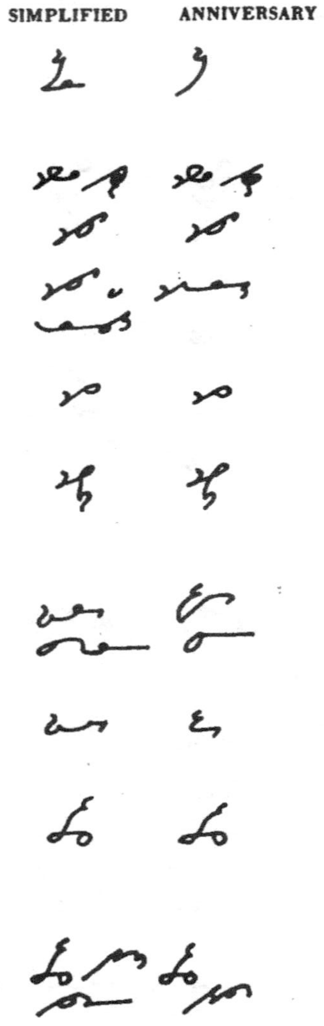

Term	Definition
sovereign	A person, body, or state in which independent and supreme authority is vested.
stare decisis	To follow decided cases.
statute	An act of the legislature.
statute of limitation	A statute limiting the time to bring an action after the right of action has arisen.
stay	To hold in abeyance an order of a court.
stipulation	Any agreement made by opposing attorneys regulating any matter incidental to the proceedings or trial.
subordination (agreement)	An agreement making one's rights inferior to or of a lower rank than another's.
subornation	The crime of procuring a person to lie or to make false statements to a court.
subpoena	A writ or order directed to a person, and requiring his attendance at a particular time and place to testify as a witness.
subpoena duces tecum	A subpoena used, not only for the purpose of compelling witnesses to attend in court, but also requiring them to bring with them books or documents which may be in their possession, and which may tend to elucidate the subject matter of the trial.

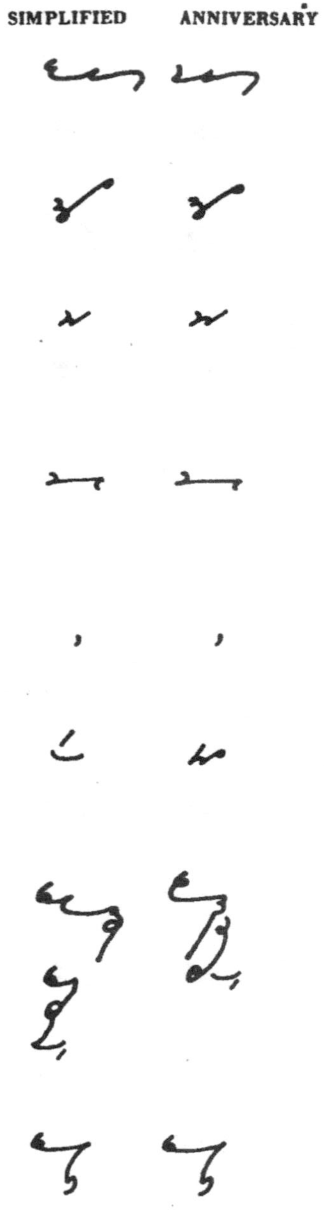

Term	Definition
subrogation	The substituting of one for another as a creditor, the new creditor succeeding to the former's rights.
subsidy	A government grant to assist a private enterprise deemed advantageous to the public.
suit	Any civil proceeding by a person or persons against another or others in a court of justice by which the plaintiff pursues the remedies afforded him by law.
summons	A notice to a defendant that an action against him has been commenced and requiring him to appear in court and answer the complaint.
supra	Above; this word occurring by itself in a book refers the reader to a previous part of the book.
surety	A person who binds himself for the payment of a sum of money, or for the performance of something else, for another.
surplusage	Extraneous or unnecessary matter.
survivorship	A term used when a person becomes entitled to property by reason of his having survived another person who had an interest in the property.
syllabus	A note prefixed to a report, especially a case, giving a brief statement of the court's ruling on different issues of the case.

S

T

Term	SIMPLIFIED / ANNIVERSARY	Definition
tenant		One who holds or possesses lands by any kind of right or title; also, one who has the temporary use and occupation of real property owned by another person (landlord), the duration and terms of his tenancy being usually fixed by an instrument called "a lease".
tender		An offer of money; an expression of willingness to perform a contract according to its terms.
term		When used with reference to a court, it signifies the period of time during which the court holds a session, usually of several weeks or months duration.
testamentary		Pertaining to a will or the administration of a will.
testator (male) **testatrix (female)**	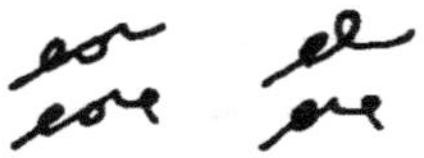	One who makes or has made a testament or will.
testify **(testimony)**		To give evidence under oath as a witness.
to wit		That is to say; namely.
tort		Wrong; injury to the person.
transitory		Passing from place to place.
trial		The examination of a cause, civil or criminal, before a judge who has jurisdiction over it, according to the laws of the land.
trust		A right of property, real or personal, held by one party for the benefit of another.

T

U

Term	SIMPLIFIED / ANNIVERSARY	Definition
ultra vires		Acts beyond the scope and power of a corporation, association, etc.
unilateral		One-sided; obligation upon, or act of one party.

V

SIMPLIFIED ANNIVERSARY

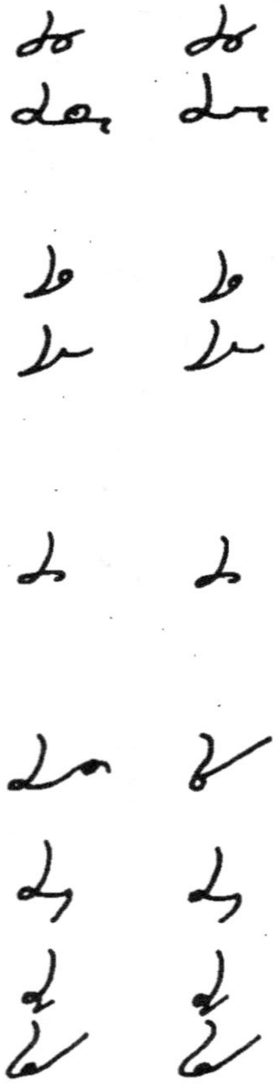

Term	Definition
vacate	To set aside; to move out.
variance	A discrepancy or disagreement between two instruments or two aspects of the same case, which by law should be consistent.
vendee	A purchaser or buyer.
vendor	The person who transfers property by sale, particularly real estate; the term "seller" is used more commonly for one who sells personal property.
venue	The place at which an action is tried, generally based on locality or judicial district in which an injury occurred or a material fact happened.
verdict	The formal decision or finding of a jury.
verify	To confirm or substantiate by oath.
vest	To accrue to.
void	Having no legal force or binding effect.

W

SIMPLIFIED ANNIVERSARY

Term	Definition
waiver	The intentional or voluntary relinquishment of a known right.
warrant (warranty)	(v.) To promise that a certain fact or state of facts, in relation to the subject matter, is, or shall be, as it is represented to be.
warrant	(n.) A writ issued by a judge, or other competent authority, addressed to a sheriff, or other officer, requiring him to arrest the person therein named, and bring him before the judge or court, to answer or be examined regarding the offense with which he is charged.
writ	An order or process issued in the name of the sovereign or in the name of a court or judicial officer, commanding the performance or nonperformance of some act.

24

V

COURT REPORTING

SOUNDS

A. <u>SHORT VOWELS</u>

It is now time for you to hear the distinct difference between words having SHORT VOWEL SOUNDS and words having LONG VOWEL SOUNDS.

The following word list of SHORT VOWEL SOUNDS are to be said out loud. Read the word. "Hear" the SHORT VOWEL SOUND. See how it is written on the machine. Write each word followed by the "Period" stroke –FPLT.

Sound	Word	Machine	Written
A	cat	A	KAT
	hat	A	HAT
	pad	A	PAD
	bad	A	BAD
	pan	A	PAN
	fan	A	FAN
E	bed	E	BED
	head	E	HED
	tell	E	TEL
	well	E	WEL
	set	E	SET
	get	E	GET
I	sit	EU	SEUT
	hit	EU	HEUT
	pin	EU	PEUN
	win	EU	WEUN
	fill	EU	FEUL
	bill	EU	BEUL
O	lot	AU	LAUT
	hot	AU	HAUT
	rod	AU	NAUD
	nod	AU	NAUD
	tall	AU	TAUL
	ball	AU	BAUL
U	love	U	LUV
	dove	U	DUV
	cuff	U	KUF
	stuff	U	STUF
	tough	U	TUF
	rough	U	RUF

Read your notes OUT LOUD. Repeat 20 times.

B. LONG VOWELS

It is now time to hear the LONG VOWEL SOUNDS.

The following word list of LONG VOWEL SOUNDS are to be said out loud. Read the word. "Hear" the LONG VOWEL SOUND. See how it is written on the machine. Write each word followed by the "Period" stroke –FPLT.

Sound	Word	Machine	Written
A	late	AEU	LAEUT
	rate	AEU	RAEUT
	made	AEU	MAEUD
	paid	AEU	PAEUD
	cane	AEU	KAEUN
	lane	AEU	LAEUN
E	meet	AE	MAET
	beat	AE	BAET
	deed	AE	DAED
	need	AE	NAED
	lean	AE	LAEN
	seen	AE	SAEN
I	kite	AOEU	KAOEUT
	bite	AOEU	BAOEUT
	time	AOEU	TAOEUM
	dime	AOEU	DAOEUM
	file	AOEU	FAOEUL
	mile	AOEU	MAOEUL
O	snow	OE	SNOE
	row	OE	ROE
	coat	OE	KOET
	wrote	OE	ROET
	load	OE	LOED
	road	OE	ROED
U	flue	AO	FLAO
	new	AO	NAO
	food	AO	FAOD
	rude	AO	RAOD
	soon	AO	SAON
	tune	AO	TAON

Read your notes OUT LOUD. Repeat 20 times.

C. OTHER SOUNDS

The following SOUNDS should be said OUT LOUD for you to hear for the very first time.

Say each word OUT LOUD before writing it on the machine. Write each word followed by the "Period" stroke –FPLT.

Sound	Word	Machine	Written
"OW"	how	OU	HOU
	now	OU	NOU
	brown	OU	BROUN
"AW"	job	AU	JAUB
	pawn	AU	PAUN
	taught	AU	TAUT
"OY"	boy	OEU	BOEU
	toy	OEU	TOEU
	ploy	OEU	PLOEU
"OI"	toil	OEU	TOEUL
	coin	OEU	KOEUN
	void	OEU	VOEUD

Read your notes OUT LOUD. Repeat 20 times.

C. OTHER SOUNDS

The following SOUNDS need to be said OUT LOUD very slowly and very distinctly before writing them on the machine.

Be sure to HEAR the SOUNDS as you are writing the outlines. Write each word followed by the "Period" stroke –FPLT.

Sound	Word	Machine	Written
"OO"	look	O	LOK
	took	O	TOK
	cook	O	KOK
	put	O	POT
	soot	O	SOT
	wood	O	WOD
	hood	O	HOD
	push	O	POSH
	bush	O	BOSH

Read your notes OUT LOUD. Repeat 20 times.

The following words SOUND alike. Be sure to HEAR the SOUNDS as you write them on the machine. Write each word followed by the "Period" stroke –FPLT.

Sound	Word	Machine	Written
"OOL"	cool	U	KUL
	tool	U	TUL
	school	U	SKUL
"UL"	pull	U	PUL
	bull	U	BUL
	full	U	FUL

Read your notes OUT LOUD. Repeat 20 times.

The following SOUND is very distinct. HEAR the SOUND as you are writing it on the machine. Write each word followed by the "Period" stroke –FPLT.

Sound	Word	Machine	Written
"AR"	art	AR	ART
	car	AR	KAR
	mark	AR	MARK
	hard	AR	HARD
	bar	AR	BAR
	guard	AR	GARD

Read your notes OUT LOUD. Repeat 20 times.

The following SOUNDS are very similar. Say the SOUNDS very slowly OUT LOUD and be sure to HEAR the SOUNDS as you are writing the outlines. Write each word followed by the "Period" stroke –FPLT.

Sound	Word	Machine	Written
"IR"	sir	EUR	SEUR
	girl	EUR	GEURL
	flirt	EUR	FLEURT
"ER"	jerk	EUR	JEURK
	term	EUR	TEURM
	herd	EUR	HEURD
"UR"	turn	EUR	TEURN
	lurk	EUR	LEURK
	purse	EUR	PEURS
"WUR"	world	UR	WURLD
	work	UR	WURK
	word	UR	WURD

Read your notes OUT LOUD. Repeat 20 times.

The following SOUNDS are the "stressed" LONG VOWEL SOUNDS of the "U" SOUND. Although these words are few in number, there is a need for distinction in the writing outline.

EXAMPLE: WHO and HUE
WHO has the LONG VOWEL SOUND of "U"
HUE has the "stressed" LONG VOWEL SOUND of "U"

These words are written as differently and as distinctly as their two SOUNDS dictate:

WHO is written: HAO
HUE is written: HAOU

Say the following words OUT LOUD very slowly and distinctly before writing that word on the machine. Be sure to HEAR the SOUNDS as you are writing the outlines. Write each word followed by the "Period" stroke –FPLT.

Sound	Word	Machine	Written
"UU—"	hue	AOU	HAOU
	cue	AOU	KAOU
	queue	AOU	KAOU
	fued	AOU	FAOUD
	fuel	AOU	FAOUL
	mule	AOU	MAOUL
	cute	AOU	KAOUT
	cube	AOU	KAOUB
	few	AOU	FAOU
	view	AOU	VAOU
	hew	AOU	HAOU
	pew	AOU	PAOU
	fuse	AOU	FAOUZ
	muse	AOU	MAOUZ
	mute	AOU	MAOUT
	puke	AOU	PAOUK
	pure	AOU	PAOUR
	cure	AOU	KAOUR

Read your notes OUT LOUD. Repeat 20 times.

6

It is now time for you to learn the "Underscore" stroke. Simply stroke all the LOWER KEYS on the INITIAL and FINAL sides of the keyboard together:

S – K – W – R   R – B – G – S

This is your "Underscore" stroke. LEARN IT WELL.

The "Underscore" stroke is used immediately after you have written a Proper Name. This SKWR RBGS outline tells you that the stroke or strokes immediately preceding it are to be capitalized.

EXAMPLE: J A U N
M A E U
S K W R R B G S

The "Underscore" stroke tells you that the preceding outlines are to be capitalized as: John May.

As you can see, if you DID NOT "Underscore" immediately after the Proper Name, the word "may" could become very confused within the sentence and make readability extremely difficult.

The Rule is: ALWAYS UNDERSCORE A PROPER NAME.

Also, the "Underscore" stroke can be used to denoted something unusual in your writing, such as an unfamiliar word, a foreign word, a slang word, etc. The "Underscore" stroke signals you that the preceding outline demands your special attention.

The "Underscore" stroke is your friend. USE IT WELL.

MOST COMMON WORDS

For our beginner's learning process, I have selected 100 of the commoner words for practice. They are listed in high usage sequence.

Write each word followed by the "Period" stroke –FPLT.

	WORD	WRITTEN		WORD	WRITTEN
1.	it	EUT	26.	some	SUM
2.	was	WAUZ	27.	great	GRAEUT
3.	as	AZ	28.	such	SUCH
4.	by	BAOEU	29.	first	FEURS
5.	at	AT	30.	how	HOU
6.	all	AUL	31.	come	KUM
7.	one	WUN	32.	us	US
8.	so	SOE	33.	then	THEN
9.	my	MAOEU	34.	like	LAOEUK
10.	me	MAE	35.	well	WEL
11.	war	WOER	36.	little	LEULGTS
12.	more	MOER	37.	say	SAEU
13.	now	NOU	38.	here	HAER
14.	its	EUTS	39.	good	GOD
15.	time	TAOEUM	40.	make	MAEUK
16.	up	UP	41.	most	MOES
17.	out	OUT	42.	way	WAEU
18.	than	THAN	43.	see	SAE
19.	made	MAEUD	44.	world	WURLD
20.	men	MEN	45.	know	NOE
21.	must	MUS	46.	day	DAEU
22.	said	SED	47.	never	NEVR
23.	may	MAEU	48.	new	NAO
24.	man	MAN	49.	down	DOUN
25.	over	OEVR	50.	years	YAERZ

Read your notes OUT LOUD. Repeat 20 times.

Let's continue with the second half.

	WORD	WRITTEN
51.	long	LAUNG
52.	right	RAOEUT
53.	get	GET
54.	life	LAOEUF/-F
55.	just	JUS
56.	take	TAEUK
57.	work	WURK
58.	things	THEUNGZ
59.	part	PART
60.	through	THRAO
61.	while**	WHAOEUL
62.	last	LA*S
63.	might	MAOEUT
64.	back	BAK
65.	old	OELD
66.	own	OEN
67.	came	KAEUM
68.	days	DAEUZ
69.	yet	YET
70.	same	SAEUM
71.	thought	THAUT
72.	each	AECH
73.	far	FAR
74.	home	HOEM
75.	put	POT
76.	per	PEUR
77.	once	WUNS
78.	peace	PAES
79.	year	YAER
80.	away	AU/WAEU
81.	fact	FAK
82.	half	HAF
83.	still	STEUL
84.	give	GEUV
85.	power	POUR
86.	found	FOUND
87.	few	FAOU
88.	food	FAOD
89.	house	HOUS
90.	less	LES
91.	oh	OE
92.	best	BES
93.	case	KAEUS
94.	line	LAOEUN
95.	place	PLAEUS
96.	says	SEZ
97.	since	SEUNS
98.	let	LET
99.	tell	TEL
100.	big	BEUG

**The few words in the English language beginning with "WH" should be written on the machine with a beginning "WH" stroke even though the "WH" is not a "true" sound. Examples: white, wheel, wheat, whirl, whistle.

Read your notes OUT LOUD. Repeat 20 times.

REMEMBER: After you have finished practicing the above 100 words, it will be time to again practice them over and over from your "lesson tape" that is made for home practice. To hear the words and all of the SOUNDS is of vital importance.

The Key to Success in learning Reporting is R-E-P-E-T-I-T-I-O-N.

Every time you HEAR a sound and WRITE it into your stenoprint outline, you are programming your computer-brain to accept that sound. Every time you READ your notes, you are programming your computer-brain that these stenoprint outlines are your new language.

If you can READ your notes, you can WRITE your notes. It is as simple as that.

CONNECTING BRIEFS – SENTENCES

Now that your vocabulary on the machine has blossomed within the last few lessons, let's put those words on the machine into SENTENCES.

In order to make SENTENCES, you will need to learn a few CONNECTING BRIEFS at this time.

A. Here are your first ten (10) "High Frequency BRIEF:

INITIAL SIDE	VOWELS	FINAL SIDE
TAO = to	AO = and	-T = the
N- = in	A = a	-F = of
P- = that		-P = that
T- = it (in phrases only)		-S = is
FOER – for		
S- = is		

NOTE: The word "it" is written: EUT.

Read your notes OUT LOUD. Repeat 20 times.

The following are some "High Frequency" PHRASES:

TAOP	=	to that
TAOT	=	to the (Conflict "toot" – very infrequent court word)
N-T	=	in the
P-A	=	that a
P-T	=	that the
P-S	=	that is
T-S	=	it is
FOER-P	=	for that
FOER-T	=	for the (Conflict "fort" – very infrequent court word)
S-A	=	is a
S-P	=	is that
S-T	=	is the
AO-P	=	and that
AO-T	=	and the
-FT	=	of the

Read your notes OUT LOUD. Repeat 20 times.

NOTE: In Dwyer's Simplified Method of Sound Writing, every time there is a Conflict of a BRIEF or a PHRASE in writing, it will be noted and stated exactly what that Conflict is.

You will see it, you will note it, and you will be aware of it.

To put it simply: "To know" of the Conflicts is your key to successful writing and reading.

B. Now, let's READ SENTENCES OUT LOUD.

NOTE: When the word "is" stands alone, it may be written with either the INITIAL S or the FINAL S.

When the word "that" stands alone, it may be written with either the INITIAL P or the FINAL P.

WUN FPLT T-S KWAOEUT A NOEN FAK P-T STAEUT –S RAOEUT FPLT

TO FPLT –T HOEL THEUNG KAEM OUT N-T MEULGTS –FT STOER FPLT

THRE FPLT AUFN T-S KAULD A BALGTS FOERT KAUZ FPLT

FOR FPLT –T DAER LEULGTS KHAOEULD –S N-T FRUNT –FT HOUS FPLT

FAOEUV FPLT KAUL MAE AO SAEU –T AUL –T RAUNG –S N-T PA*S FPLT

SEUX FPLT AECH MAN –S TAO TAEUK LAOEUF/F DAEU BAOEU DAEU FPLT

SEVN FPLT JUS TAEUK –T BOKZ BAK AO SAEUV FAEUS FPLT

AEUT FPLT –T BES TAO HOEP FOER S-A WURLD FUL –F PAES FPLT

NOTE: The "Question Mark" is written: STPH

NAOEUN FPLT HOU S-T BEUG POEUNT N-T KAEUS TAO KUM OUT STPH

TEN FPLT –T GROUND –S TAOE HARD TAO PLANT –T TRAEZ AU FLOURZ FPLT

LEVN FPLT –T FAEL TRAOGT –FT PLAEU –S AUFN LAU*S AU/LAUNG –T WAEU FPLT

TWEVL FPLT EUT TOK AUL NAOEUT LAUNG FOERT WURK TAO GET DUN FPLT

THAEN FPLT TAO FAEL SAEUF/F AO SOUND –S AUL –T LEULGTS GEURL WUNTD FPLT

FRAEN FPLT –T PLAEUN TOK AUF N-T AEUR AO SAON EUT WENT OUT –F SAOEUT FPLT

GLAEN FPLT –T LAU/SAOT MAEU KUM TAO A KOERT KAEUS N-A FAOU DAEUZ FPLT

SKAEN FPLT –T OELD MAN DROEV DOUN –T STRAET TEURND TAOT LEFT AO WENT STRAEUT FOERT HAOEU/WAEU FLT

STPAEN FPLT –T KAUS –F A POUND –F TAE –S HAOEUR THAN –T PRAOEUS –F A FAOEUN BAULGTS –F WAOEUN FPLT

AEN FPLT –T BOEUZ TOELD US P-T SAEUM LA*S NAEUM –S N-T FOEN BOK TWEVL TAOEUMZ FPLT

STPHRAEN FPLT FRENDZ –F MAOEUN KAEUM OEVR FOER A STAEUK AO BAEUKD BAENZ KOK/OUT LA*S NAOEUT FPLT

TWEU FPLT NOU S-T TAOEUM FOER AUL GOD MEN TAO KUM TAOT AEUD –F US AUL FPLT

Finally, before turning to the MASTER KEY section, let's TRANSCRIBE SENTENCES.

Take a pencil and paper – TRANSCRIBE the above SENTENCES – include all the punctuation. This section is to be done only once.

After you have read and transcribed all of the SENTENCES, turn to the MASTER KEY section and check your SENTENCES for spelling, punctuation, and correctness.

Read Part B OUT LOUD. Repeat 20 times.

1. It is quite a known fact that the state is right.
2. The whole thing came out in the middle of the store.
3. Often it is called a battle for the cause.
4. The dear little child is in the front of the house.
5. Call me and say that all the wrong is in the past.
6. Each man is to take life day by day.
7. Just take the books back and save face.
8. The best to hope for is a world full of peace.
9. How is the big point in the case to come out?
10. The ground is too hard to plant the trees and flowers.
11. The real truth of the lay is often lost along the way.
12. It took all night long for the work to get done.
13. To feel safe and sound is all the little girl wanted.
14. The plane took off in the air and soon it went out of sight.
15. The lawsuit may come to a court case in a few days.

16. The old man drove down the street, turned to the left, and went straight for the highway.

17. The cost of a pound of tea is higher than the price of a fine bottle of wine.

18. The boys told us that the same last name is in the phone book twelve times.

19. Friends of mine came over for a steak and baked beans cookout last night.

20. Now is the time for all good men to come to the aid of us all.

C. Now, let's WRITE SENTENCES.

Write each SENTENCE beginning with the NUMBER, followed by a "Period." End each SENTENCE with the proper punctuation, which will usually be a "Period."

At this stage of your writing, you will NOT be writing any punctuation <u>within</u> the SENTENCE, such as the "Comma." Your only concern is to write what the Speaker has said.

Use this simple procedure for all the WRITE SENTENCES sections.

After you have written all the SENTENCES, please turn to the MASTER KEY section and check you outlines.

1. Great men come to show us that life is full of good.

2. It is now time to get up and make the best of it.

3. The little boy hit the ball all the way to the right side of the field and made it to first base.

4. To buy the wheat and flour at that price is part of the terms.

5. Is that the best way to clean mud and dirt off shoes?

6. The food got turned over and down it went, all over the books.

7. Less light is given to the plants in the P.M. than in the A.M.

8. The young girls told us that the school is at least four more blocks away.

9. To check the plans and list the needs of the whole town is a lot of work for just one man.

10. The rest of the boys ought to stay out of sight for now.

11. Write to me and tell me all the news of the guys in the troops.

12. The old man told me it is miles away and the name of the place is High View.

13. Get the name of the case, the date and time of the trial, and then put the files away.

14. The second time the girls saw the play, the lines seemed to make more sense.

15. Turn the lights out in the room and close the door.

16. The fair is held in the hillsides of the small town in June.

17. To force the truth out of the old man seems like a hard job.

18. The price of the car in the lot is higher than the one in the showroom.

19. My feet hurt, my back aches, and my head feels like it weighs a ton.

20. The eyes of the young girl held the look of love.

Read your notes OUT LOUD. Repeat 20 times.

NOTE: When the word “is” stands alone, it may be written with either the INITIAL S or the FINAL S.

When the word “that” stands alone, it may be written with either the INITIAL P or the FINAL P.

WUN FPLT GRAEUT MEN KUM TAO SHOE US –P LAOEUF/F –S FUL –F GOD FPLT

TO FPLT T-S NOU TAOEUM TAO GET UP AO MAEUK –T BES –F EUT FPLT

THRE FPLT –T LEULGTS BOEU HEUT –T BAUL AUL –T WAEU TAOL RAOEUT SAOEUD –FT FAELD AO MAEUD EUT TAO FEURS BAEUS FPLT

FOR FPLT TAO BAOEU –T WHAET AO FLOUR AT –T PRAOEUS –S PART –FT TEURMZ FPLT

FAOEUV FPLT S-P –T BES WAEU TAO KLAEN MUD AO DEURT AUF SHAOZ STPH

SEUX FPLT –T FAOD GAUT TEURND OEVR AO DOUN EUT WENT AUL OEVR –T BOKZ FPLT

SEVN FPLT LES LAOEUT –S GEUVN TAOT PLANTS N-T P-M THAN N-T A-M FPLT

AEUT FPLT –T YUNG GEURLZ TOELD US P-T SKUL –S AT LAE*S FOR MOER BLAUKS AU/WAEU FPLT

NAOEUN FPLT TAO KHEK –T PLANZ AO LEUS –T NAEDZ –FT HOEL TOUN S-A LAUT –F WURK FOER JUS WUN MAN FPLT

TEN FPLT –T RES –FT BOEUZ AUT TAO STAEU OUT –F SAOEUT FOER NOU FPLT

LEVN FPLT RAOEUT TAO MAE AO TEL MAE AUL –T NAOZ –FT GAOEUZ N-T TRAOPS FPLT

TWEVL FPLT –T OELD MAN TOELD MAE T-S MAOEULZ AU/WAEU AO-T NAEUM –FT PLAEUS –S HAOEU VAOU SKWR-RBGS FPLT

THAEN FPLT GET –T NAEUM –FT KAEUS –T DAEUT AO TAOEUM –FT TRAOEUL AO THEN POT –T FAOEULZ AU/WAEU FPLT

FRAEN FPLT –T SEKD TAOEUM –T GEURLZ SAU –T PLAEU –T LAOEUNZ SAEUMD TAO MAEUK MOER SENS FPLT

GLAEN FPLT TEURN –T LAOEUTS OUT N-T RAOM AO KLOEZ –T DOER FPLT

SKAEN FPLT –T FAEUR –S HELD N-T HEUL/SAOEUDZ –FT SMAUL TOUN N- JAON SKWR-RBGS FPLT

STPAEN FPLT TAO FOERS –T TRAOGT OUT –FT OELD MAN SAEMZ LAOEUK A HARD JAUB FPLT

AEN FPLT –T PRAOEUS –FT KA N-T LAUT –S HAOEUR THAN –T WUN N-T SHOE/RAOM FPLT

STPHRAEN FPLT MAOEU FAET HEURT MAOEU BAK AEUKZ AO MAOEU HED FAELZ LAOEUK EUT WAEUZ A TUN FPLT

TWEU FPLT –T AOEUZ –FT YUNG GEURL HELD –T LOK –F LUV FPLT

JURY CHARGE #1 – BRIEF AND PHRASES

To achieve the status of RPR, which signifi8es Registered Professional Reporter, a test is given by the National Shorthand Reporters Association. This test is given twice a year; once in May and once in November.

The test consists of two parts:

1. Written Knowledge Test (WKT)
2. Machine Shorthand Tests

Simply stated: The WKT is a test of the student's knowledge of the "academics" of the profession such as legal and medical terminology, transcription, and English.

The Machine Shorthand Tests are the actual "speed-writing" sections.

The machine portion consists of three categories:

1. Literary
2. Jury Charge
3. Q & A (Testimony)

A five minute test is given in each category at the following speeds:

1. Literary – 180 wpm
2. Jury Charge – 200 wpm
3. Q & A (Testimony) – 225 wpm

The above speeds represent "Reporting" status. Strive for perfection to obtain them. This is your final goal.

Now, it is time to learn to write JURY CHARGE material.

What is a JURY CHARGE?

Simply stated: A JURY CHARGE or Judge's Charge is a "charge to the jury" by the Court of a set of instructions that must be followed in this particular case, based upon the evidence produced at trial and the applicable laws.

These instructions are given at the end of the case.

JURY CHARGE material can be very repetitive in nature simply because the same instructions apply from one case to another.

The proper way to study the following JURY CHARGE will be:

1. READ each word of the JURY CHARGE in Section A, paying special attention to the new Briefs and Phrases -- 5 times.

2. WRITE the JURY CHARGE in Section B -- 5 times; and READ your notes each time.

3. WRITE the JURY CHARGE in Section B -- 1 final time and use this "Perfect Outline Stenoprint Notes" for reading practice; READ your notes -- 10 times.

Here are the new BRIEFS AND PHRASES that will appear in JURY CHARGE #1. Derivatives will also be listed where applicable, for ease in learning.

WORD	WRITTEN
Ladies and Gentlemen of the Jury	LAEUDZ/JEJ
follow	FOL
consider	K-R
consideration	K-RGS
instruct	STRUKT
instruction	STRUKGS
duty	DAOUT
also	-LS
determine	DERM
determination	DERM/AEUGS
evidence	EV
evident	EVT
produce	PRAO

about	B-
influence	FLU
sympathy	SEUGT
prejudice	PREJ
judge	J-
judgment	J-MT
regard	RARD
however	HOUVR
after	AFR
apply	PLEU
applicable	PLEUBL
together	TOEGT
as you have	ZUV
decide	SDAOEUD (Inverted "DS")
decision	SDEUGS (Inverted "DS")
these	THAEZ

A. Now, let's READ JURY CHARGE #1. (All new BRIEFS AND PHRASES are underlined.)

LAEUDZ/JEJ EUL NOU TEL U SUM -FT RULZ U MUS FOL N- K-R/-G TH-KAEUS FPLT EUL STRUKT U OT LAU FPLT T-S UR DAOUT TAO FOL -T LAU FPLT T-S -LS UR DAOUT TAO DERM -T FAKZ FPLT U MUS DERM -T FAKZ ONL FR-T EV PRAOD N- KOERT FPLT U SHON GES B- NEU FAK FPLT U MUS -N -B FLUD BAOEU SEUGT OER PREJ FPLT U -R -T DOEL J-Z -FT FAKZ FPLT U MUS TAEUK AU/KOUNT -F AUL MAOEU STRUKGSZ OT LAU FPLT U -R -N TAO PEUK OUT WUN STRUKGS OER PART -F WUN AO DEUS/RARD -T UGTS FPLT HOUVR AFR UV DERMD -T FAKZ U MAEU FAOEUND -P SUM STRUKGSZ DAON PLEU FPLT U MUS THEN K-R -T STRUKGSZ -P DAO PLEU TOEGT W-T FAKZ ZUV DERMD THEM FPLT SDAOEUD -T KAEUS BAOEU PLEUG -T LAU N- THAEZ STRUKGSZ TAOT FAKZ FPLT

B. Now, let's WRITE JURY CHARGE #1. (All new BRIEFS AND PHRASES are underlined.)

Ladies and Gentlemen of the Jury:

I will now tell you some of the rules you must follow in considering this case. I will instruct you on the law. It is your duty to follow the law.

It is also your duty to determine the facts. You must determine the facts only from the evidence produced in court. You should not guess about any fact. You must not be influenced by sympathy or prejudice.

You are the sole judges of the facts.

You must take account of all my instructions on the law. You are not to pick out one instruction or part of one and disregard the others. However, after you have determined the facts, you may find that some instructions do not apply. You must then consider the instructions that do apply, together with the facts as you have determined them. Decide the case by applying the law in these instructions to the facts.

C. This section will contain a list of ten (10) new BRIEFS and ten (10) new PHRASES.

BRIEFS	WRITTEN
abdomen	ABD
above	BUV (Conflict "buff" – very infrequent court word)
absolute	SLAOT
accept	SEP
accident	SDENT
accomplish	PLEUSH
acknowledge	AK/-J
actual	ACH
address	DREUS
advance	VANS

PHRASES	WRITTEN
accident happened	SDAPD
accident occurred	SDURD
all right	L-RT
are you married	RUMD
as a matter of fact	ZMAFT
as a result	ZARLT
as the result	ZERLT
as long as	Z-LGZ
ask you	SK-U (SK = "ask)
ask your	SK-UR (SK = "ask)

Read your notes OUT LOUD. Repeat 20 times.

The following sentences contain the new BRIEFS AND PHRASES of Section C. As you practice writing, read each sentence OUT LOUD. All new BRIEFS AND PHRASES are underlined.

1. As long as you're going to the store, will you please get me a change of address card?

2. When the accident happened, I had no actual fear of danger.

3. As a result of all his hard studying, he was able to accomplish his goal.

4. Her pain was just above the abdomen.

5. As a matter of fact, I need you to ask your boss about the new job.

6. All right, are you married or single?

7. Please acknowledge that the advance classes will be taught this fall.

8. When the accident occurred, did you accept any ticket?

9. As the result of testing, we now have absolute proof it will work.

10. I would like to ask you about the accident if you are not too busy.

Read your notes OUT LOUD. Repeat 20 times.

GLOSSARY OF LEGAL TERMS

TABLE OF CONTENTS

GLOSSARY OF LEGAL TERMS

A

ACTION - "Action" includes a civil action and a criminal action.
A FORTIORI - A term meaning you can reason one thing from the existence of certain facts.
A POSTERIORI - From what goes after; from effect to cause.
A PRIORI - From what goes before; from cause to effect.
AB INITIO - From the beginning.
ABATE - To diminish or put an end to.
ABET - To encourage the commission of a crime.
ABEYANCE - Suspension, temporary suppression.
ABIDE - To accept the consequences of.
ABJURE - To renounce; give up.
ABRIDGE - To reduce; contract; diminish.
ABROGATE - To annul, repeal, or destroy.
ABSCOND - To hide or absent oneself to avoid legal action.
ABSTRACT - A summary.
ABUT - To border on, to touch.
ACCESS - Approach; in real property law it means the right of the owner of property to the use of the highway or road next to his land, without obstruction by intervening property owners.
ACCESSORY - In criminal law, it means the person who contributes or aids in the commission of a crime.
ACCOMMODATED PARTY - One to whom credit is extended on the strength of another person signing a commercial paper.
ACCOMMODATION PAPER - A commercial paper to which the accommodating party has put his name.
ACCOMPLICE - In criminal law, it means a person who together with the principal offender commits a crime.
ACCORD - An agreement to accept something different or less than that to which one is entitled, which extinguishes the entire obligation.
ACCOUNT - A statement of mutual demands in the nature of debt and credit between parties.
ACCRETION - The act of adding to a thing; in real property law, it means gradual accumulation of land by natural causes.
ACCRUE - To grow to; to be added to.
ACKNOWLEDGMENT - The act of going before an official authorized to take acknowledgments, and acknowledging an act as one's own.
ACQUIESCENCE - A silent appearance of consent.
ACQUIT - To legally determine the innocence of one charged with a crime.
AD INFINITUM - Indefinitely.
AD LITEM - For the suit.
AD VALOREM - According to value.
ADJECTIVE LAW - Rules of procedure.
ADJUDICATION - The judgment given in a case.
ADMIRALTY - Court having jurisdiction over maritime cases.
ADULT - Sixteen years old or over (in criminal law).
ADVANCE - In commercial law, it means to pay money or render other value before it is due.
ADVERSE - Opposed; contrary.
ADVOCATE - (v.) To speak in favor of;
(n.) One who assists, defends, or pleads for another.
AFFIANT - A person who makes and signs an affidavit.

AFFIDAVIT - A written and sworn to declaration of facts, voluntarily made.
AFFINITY- The relationship between persons through marriage with the kindred of each other; distinguished from consanguinity, which is the relationship by blood.
AFFIRM - To ratify; also when an appellate court affirms a judgment, decree, or order, it means that it is valid and right and must stand as rendered in the lower court.
AFOREMENTIONED; AFORESAID - Before or already said.
AGENT - One who represents and acts for another.
AID AND COMFORT - To help; encourage.
ALIAS - A name not one's true name.
ALIBI - A claim of not being present at a certain place at a certain time.
ALLEGE - To assert.
ALLOTMENT - A share or portion.
AMBIGUITY - Uncertainty; capable of being understood in more than one way.
AMENDMENT - Any language made or proposed as a change in some principal writing.
AMICUS CURIAE - A friend of the court; one who has an interest in a case, although not a party in the case, who volunteers advice upon matters of law to the judge. For example, a brief amicus curiae.
AMORTIZATION - To provide for a gradual extinction of (a future obligation) in advance of maturity, especially, by periodical contributions to a sinking fund which will be adequate to discharge a debt or make a replacement when it becomes necessary.
ANCILLARY - Aiding, auxiliary.
ANNOTATION - A note added by way of comment or explanation.
ANSWER - A written statement made by a defendant setting forth the grounds of his defense.
ANTE - Before.
ANTE MORTEM - Before death.
APPEAL - The removal of a case from a lower court to one of superior jurisdiction for the purpose of obtaining a review.
APPEARANCE - Coming into court as a party to a suit.
APPELLANT - The party who takes an appeal from one court or jurisdiction to another (appellate) court for review.
APPELLEE - The party against whom an appeal is taken.
APPROPRIATE - To make a thing one's own.
APPROPRIATION - Prescribing the destination of a thing; the act of the legislature designating a particular fund, to be applied to some object of government expenditure.
APPURTENANT - Belonging to; accessory or incident to.
ARBITER - One who decides a dispute; a referee.
ARBITRARY - Unreasoned; not governed by any fixed rules or standard.
ARGUENDO - By way of argument.
ARRAIGN - To call the prisoner before the court to answer to a charge.
ASSENT - A declaration of willingness to do something in compliance with a request.
ASSERT - Declare.
ASSESS - To fix the rate or amount.
ASSIGN - To transfer; to appoint; to select for a particular purpose.
ASSIGNEE - One who receives an assignment.
ASSIGNOR - One who makes an assignment.
AT BAR - Before the court.

AT ISSUE - When parties in an action come to a point where one asserts something and the other denies it.
ATTACH - Seize property by court order and sometimes arrest a person.
ATTEST - To witness a will, etc.; act of attestation.
AVERMENT - A positive statement of facts.

B

BAIL - To obtain the release of a person from legal custody by giving security and promising that he shall appear in court; to deliver (goods, etc.) in trust to a person for a special purpose.
BAILEE - One to whom personal property is delivered under a contract of bailment.
BAILMENT - Delivery of personal property to another to be held for a certain purpose and to be returned when the purpose is accomplished.
BAILOR - The party who delivers goods to another, under a contract of bailment.
BANC (OR BANK) - Bench; the place where a court sits permanently or regularly; also the assembly of all the judges of a court.
BANKRUPT - An insolvent person, technically, one declared to be bankrupt after a bankruptcy proceeding.
BAR - The legal profession.
BARRATRY - Exciting groundless judicial proceedings.
BARTER - A contract by which parties exchange goods for other goods.
BATTERY - Illegal interfering with another's person.
BEARER - In commercial law, it means the person in possession of a commercial paper which is payable to the bearer.
BENCH - The court itself or the judge.
BENEFICIARY - A person benefiting under a will, trust, or agreement.
BEST EVIDENCE RULE,THE - Except as otherwise provided by statute, no evidence other than the writing itself is admissible to prove the content of a writing. This section shall be known and may be cited as the best evidence rule.
BEQUEST - A gift of personal property under a will.
BILL - A formal written statement of complaint to a court of justice; also, a draft of an act of the legislature before it becomes a law; also, accounts for goods sold, services rendered, or work done.
BONA FIDE - In or with good faith; honestly.
BOND - An instrument by which the maker promises to pay a sum of money to another, usually providing that upon performances of a certain condition the obligation shall be void.
BOYCOTT - A plan to prevent the carrying on of a business by wrongful means.
BREACH - The breaking or violating of a law, or the failure to carry out a duty.
BRIEF - A written document, prepared by a lawyer to serve as the basis of an argument upon a case in court, usually an appellate court.
BURDEN OF PRODUCING EVIDENCE - The obligation of a party to introduce evidence sufficient to avoid a ruling against him on the issue.
BURDEN OF PROOF - The obligation of a party to establish by evidence a requisite degree of belief concerning a fact in the mind of the trier of fact or the court. The burden of proof may require a party to raise a reasonable doubt concerning the existence of nonexistence of a fact or that he establish the existence or nonexistence of a fact by a preponderance of the evidence, by clear and convincing proof, or by proof beyond a reasonable doubt.

Except as otherwise provided by law, the burden of proof requires proof by a preponderance of the evidence.

BUSINESS, A - Shall include every kind of business, profession, occupation, calling or operation of institutions, whether carried on for profit or not.
BY-LAWS - Regulations, ordinances, or rules enacted by a corporation, association, etc., for its own government.

C

CANON - A doctrine; also, a law or rule, of a church or association in particular.
CAPIAS - An order to arrest.
CAPTION - In a pleading, deposition or other paper connected with a case in court, it is the heading or introductory clause which shows the names of the parties, name of the court, number of the case on the docket or calendar, etc.
CARRIER - A person or corporation undertaking to transport persons or property.
CASE - A general term for an action, cause, suit, or controversy before a judicial body.
CAUSE - A suit, litigation or action before a court.
CAVEAT EMPTOR - Let the buyer beware. This term expresses the rule that the purchaser of an article must examine, judge, and test it for himself, being bound to discover any obvious defects or imperfections.
CERTIFICATE - A written representation that some legal formality has been complied with.
CERTIORARI - To be informed of; the name of a writ issued by a superior court directing the lower court to send up to the former the record and proceedings of a case.
CHANGE OF VENUE - To remove place of trial from one place to another.
CHARGE - An obligation or duty; a formal complaint; an instruction of the court to the jury upon a case.
CHARTER - (n.) The authority by virtue of which an organized body acts;
(v.) in mercantile law, it means to hire or lease a vehicle or vessel for transportation.
CHATTEL - An article of personal property.
CHATTEL MORTGAGE - A mortgage on personal property.
CIRCUIT - A division of the country, for the administration of justice; a geographical area served by a court.
CITATION - The act of the court by which a person is summoned or cited; also, a reference to legal authority.
CIVIL (ACTIONS)- It indicates the private rights and remedies of individuals in contrast to the word "criminal" (actions) which relates to prosecution for violation of laws.
CLAIM (n.) - Any demand held or asserted as of right.
CODICIL - An addition to a will.
CODIFY - To arrange the laws of a country into a code.
COGNIZANCE - Notice or knowledge.
COLLATERAL - By the side; accompanying; an article or thing given to secure performance of a promise.
COMITY - Courtesy; the practice by which one court follows the decision of another court on the same question.
COMMIT - To perform, as an act; to perpetrate, as a crime; to send a person to prison.
COMMON LAW - As distinguished from law created by the enactment of the legislature (called statutory law), it relates to those principles and rules of action which derive their authority solely from usages and customs of immemorial antiquity, particularly with reference to the ancient unwritten law of England. The written pronouncements of the common law are found in court decisions.
COMMUTE - Change punishment to one less severe.

COMPLAINANT - One who applies to the court for legal redress.
COMPLAINT - The pleading of a plaintiff in a civil action; or a charge that a person has committed a specified offense.
COMPROMISE - An arrangement for settling a dispute by agreement.
CONCUR - To agree, consent.
CONCURRENT - Running together, at the same time.
CONDEMNATION - Taking private property for public use on payment therefor.
CONDITION - Mode or state of being; a qualification or restriction.
CONDUCT - Active and passive behavior; both verbal and nonverbal.
CONFESSION - Voluntary statement of guilt of crime.
CONFIDENTIAL COMMUNICATION BETWEEN CLIENT AND LAWYER - Information transmitted between a client and his lawyer in the course of that relationship and in confidence by a means which, so far as the client is aware, discloses the information to no third persons other than those who are present to further the interest of the client in the consultation or those to whom disclosure is reasonably necessary for the transmission of the information or the accomplishment of the purpose for which the lawyer is consulted, and includes a legal opinion formed and the advice given by the lawyer in the course of that relationship.
CONFRONTATION - Witness testifying in presence of defendant.
CONSANGUINITY - Blood relationship.
CONSIGN - To give in charge; commit; entrust; to send or transmit goods to a merchant, factor, or agent for sale.
CONSIGNEE - One to whom a consignment is made.
CONSIGNOR - One who sends or makes a consignment.
CONSPIRACY - In criminal law, it means an agreement between two or more persons to commit an unlawful act.
CONSPIRATORS - Persons involved in a conspiracy.
CONSTITUTION - The fundamental law of a nation or state.
CONSTRUCTION OF GENDERS - The masculine gender includes the feminine and neuter.
CONSTRUCTION OF SINGULAR AND PLURAL - The singular number includes the plural; and the plural, the singular.
CONSTRUCTION OF TENSES - The present tense includes the past and future tenses; and the future, the present.
CONSTRUCTIVE - An act or condition assumed from other parts or conditions.
CONSTRUE - To ascertain the meaning of language.
CONSUMMATE - To complete.
CONTIGUOUS - Adjoining; touching; bounded by.
CONTINGENT - Possible, but not assured; dependent upon some condition.
CONTINUANCE - The adjournment or postponement of an action pending in a court.
CONTRA - Against, opposed to; contrary.
CONTRACT - An agreement between two or more persons to do or not to do a particular thing.
CONTROVERT - To dispute, deny.
CONVERSION - Dealing with the personal property of another as if it were one's own, without right.
CONVEYANCE - An instrument transferring title to land.
CONVICTION - Generally, the result of a criminal trial which ends in a judgment or sentence that the defendant is guilty as charged.

COOPERATIVE - A cooperative is a voluntary organization of persons with a common interest, formed and operated along democratic lines for the purpose of supplying services at cost to its members and other patrons, who contribute both capital and business.
CORPUS DELICTI - The body of a crime; the crime itself.
CORROBORATE - To strengthen; to add weight by additional evidence.
COUNTERCLAIM - A claim presented by a defendant in opposition to or deduction from the claim of the plaintiff.
COUNTY - Political subdivision of a state.
COVENANT - Agreement.
CREDIBLE - Worthy of belief.
CREDITOR - A person to whom a debt is owing by another person, called the "debtor."
CRIMINAL ACTION - Includes criminal proceedings.
CRIMINAL INFORMATION - Same as complaint.
CRITERION (sing.)
CRITERIA (plural) - A means or tests for judging; a standard or standards.
CROSS-EXAMINATION - Examination of a witness by a party other than the direct examiner upon a matter that is within the scope of the direct examination of the witness.
CULPABLE - Blamable.
CY-PRES - As near as (possible). The rule of *cy-pres* is a rule for the construction of instruments in equity by which the intention of the party is carried out *as near as may be*, when it would be impossible or illegal to give it literal effect.

D

DAMAGES - A monetary compensation, which may be recovered in the courts by any person who has suffered loss, or injury, whether to his person, property or rights through the unlawful act or omission or negligence of another.
DECLARANT - A person who makes a statement.
DE FACTO - In fact; actually but without legal authority.
DE JURE - Of right; legitimate; lawful.
DE MINIMIS - Very small or trifling.
DE NOVO - Anew; afresh; a second time.
DEBT - A specified sum of money owing to one person from another, including not only the obligation of the debtor to pay, but the right of the creditor to receive and enforce payment.
DECEDENT - A dead person.
DECISION - A judgment or decree pronounced by a court in determination of a case.
DECREE - An order of the court, determining the rights of all parties to a suit.
DEED - A writing containing a contract sealed and delivered; particularly to convey real property.
DEFALCATION - Misappropriation of funds.
DEFAMATION - Injuring one's reputation by false statements.
DEFAULT - The failure to fulfill a duty, observe a promise, discharge an obligation, or perform an agreement.
DEFENDANT - The person defending or denying; the party against whom relief or recovery is sought in an action or suit.
DEFRAUD - To practice fraud; to cheat or trick.
DELEGATE (v.)- To entrust to the care or management of another.
DELICTUS - A crime.
DEMUR (v.) - To dispute the sufficiency in law of the pleading of the other side.

DEMURRAGE - In maritime law, it means, the sum fixed or allowed as remuneration to the owners of a ship for the detention of their vessel beyond the number of days allowed for loading and unloading or for sailing; also used in railroad terminology.
DENIAL - A form of pleading; refusing to admit the truth of a statement, charge, etc.
DEPONENT - One who gives testimony under oath reduced to writing.
DEPOSITION - Testimony given under oath outside of court for use in court or for the purpose of obtaining information in preparation for trial of a case.
DETERIORATION - A degeneration such as from decay, corrosion or disintegration.
DETRIMENT - Any loss or harm to person or property.
DEVIATION - A turning aside.
DEVISE - A gift of real property by the last will and testament of the donor.
DICTUM (sing.)
DICTA (plural) - Any statements made by the court in an opinion concerning some rule of law not necessarily involved nor essential to the determination of the case.
DIRECT EVIDENCE - Evidence that directly proves a fact, without an inference or presumption, and which in itself if true, conclusively establishes that fact.
DIRECT EXAMINATION - The first examination of a witness upon a matter that is not within the scope of a previous examination of the witness.
DISAFFIRM - To repudiate.
DISMISS - In an action or suit, it means to dispose of the case without any further consideration or hearing.
DISSENT - To denote disagreement of one or more judges of a court with the decision passed by the majority upon a case before them.
DOCKET (n.) - A formal record, entered in brief, of the proceedings in a court.
DOCTRINE - A rule, principle, theory of law.
DOMICILE - That place where a man has his true, fixed and permanent home to which whenever he is absent he has the intention of returning.
DRAFT (n.) - A commercial paper ordering payment of money drawn by one person on another.
DRAWEE - The person who is requested to pay the money.
DRAWER - The person who draws the commercial paper and addresses it to the drawee.
DUPLICATE - A counterpart produced by the same impression as the original enlargements and miniatures, or by mechanical or electronic re-recording, or by chemical reproduction, or by other equivalent technique which accurately reproduces the original.
DURESS - Use of force to compel performance or non-performance of an act.

E

EASEMENT - A liberty, privilege, or advantage without profit, in the lands of another.
EGRESS - Act or right of going out or leaving; emergence.
EIUSDEM GENERIS - Of the same kind, class or nature. A rule used in the construction of language in a legal document.
EMBEZZLEMENT - To steal; to appropriate fraudulently to one's own use property entrusted to one's care.
EMBRACERY - Unlawful attempt to influence jurors, etc., but not by offering value.
EMINENT DOMAIN - The right of a state to take private property for public use.
ENACT - To make into a law.
ENDORSEMENT - Act of writing one's name on the back of a note, bill or similar written instrument.

ENJOIN - To require a person, by writ of injunction from a court of equity, to perform or to abstain or desist from some act.
ENTIRETY - The whole; that which the law considers as one whole, and not capable of being divided into parts.
ENTRAPMENT - Inducing one to commit a crime so as to arrest him.
ENUMERATED - Mentioned specifically; designated.
ENURE - To operate or take effect.
EQUITY - In its broadest sense, this term denotes the spirit and the habit of fairness, justness, and right dealing which regulate the conduct of men.
ERROR - A mistake of law, or the false or irregular application of law as will nullify the judicial proceedings.
ESCROW - A deed, bond or other written engagement, delivered to a third person, to be delivered by him only upon the performance or fulfillment of some condition.
ESTATE - The interest which any one has in lands, or in any other subject of property.
ESTOP - To stop, bar, or impede.
ESTOPPEL - A rule of law which prevents a man from alleging or denying a fact, because of his own previous act.
ET AL. (alii) - And others.
ET SEQ. (sequential) - And the following.
ET UX. (uxor) - And wife.
EVIDENCE - Testimony, writings, material objects, or other things presented to the senses that are offered to prove the existence or non-existence of a fact.

Means from which inferences may be drawn as a basis of proof in duly constituted judicial or fact finding tribunals, and includes testimony in the form of opinion and hearsay.

EX CONTRACTU
EX DELICTO - In law, rights and causes of action are divided into two classes, those arising *ex contractu* (from a contract) and those arising *ex delicto* (from a delict or tort).
EX OFFICIO - From office; by virtue of the office.
EX PARTE - On one side only; by or for one.
EX POST FACTO - After the fact.
EX POST FACTO LAW - A law passed after an act was done which retroactively makes such act a crime.
EX REL. (relations) - Upon relation or information.
EXCEPTION - An objection upon a matter of law to a decision made, either before or after judgment by a court.
EXECUTOR (male)
EXECUTRIX (female) - A person who has been appointed by will to execute the will.
EXECUTORY - That which is yet to be executed or performed.
EXEMPT - To release from some liability to which others are subject.
EXONERATION - The removal of a burden, charge or duty.
EXTRADITION - Surrender of a fugitive from one nation to another.

F

F.A.S.- "Free alongside ship"; delivery at dock for ship named.
F.O.B.- "Free on board"; seller will deliver to car, truck, vessel, or other conveyance by which goods are to be transported, without expense or risk of loss to the buyer or consignee.
FABRICATE - To construct; to invent a false story.
FACSIMILE - An exact or accurate copy of an original instrument.

FACTOR - A commercial agent.
FEASANCE - The doing of an act.
FELONIOUS - Criminal, malicious.
FELONY - Generally, a criminal offense that may be punished by death or imprisonment for more than one year as differentiated from a misdemeanor.
FEME SOLE - A single woman.
FIDUCIARY - A person who is invested with rights and powers to be exercised for the benefit of another person.
FIERI FACIAS - A writ of execution commanding the sheriff to levy and collect the amount of a judgment from the goods and chattels of the judgment debtor.
FINDING OF FACT - Determination from proof or judicial notice of the existence of a fact. A ruling implies a supporting finding of fact; no separate or formal finding is required unless required by a statute of this state.
FISCAL - Relating to accounts or the management of revenue.
FORECLOSURE (sale) - A sale of mortgaged property to obtain satisfaction of the mortgage out of the sale proceeds.
FORFEITURE - A penalty, a fine.
FORGERY - Fabricating or producing falsely, counterfeited.
FORTUITOUS - Accidental.
FORUM - A court of justice; a place of jurisdiction.
FRAUD - Deception; trickery.
FREEHOLDER - One who owns real property.
FUNGIBLE - Of such kind or nature that one specimen or part may be used in the place of another.

G

GARNISHEE - Person garnished.
GARNISHMENT - A legal process to reach the money or effects of a defendant, in the possession or control of a third person.
GRAND JURY - Not less than 16, not more than 23 citizens of a county sworn to inquire into crimes committed or triable in the county.
GRANT - To agree to; convey, especially real property.
GRANTEE - The person to whom a grant is made.
GRANTOR - The person by whom a grant is made.
GRATUITOUS - Given without a return, compensation or consideration.
GRAVAMEN - The grievance complained of or the substantial cause of a criminal action.
GUARANTY (n.) - A promise to answer for the payment of some debt, or the performance of some duty, in case of the failure of another person, who, in the first instance, is liable for such payment or performance.
GUARDIAN - The person, committee, or other representative authorized by law to protect the person or estate or both of an incompetent (or of a *sui juris* person having a guardian) and to act for him in matters affecting his person or property or both. An incompetent is a person under disability imposed by law.
GUILTY - Establishment of the fact that one has committed a breach of conduct; especially, a violation of law.

H

HABEAS CORPUS - You have the body; the name given to a variety of writs, having for their object to bring a party before a court or judge for decision as to whether such person is being lawfully held prisoner.
HABENDUM - In conveyancing; it is the clause in a deed conveying land which defines the extent of ownership to be held by the grantee.
HEARING - A proceeding whereby the arguments of the interested parties are heared.
HEARSAY - A type of testimony given by a witness who relates, not what he knows personally, but what others have told hi, or what he has heard said by others.
HEARSAY RULE, THE - (a) "Hearsay evidence" is evidence of a statement that was made other than by a witness while testifying at the hearing and that is offered to prove the truth of the matter stated; (b) Except as provided by law, hearsay evidence is inadmissible; (c) This section shall be known and may be cited as the hearsay rule.
HEIR - Generally, one who inherits property, real or personal.
HOLDER OF THE PRIVILEGE - (a) The client when he has no guardian or conservator; (b) A guardian or conservator of the client when the client has a guardian or conservator; (c) The personal representative of the client if the client is dead; (d) A successor, assign, trustee in dissolution, or any similar representative of a firm, association, organization, partnership, business trust, corporation, or public entity that is no longer in existence.
HUNG JURY - One so divided that they can't agree on a verdict.
HUSBAND-WIFE PRIVILEGE - An accused in a criminal proceeding has a privilege to prevent his spouse from testifying against him.
HYPOTHECATE - To pledge a thing without delivering it to the pledgee.
HYPOTHESIS - A supposition, assumption, or toehry.

I

I.E. (id est) - That is.
IB., OR IBID.(ibidem) - In the same place; used to refer to a legal reference previously cited to avoid repeating the entire citation.
ILLICIT - Prohibited; unlawful.
ILLUSORY - Deceiving by false appearance.
IMMUNITY - Exemption.
IMPEACH - To accuse, to dispute.
IMPEDIMENTS - Disabilities, or hindrances.
IMPLEAD - To sue or prosecute by due course of law.
IMPUTED - Attributed or charged to.
IN LOCO PARENTIS - In place of parent, a guardian.
IN TOTO - In the whole; completely.
INCHOATE - Imperfect; unfinished.
INCOMMUNICADO - Denial of the right of a prisoner to communicate with friends or relatives.
INCOMPETENT - One who is incapable of caring for his own affairs because he is mentally deficient or undeveloped.
INCRIMINATION - A matter will incriminate a person if it constitutes, or forms an essential part of, or, taken in connection with other matters disclosed, is a basis for a reasonable inference of such a violation of the laws of this State as to subject him to liability to punishment therefor, unless he has become for any reason permanently immune from punishment for such violation.
INCUMBRANCE - Generally a claim, lien, charge or liability attached to and binding real property.

INDEMNIFY - To secure against loss or damage; also, to make reimbursement to one for a loss already incurred by him.
INDEMNITY - An agreement to reimburse another person in case of an anticipated loss falling upon him.
INDICIA - Signs; indications.
INDICTMENT - An accusation in writing found and presented by a grand jury charging that a person has committed a crime.
INDORSE - To write a name on the back of a legal paper or document, generally, a negotiable instrument
INDUCEMENT - Cause or reason why a thing is done or that which incites the person to do the act or commit a crime; the motive for the criminal act.
INFANT - In civil cases one under 21 years of age.
INFORMATION - A formal accusation of crime made by a prosecuting attorney.
INFRA - Below, under; this word occurring by itself in a publication refers the reader to a future part of the publication.
INGRESS - The act of going into.
INJUNCTION - A writ or order by the court requiring a person, generally, to do or to refrain from doing an act.
INSOLVENT - The condition of a person who is unable to pay his debts.
INSTRUCTION - A direction given by the judge to the jury concerning the law of the case.
INTERIM - In the meantime; time intervening.
INTERLOCUTORY - Temporary, not final; something intervening between the commencement and the end of a suit which decides some point or matter, but is not a final decision of the whole controversy.
INTERROGATORIES - A series of formal written questions used in the examination of a party or a witness usually prior to a trial.
INTESTATE - A person who dies without a will.
INURE - To result, to take effect.
IPSO FACTO - By the fact iself; by the mere fact.
ISSUE (n.) The disputed point or question in a case,

J

JEOPARDY - Danger, hazard, peril.
JOINDER - Joining; uniting with another person in some legal steps or proceeding.
JOINT - United; combined.
JUDGE - Member or members or representative or representatives of a court conducting a trial or hearing at which evidence is introduced.
JUDGMENT - The official decision of a court of justice.
JUDICIAL OR JUDICIARY - Relating to or connected with the administration of justice.
JURAT - The clause written at the foot of an affidavit, stating when, where and before whom such affidavit was sworn.
JURISDICTION - The authority to hear and determine controversies between parties.
JURISPRUDENCE - The philosophy of law.
JURY - A body of persons legally selected to inquire into any matter of fact, and to render their verdict according to the evidence.

L

LACHES - The failure to diligently assert a right, which results in a refusal to allow relief.

LANDLORD AND TENANT - A phrase used to denote the legal relation existing between the owner and occupant of real estate.
LARCENY - Stealing personal property belonging to another.
LATENT - Hidden; that which does not appear on the face of a thing.
LAW - Includes constitutional, statutory, and decisional law.
LAWYER-CLIENT PRIVILEGE - (1) A "client" is a person, public officer, or corporation, association, or other organization or entity, either public or private, who is rendered professional legal services by a lawyer, or who consults a lawyer with a view to obtaining professional legal services from him; (2) A "lawyer" is a person authorized, or reasonably believed by the client to be authorized, to practice law in any state or nation; (3) A "representative of the lawyer" is one employed to assist the lawyer in the rendition of professional legal services; (4) A communication is "confidential" if not intended to be disclosed to third persons other than those to whom disclosure is in furtherance of the rendition of professional legal services to the client or those reasonably necessary for the transmission of the communication.

General rule of privilege - A client has a privilege to refuse to disclose and to prevent any other person from disclosing confidential communications made for the purpose of facilitating the rendition of professional legal services to the client, (1) between himself or his representative and his lawyer or his lawyer's representative, or (2) between his lawyer and the lawyer's representative, or (3) by him or his lawyer to a lawyer representing another in a matter of common interest, or (4) between representatives of the client or between the client and a representative of the client, or (5) between lawyers representing the client.
LEADING QUESTION - Question that suggests to the witness the answer that the examining party desires.
LEASE - A contract by which one conveys real estate for a limited time usually for a specified rent; personal property also may be leased.
LEGISLATION - The act of enacting laws.
LEGITIMATE - Lawful.
LESSEE - One to whom a lease is given.
LESSOR - One who grants a lease
LEVY - A collecting or exacting by authority.
LIABLE - Responsible; bound or obligated in law or equity.
LIBEL (v.) - To defame or injure a person's reputation by a published writing.
(n.) - The initial pleading on the part of the plaintiff in an admiralty proceeding.
LIEN - A hold or claim which one person has upon the property of another as a security for some debt or charge.
LIQUIDATED - Fixed; settled.
LIS PENDENS - A pending civil or criminal action.
LITERAL - According to the language.
LITIGANT - A party to a lawsuit.
LITATION - A judicial controversy.
LOCUS - A place.
LOCUS DELICTI - Place of the crime.
LOCUS POENITENTIAE - The abandoning or giving up of one's intention to commit some crime before it is fully completed or abandoning a conspiracy before its purpose is accomplished.

M

MALFEASANCE - To do a wrongful act.
MALICE - The doing of a wrongful act Intentionally without just cause or excuse.

MANDAMUS - The name of a writ issued by a court to enforce the performance of some public duty.
MANDATORY (adj.) Containing a command.
MARITIME - Pertaining to the sea or to commerce thereon.
MARSHALING - Arranging or disposing of in order.
MAXIM - An established principle or proposition.
MINISTERIAL - That which involves obedience to instruction, but demands no special discretion, judgment or skill.
MISAPPROPRIATE - Dealing fraudulently with property entrusted to one.
MISDEMEANOR - A crime less than a felony and punishable by a fine or imprisonment for less than one year.
MISFEASANCE - Improper performance of a lawful act.
MISREPRESENTATION - An untrue representation of facts.
MITIGATE - To make or become less severe, harsh.
MITTIMUS - A warrant of commitment to prison.
MOOT (adj.) Unsettled, undecided, not necessary to be decided.
MORTGAGE - A conveyance of property upon condition, as security for the payment of a debt or the performance of a duty, and to become void upon payment or performance according to the stipulated terms.
MORTGAGEE - A person to whom property is mortgaged.
MORTGAGOR - One who gives a mortgage.
MOTION - In legal proceedings, a "motion" is an application, either written or oral, addressed to the court by a party to an action or a suit requesting the ruling of the court on a matter of law.
MUTUALITY - Reciprocation.

N

NEGLIGENCE - The failure to exercise that degree of care which an ordinarily prudent person would exercise under like circumstances.
NEGOTIABLE (instrument) - Any instrument obligating the payment of money which is transferable from one person to another by endorsement and delivery or by delivery only.
NEGOTIATE - To transact business; to transfer a negotiable instrument; to seek agreement for the amicable disposition of a controversy or case.
NOLLE PROSEQUI - A formal entry upon the record, by the plaintiff in a civil suit or the prosecuting officer in a criminal action, by which he declares that he "will no further prosecute" the case.
NOLO CONTENDERE - The name of a plea in a criminal action, having the same effect as a plea of guilty; but not constituting a direct admission of guilt.
NOMINAL - Not real or substantial.
NOMINAL DAMAGES - Award of a trifling sum where no substantial injury is proved to have been sustained.
NONFEASANCE - Neglect of duty.
NOVATION - The substitution of a new debt or obligation for an existing one.
NUNC PRO TUNC - A phrase applied to acts allowed to be done after the time when they should be done, with a retroactive effect.("Now for then.")

O

OATH - Oath includes affirmation or declaration under penalty of perjury.
OBITER DICTUM - Opinion expressed by a court on a matter not essentially involved in a case and hence not a decision; also called dicta, if plural.

OBJECT (v.) - To oppose as improper or illegal and referring the question of its propriety or legality to the court.
OBLIGATION - A legal duty, by which a person is bound to do or not to do a certain thing.
OBLIGEE - The person to whom an obligation is owed.
OBLIGOR - The person who is to perform the obligation.
OFFER (v.) - To present for acceptance or rejection.
(n.) - A proposal to do a thing, usually a proposal to make a contract.
OFFICIAL INFORMATION - Information within the custody or control of a department or agency of the government the disclosure of which is shown to be contrary to the public interest.
OFFSET - A deduction.
ONUS PROBANDI - Burden of proof.
OPINION - The statement by a judge of the decision reached in a case, giving the law as applied to the case and giving reasons for the judgment; also a belief or view.
OPTION - The exercise of the power of choice; also a privilege existing in one person, for which he has paid money, which gives him the right to buy or sell real or personal property at a given price within a specified time.
ORDER - A rule or regulation; every direction of a court or judge made or entered in writing but not including a judgment.
ORDINANCE - Generally, a rule established by authority; also commonly used to designate the legislative acts of a municipal corporation.
ORIGINAL - Writing or recording itself or any counterpart intended to have the same effect by a person executing or issuing it. An "original" of a photograph includes the negative or any print therefrom. If data are stored in a computer or similar device, any printout or other output readable by sight, shown to reflect the data accurately, is an "original."
OVERT - Open, manifest.

<u>P</u>

PANEL - A group of jurors selected to serve during a term of the court.
PARENS PATRIAE - Sovereign power of a state to protect or be a guardian over children and incompetents.
PAROL - Oral or verbal.
PAROLE - To release one in prison before the expiration of his sentence, conditionally.
PARITY - Equality in purchasing power between the farmer and other segments of the economy.
PARTITION - A legal division of real or personal property between one or more owners.
PARTNERSHIP - An association of two or more persons to carry on as co-owners a business for profit.
PATENT (adj.) - Evident.
(n.) - A grant of some privilege, property, or authority, made by the government or sovereign of a country to one or more individuals.
PECULATION - Stealing.
PECUNIARY - Monetary.
PENULTIMATE - Next to the last.
PER CURIAM - A phrase used in the report of a decision to distinguish an opinion of the whole court from an opinion written by any one judge.
PER SE - In itself; taken alone.
PERCEIVE - To acquire knowledge through one's senses.
PEREMPTORY - Imperative; absolute.
PERJURY - To lie or state falsely under oath.

PERPETUITY - Perpetual existence; also the quality or condition of an estate limited so that it will not take effect or vest within the period fixed by law.
PERSON - Includes a natural person, firm, association, organization, partnership, business trust, corporation, or public entity.
PERSONAL PROPERTY - Includes money, goods, chattels, things in action, and evidences of debt.
PERSONALTY - Short term for personal property.
PETITION - An application in writing for an order of the court, stating the circumstances upon which it is founded and requesting any order or other relief from a court.
PLAINTIFF - A person who brings a court action.
PLEA - A pleading in a suit or action.
PLEADINGS - Formal allegations made by the parties of their respective claims and defenses, for the judgment of the court.
PLEDGE - A deposit of personal property as a security for the performance of an act.
PLEDGEE - The party to whom goods are delivered in pledge.
PLEDGOR - The party delivering goods in pledge.
PLENARY - Full; complete.
POLICE POWER - Inherent power of the state or its political subdivisions to enact laws within constitutional limits to promote the general welfare of society or the community.
POLLING THE JURY - Call the names of persons on a jury and requiring each juror to declare what his verdict is before it is legally recorded.
POST MORTEM - After death.
POWER OF ATTORNEY - A writing authorizing one to act for another.
PRECEPT - An order, warrant, or writ issued to an officer or body of officers, commanding him or them to do some act within the scope of his or their powers.
PRELIMINARY FACT - Fact upon the existence or nonexistence of which depends the admissibility or inadmissibility of evidence. The phrase "the admissibility or inadmissibility of evidence" includes the qualification or disqualification of a person to be a witness and the existence or nonexistence of a privilege.
PREPONDERANCE - Outweighing.
PRESENTMENT - A report by a grand jury on something they have investigated on their own knowledge.
PRESUMPTION - An assumption of fact resulting from a rule of law which requires such fact to be assumed from another fact or group of facts found or otherwise established in the action.
PRIMA FACUE - At first sight.
PRIMA FACIE CASE - A case where the evidence is very patent against the defendant.
PRINCIPAL - The source of authority or rights; a person primarily liable as differentiated from "principle" as a primary or basic doctrine.
PRO AND CON - For and against.
PRO RATA - Proportionally.
PROBATE - Relating to proof, especially to the proof of wills.
PROBATIVE - Tending to prove.
PROCEDURE - In law, this term generally denotes rules which are established by the Federal, State, or local Governments regarding the types of pleading and courtroom practice which must be followed by the parties involved in a criminal or civil case.
PROCLAMATION - A public notice by an official of some order, intended action, or state of facts.

PROFFERED EVIDENCE - The admissibility or inadmissibility of which is dependent upon the existence or nonexistence of a preliminary fact.
PROMISSORY (NOTE) - A promise in writing to pay a specified sum at an expressed time, or on demand, or at sight, to a named person, or to his order, or bearer.
PROOF - The establishment by evidence of a requisite degree of belief concerning a fact in the mind of the trier of fact or the court.
PROPERTY - Includes both real and personal property.
PROPRIETARY (adj.) - Relating or pertaining to ownership; usually a single owner.
PROSECUTE - To carry on an action or other judicial proceeding; to proceed against a person criminally.
PROVISO - A limitation or condition in a legal instrument.
PROXIMATE - Immediate; nearest
PUBLIC EMPLOYEE - An officer, agent, or employee of a public entity.
PUBLIC ENTITY - Includes a national, state, county, city and county, city, district, public authority, public agency, or any other political subdivision or public corporation, whether foreign or domestic.
PUBLIC OFFICIAL - Includes an official of a political dubdivision of such state or territory and of a municipality.
PUNITIVE - Relating to punishment.

Q

QUASH - To make void.
QUASI - As if; as it were.
QUID PRO QUO - Something for something; the giving of one valuable thing for another.
QUITCLAIM (v.) - To release or relinquish claim or title to, especially in deeds to realty.
QUO WARRANTO - A legal procedure to test an official's right to a public office or the right to hold a franchise, or to hold an office in a domestic corporation.

R

RATIFY - To approve and sanction.
REAL PROPERTY - Includes lands, tenements, and hereditaments.
REALTY - A brief term for real property.
REBUT - To contradict; to refute, especially by evidence and arguments.
RECEIVER - A person who is appointed by the court to receive, and hold in trust property in litigation.
RECIDIVIST - Habitual criminal.
RECIPROCAL - Mutual.
RECOUPMENT - To keep back or get something which is due; also, it is the right of a defendant to have a deduction from the amount of the plaintiff's damages because the plaintiff has not fulfilled his part of the same contract.
RECROSS EXAMINATION - Examination of a witness by a cross-examiner subsequent to a redirect examination of the witness.
REDEEM - To release an estate or article from mortgage or pledge by paying the debt for which it stood as security.
REDIRECT EXAMINATION - Examination of a witness by the direct examiner subsequent to the cross-examination of the witness.
REFEREE - A person to whom a cause pending in a court is referred by the court, to take testimony, hear the parties, and report thereon to the court.

REFERENDUM - A method of submitting an important legislative or administrative matter to a direct vote of the people.
RELEVANT EVIDENCE - Evidence including evidence relevant to the credulity of a witness or hearsay declarant, having any tendency in reason to prove or disprove any disputed fact that is of consequence to the determination of the action.
REMAND - To send a case back to the lower court from which it came, for further proceedings.
REPLEVIN - An action to recover goods or chattels wrongfully taken or detained.
REPLY (REPLICATION) - Generally, a reply is what the plaintiff or other person who has instituted proceedings says in answer to the defendant's case.
RE JUDICATA - A thing judicially acted upon or decided.
RES ADJUDICATA - Doctrine that an issue or dispute litigated and determined in a case between the opposing parties is deemed permanently decided between these parties.
RESCIND (RECISSION) - To avoid or cancel a contract.
RESPONDENT - A defendant in a proceeding in chancery or admiralty; also, the person who contends against the appeal in a case.
RESTITUTION - In equity, it is the restoration of both parties to their original condition (when practicable), upon the rescission of a contract for fraud or similar cause.
RETROACTIVE (RETROSPECTIVE) - Looking back; effective as of a prior time.
REVERSED - A term used by appellate courts to indicate that the decision of the lower court in the case before it has been set aside.
REVOKE - To recall or cancel.
RIPARIAN (RIGHTS) - The rights of a person owning land containing or bordering on a water course or other body of water, such as lakes and rivers.

S

SALE - A contract whereby the ownership of property is transferred
from one person to another for a sum of money or for any consideration.
SANCTION - A penalty or punishment provided as a means of enforcing obedience to a law; also, an authorization.
SATISFACTION - The discharge of an obligation by paying a party what is due to him; or what is awarded to him by the judgment of a court or otherwise.
SCIENTER - Knowingly; also, it is used in pleading to denote the defendant 's guilty knowledge.
SCINTILLA - A spark; also the least particle.
SECRET OF STATE - Governmental secret relating to the national defense or the international relations of the United States.
SECURITY - Indemnification; the term is applied to an obligation, such as a mortgage or deed of trust, given by a debtor to insure the payment or performance of his debt, by furnishing the creditor with a resource to be used in case of the debtor's failure to fulfill the principal obligation.
SENTENCE - The judgment formally pronounced by the court or judge upon the defendant after his conviction in a criminal prosecution.
SET-OFF - A claim or demand which one party in an action credits against the claim of the opposing party.
SHALL and MAY - "Shall" is mandatory and "may" is permissive.
SITUS - Location.
SOVEREIGN - A person, body or state in which independent and supreme authority is vested.
STARE DECISIS - To follow decided cases.

STATE - "State" means this State, unless applied to the different parts of the United States. In the latter case, it includes any state, district, commonwealth, territory or insular possession of the United States, including the District of Columbia.
STATEMENT - (a) Oral or written verbal expression or (b) nonverbal conduct of a person intended by him as a substitute for oral or written verbal expression.
STATUTE - An act of the legislature. Includes a treaty.
STATUTE OF LIMITATION - A statute limiting the time to bring an action after the right of action has arisen.
STAY - To hold in abeyance an order of a court.
STIPULATION - Any agreement made by opposing attorneys regulating any matter incidental to the proceedings or trial.
SUBORDINATION (AGREEMENT) - An agreement making one's rights inferior to or of a lower rank than another's.
SUBORNATION - The crime of procuring a person to lie or to make false statements to a court.
SUBPOENA - A writ or order directed to a person, and requiring his attendance at a particular time and place to testify as a witness.
SUBPOENA DUCES TECUM - A subpoena used, not only for the purpose of compelling witnesses to attend in court, but also requiring them to bring with them books or documents which may be in their possession, and which may tend to elucidate the subject matter of the trial.
SUBROGATION - The substituting of one for another as a creditor, the new creditor succeeding to the former's rights.
SUBSIDY - A government grant to assist a private enterprise deemed advantageous to the public.
SUI GENERIS - Of the same kind.
SUIT - Any civil proceeding by a person or persons against another or others in a court of justice by which the plaintiff pursues the remedies afforded him by law.
SUMMONS - A notice to a defendant that an action against him has been commenced and requiring him to appear in court and answer the complaint.
SUPRA - Above; this word occurring by itself in a book refers the reader to a previous part of the book.
SURETY - A person who binds himself for the payment of a sum of money, or for the performance of something else, for another.
SURPLUSAGE - Extraneous or unnecessary matter.
SURVIVORSHIP - A term used when a person becomes entitled to property by reason of his having survived another person who had an interest in the property.
SUSPEND SENTENCE - Hold back a sentence pending good behavior of prisoner.
SYLLABUS - A note prefixed to a report, especially a case, giving a brief statement of the court's ruling on different issues of the case.

<u>T</u>

TALESMAN - Person summoned to fill a panel of jurors.
TENANT - One who holds or possesses lands by any kind of right or title; also, one who has the temporary use and occupation of real property owned by another person (landlord), the duration and terms of his tenancy being usually fixed by an instrument called "a lease."
TENDER - An offer of money; an expression of willingness to perform a contract according to its terms.
TERM - When used with reference to a court, it signifies the period of time during which the court holds a session, usually of several weeks or months duration.

TESTAMENTARY - Pertaining to a will or the administration of a will.
TESTATOR (male)
TESTATRIX (female) - One who makes or has made a testament or will.
TESTIFY (TESTIMONY) - To give evidence under oath as a witness.
TO WIT - That is to say; namely.
TORT - Wrong; injury to the person.
TRANSITORY - Passing from place to place.
TRESPASS - Entry into another's ground, illegally.
TRIAL - The examination of a cause, civil or criminal, before a judge who has jurisdiction over it, according to the laws of the land.
TRIER OF FACT - Includes (a) the jury and (b) the court when the court is trying an issue of fact other than one relating to the admissibility of evidence.
TRUST - A right of property, real or personal, held by one party for the benefit of another.
TRUSTEE - One who lawfully holds property in custody for the benefit of another.

U

UNAVAILABLE AS A WITNESS - The declarant is (1) Exempted or precluded on the ground of privilege from testifying concerning the matter to which his statement is relevant; (2) Disqualified from testifying to the matter; (3) Dead or unable to attend or to testify at the hearing because of then existing physical or mental illness or infirmity; (4) Absent from the hearing and the court is unable to compel his attendance by its process; or (5) Absent from the hearing and the proponent of his statement has exercised reasonable diligence but has been unable to procure his attendance by the court's process.
ULTRA VIRES - Acts beyond the scope and power of a corporation, association, etc.
UNILATERAL - One-sided; obligation upon, or act of one party.
USURY - Unlawful interest on a loan.

V

VACATE - To set aside; to move out.
VARIANCE - A discrepancy or disagreement between two instruments or two aspects of the same case, which by law should be consistent.
VENDEE - A purchaser or buyer.
VENDOR - The person who transfers property by sale, particularly real estate; the term "seller" is used more commonly for one who sells personal property.
VENIREMEN - Persons ordered to appear to serve on a jury or composing a panel of jurors.
VENUE - The place at which an action is tried, generally based on locality or judicial district in which an injury occurred or a material fact happened.
VERDICT - The formal decision or finding of a jury.
VERIFY - To confirm or substantiate by oath.
VEST - To accrue to.
VOID - Having no legal force or binding effect.
VOIR DIRE - Preliminary examination of a witness or a juror to test competence, interest, prejudice, etc.

W

WAIVE - To give up a right.
WAIVER - The intentional or voluntary relinquishment of a known right.
WARRANT (WARRANTY) (v.) - To promise that a certain fact or state of facts, in relation to the subject matter, is, or shall be, as it is represented to be.

WARRANT (n.) - A writ issued by a judge, or other competent authority, addressed to a sheriff, or other officer, requiring him to arrest the person therein named, and bring him before the judge or court to answer or be examined regarding the offense with which he is charged.

WRIT - An order or process issued in the name of the sovereign or in the name of a court or judicial officer, commanding the performance or nonperformance of some act.

WRITING - Handwriting, typewriting, printing, photostating, photographing and every other means of recording upon any tangible thing any form of communication or representation, including letters, words, pictures, sounds, or symbols, or combinations thereof.

WRITINGS AND RECORDINGS - Consists of letters, words, or numbers, or their equivalent, set down by handwriting, typewriting, printing, photostating, photographing, magnetic impulse, mechanical or electronic recording, or other form of data compilation.

Y

YEA AND NAY - Yes and no.

YELLOW DOG CONTRACT - A contract by which employer requires employee to sign an instrument promising as condition that he will not join a union during its continuance, and will be discharged if he does join.

Z

ZONING - The division of a city by legislative regulation into districts and the prescription and application in each district of regulations having to do with structural and architectural designs of buildings and of regulations prescribing use to which buildings within designated districts may be put.

GLOSSARY OF MEDICAL TERMS

Contents

GLOSSARY OF MEDICAL TERMS

A

ABSCESS

Collection of pus in a tissue cavity resulting from a localized infection associated with cellular disintegration.

ALLERGY

Hypersensitive state stemming from exposure to a substance foreign to the body or to a physical agent (allergen) following a first contact. Subsequential exposure produces a reaction far more intense than the first one and entirely different.

ANEMIA

Decrease in the number of circulating red blood cells or in their hemoglobin (oxygen-carrying pigment) content. Can result from excessive bleeding or blood destruction (either inherited or disease caused) or from decreased blood formation (either nutritional deficiency or disease).

ANGINA

Choking pain. Angina pectoris: chest pain resulting from insufficient blood circulation through the hear vessels (coronaries), precipiated by exertion or emotion and usually relieved by a vasodilator drug.

ARTERIOSCLEROSIS

Generalized thickening, loss of elasticity, and hardening of the body's small and medium-size arteries.

ASTHMA

Disease characterized by repeated attacks of breath shortness, with wheezing, cough, and choking feeling due to a spasmodic narrowing of the small bronchi (small air tubes opening into the lung respiratory alveoli or cavities).

B

BIOPSY

Removal of a small piece of tissue or organ from the living body for microscopic or chemical examination to assist in disease diagnosis.

BRONCHITIS

Inflammation of the bronchi (tubular passages leading to lung cavities). It may be acute or chronic and caused by infection or the action of physical or chemical agents.

BLOOD COUNT
See: LABORATORY PROCEDURES

BLOOD GROUPING
See: LABORATORY PROCEDURES

BLOOD CHEMISTRY
See: LABORATORY PROCEDURES

BLOOD CULTURE
See: LABORATORY PROCEDURES

C

CANCER (NEOPLASM)
A cellular tumor (swelling) resulting from uncontrolled tissue growth. Its natural evolution is to spread locally and to other body locations through the blood and lymph stream.

CATARACT
Opacity of the normally transparent eye lens; this condition leads to impaired vision and stems from hereditary, nutritional, inflammatory, toxic, traumatic, or degenerative causes.

CATHETERIZATION
Introduction of a narrow tubular instrument called a catheter into a body cavity to withdraw liquids (usually into the bladder for urine withdrawal).

CEREBROSPINAL FLUID EXAMINATION
Chemical, microscopic, and bacteriological examination of a sample of the usually clear and colorless liquid bathing the brain and spinal cord. The sample is usually removed by needle puncture of the lumbar spine.

CIRRHOSIS
Chronic liver ailment, characterized by an increase in its fibrous support tissue that results in a progressive destruction of liver cells and impairment of the organ's function.

CONJUNCTIVITIS
Acute or chronic inflammation of the conjuctiva the delicate transparent membrane lining the eyelids and covering the exposed surface of the eyeball. It results from the action of bacteria, allergens, and physical or chemical irritants.

CYST
Any normal or abnormal sac in the body, especially one containing a liquid or semiliquid material.

CYSTIC FIBROSIS
An inherited disease of the glands of external secretion, affecting mostly the pancreas, respiratory tract, and sweat glands. It usually manifests itself in infancy.

CYSTITIS
Acute or chronic inflammation of the urinary bladder, caused by infection or irritation from foreign bodies (kidney stones) or chemicals. Its symptoms are frequent voiding accompanied by burning sensation

3

D

DIABETES (MELLITUS)

Hereditary or acquired disorder in which there is a sugar-utilization deficiency in the body, caused by an absolute or relative insufficiency of the normal internal secretion of the pancreas (insulin). Symptoms are thirst, hunger, itching, weakness, and increased frequency of urination. Diabetes can be controlled by diet drugs, or the administration of insulin. Lack of treatment leads to various complications, including death.

E

ECZEMA

Inflammatory skin disease that produces a great variety of lesions, such as vesicles, thickening of skin, watery discharge, and scales and crusts, with itching and burning sensations. Eczema is caused by allergy, infections, and nutritional, physical, and sometimes unknown factors.

EDEMA

Excessive accumulation of water and salt in the tissue spaces, caused by kidney or heart disease (generalized edema) or by local circulatory impairment stemming from inflammation, trauma, or neoplasm (localized edema).

ELECTROCARDIOGRAM (ECG or EKG)

Graphic tracing of the electric current that is produced by the rhythmic contraction of the heart muscle. Visually, a periodic wave pattern is produced. Changes in the wave pattern may appear in the course of various heart diseases; the tracing is obtained by applying electrodes on the skin of the chest and limbs.

ELECTROENCEPHALOGRAM (EEG)

Graphic recording of the electric current created by the activity of the brain. The electrodes are placed on the scalp. It is used in the diagnosis of organic brain disease.

EMBOLISM

Sudden blocking of an artery by a dislodged blood clot (after surgery), a fat globule (after a fracture), gas bubbles (after sudden decompression), bacterial clumps (bacterial endocarditis), or other foreign matter. The arteries most usually affected are those of the brain, heart, lungs, and extremities.

EMPHYSEMA

Lung disease characterized by overdistention of the chest and destruction of the walls separating the lung air sacs (alveoli). It results in a reduction of the respiratory surface, chronic shortness of breath, wheezing, and cough.

EPILEPSY

Disease characterized by sudden and brief attacks of convulsions, which are associated with impairment or loss of consciousness, psychic or sensory disturbances, and autonomic nervous system perturbations. Epilepsy causes the EEG to show characteristic brain wave alterations.

F

FURUNCLE (BOIL)

Acute and painful infection of the skin surrounding a hair root. Its center contains pus and dead tissue (core) that has to be discharged either spontaneously or surgically for proper cure.

G

GANGRENE

Localized tissue death, following interruption of the blood supply to the area; gangrene is associated with bacterial infection and putrefaction.

GASTRITIS

Acute or chronic inflammation of the lining of the stomach. It may be caused by the ingestion of alcohol, spices, medicines, chemicals, foods, as well as by infections or allergy.

GASTROSCOPY

Diret visualization of the stomach interior by means of an optical instrument called a gastroscope.

GASTROINTESTINAL SERIES (G.I. SERIES)

Serial X-ray examination of the stomach and intestines to detect, organic or functional alterations, enabling proper diagnosis and treatment of disease.

GLAUCOMA

Eye disease characterized by an increase in its internal pressure, caused by alteration of the intra-ocular fluid flow, and resulting in visual impairment, and if untreated, blindness.

GOITER

Enlargement of the thyroid gland that shows as a well-defined swelling at the base of the neck. Goiter is usually associated with iodine deficiency (endemic goiter), or with excessive secretion of thyroid hormones (exopthalmic goiter).

GOUT

A disturbance of body chemistry, manifested by elevated uric acid blood levels and excessive deposits in tissues, particularly joints and cartilages. It is characterized by repeated attacks of acute and very painful inflammation of joints, especially those of the big toe but also of ankles, knees, wrists, and elbows.

H

HEMATOMA

Swelling produced by a collection of blood escaping from a ruptured blood vessel, resulting from trauma or injury. It is generally located under the skin and subcutaneous tissue, or under the bony structure of the skull.

HEMORRHAGE (BLEEDING)

Any copious blood loss from the circulation. If sufficently severe or unchecked, it may lead to anemia or shock.

HEMORRHOIDS (PILES)

Abnormal dilation of the veins of the rectum and anus, causing local swelling, pain, itching, bleeding, and induration.

HEPATITIS

Liver inflammation, caused by infection or toxics. It is characterized by jaundice (yellow coloration of skin and membranes, especially of the eye) and is usually accompanied by fever and other disease manifestations.

HERNIA

Protrusion of a portion of an organ or tissue through an abnormal body opening. Inguinal hernia is one of the most common and consists of an intestinal loop protruding at the groin.

HYPERTENSION

Disease characterized by elevated blood pressure, resulting from the functional or pathological narrowing of the peripheral small arteries. Except in limited instances, its cause is generally unknown.

I

INFARCT

A circumscribed portion of tissue which has suddenly been deprived of its blood supply by embolism or thrombosis and which, as a result, is undergoing death (necrosis), to be replaced by scar tissue.

INFARCTION

The formation of an infarct; an infarct.

INTESTINAL OBSTRUCTION

Blocking of the normal flow of the intestinal contents, caused by twisting of a gut loop, benign tumor, cancer, or foreign body.

INTRADERMAL INJECTION

Injection into the skin proper. It is used less than hypodermic injection, which is done into the loose subcutaneous (under the skin) tissue.

K

KIDNEY FAILURE (RENAL FAILURE)

Severe reduction or impairment of the excretory function of the kidney. The acute form occurs most frequently after crushing injuries, transfusion of mismatched blood, severe burns or shock, generalized infections, obstetric accidents, and certain chemical poisoning.

6

L

LABORATORY PROCEDURES

Laboratory tests performed to assist in disease diagnosis and treatment, Usually these tests are carried out on samples of blood, urine, or other body fluids.

The MOST common are:

Blood Count

Determination of the number and percentage of red and white blood cells from a blood sample that is obtained by puncturing a vein or the skin. It consists of a red blood cell count (RBC), white blood count (WBC), and platelet count.

Blood Grouping

Blood typing for selecting and matching blood transfusion donors and for the diagnosis of various diseases.

Blood Chemistry

Determination of the content of various blood chemicals; the most usual are: sugar, for diabetes; urea nitrogen (BUN), for kidney or liver disease; uric acid, for gout; and cholesterol, for vascular and liver disease.

Blood Culture

Investigation to detect the presence of pathogenic germs by special culturing in artificial media.

Urinalysis (Urine Analysis)

Examination of urine constituents, both normal (urea, uric acid, total nitrogen, ammonia, chlorides, phosphate, and others) and abnormal (albumin, glucose, acetone, bile, blood, cells, and bacteria).

M

MENINGITIS

Inflammation of the enveloping membranes of the brain or spinal cord, caused by virus, bacteria, yeasts, fungi, or protozoa. It is a serious disease and may be a complication of another bodily infection.

METABOLISM

The total of the physical and chemical processes occuring in the living organism by which its substance is produced, maintained, and exchanged with transformation of energy; this energy itself provides fuel for all body functions and heat production.

METASTASIS

Transfer of a disease (usually cancer) from one part of the body to another that is not immediately connected with it.

MULTIPLE SCLEROSIS

A chronic and slowly progressive disease of unknown cause that is characterized by patches of fibrous tissue degeneration in brain and spinal cord, causing various nervous system symptoms; the disease's course is marked by occasional periods of worsening or improvement.

MUSCULAR DYSTROPHY

An inherited disease that involves the progressive weakness and degeneration of voluntary skeletal muscle fibers without nerve involvement.

MYOCARDITIS

Inflammation of the heart muscle that is associated with or caused by a number of infectious diseases, toxic chemicals, drugs and traumatic agents.

MYOCARDIUM

The muscular substance of the heart; adj., myocardial.

N

NEPHRITIS

Inflammatory, acute or chronic disease of the kidneys, which usually follows some form of infection or toxic chemical poisoning. It impairs renal function, causing headache, dropsy, elevated blood pressure, and appearance of albumin in urine.

NEURALGIA

Brief attach of acute and severe shooting pain along the course of one or more peripheral nerves, usually with clear cause.

NEURITIS

Inflammation or degeneration of one or more peripheral nerves, causing pain, tenderness, tingling, sensations, numbness, paralysis, muscle weakness, and wasting and disappearance of reflexes in the area involved. The cause may be infectious, toxic, nutritional (vitamin BI deficiency), or unknown.

P

PANCREATITIS

Inflammation of the pancreas, either mild or acute, and fulminating. The chronic form is characterized by recurrent attacks of diverse severity. Symptoms are sudden abdominal pain, tenderness and distention, vomiting and, in severe cases, shock and circulatory collapse.

PAP SMEARS (PAPANICOLAU SMEARS)

Method of staining smears of various body secretions -- especially vaginal but also respiratory, digestive, or genitourinary -- to detect cancer by examining the normally shed cells in the smear. The procedure is named for its developer.

PARKINSONISM (PARALYSIS AGITANS)

A usually chronic condition, marked by muscular rigidity, immobile face, excessive salivation, and tremor. These symptoms characterize Parkinson's disease; however, they are also observed in the course of treatment with psycho-pharmaceutical drugs or following encephalitis or trauma.

PELLAGRA

A disease caused by a vitamin (niacin) deficiency and characterized by skin, alimentary tract, and nervous system disturbances.

PERICARDITIS

Acute or chronic inflammation of the pericardium (fibrous sac surrounding the heart), caused by infection, trauma, myocardial infarction, cancer, or complication from other diseases.

PERITONITIS

Acute or chronic inflammation of the serous membrane lining abdominal walls and covering the contained viscerae. Its symptoms are abdominal pain and tenderness, nausea, vomiting, moderate fever, and constipation. It is usually caused by infectious agents or foreign matter entering the abdominal cavity from the intestinal tract (perforation), female genital tract, blood dissemination, or the outside (wounds, surgery).

PERNICIOUS ANEMIA

A chronic anemia, characterized by gastrointestinal and neurological disturbances that usually occur in late adult life and are caused by a deficiency (Biz).

PHLEBITIS

Condition caused by inflammation of a vein wall, resulting in the formation of a blood clot inside its cavity. Phlebitis produces pain, swelling, and stiffness of the affected part, generally a limb.

PLEURISY

Acute or chronic inflammation of the pleura (serous membrane lining the thoracic cavity and lungs). It often accompanies inflammatory lung diseases and may be caused by infection (tuberculous, viral or other), cancer, or cardiac infarction. Symptoms are stabbling pain in the thorax, aggravated by respiratory movements and shortness of breath.

PNEUMONIA

An acute inflammation or infection of the lung, caused by bacteria or virus. Chills, sharp chest pain, shortness of breath, cough, rusty sputum, fever, and headache are primary symptoms.

PNEUMOTHORAX

Accumulation of air or gas in the pleural cavity (between the chest wall and the lung), resulting in lung collapse. It may be spontaneous, following a penetrating chest wound or some diseases, or may be deliberately induced for treatment of lung ailments (tuberculosis).

POLYP

A protruding excrescence or growth from a mucous membrane, usually of the nasal passages but also of the uterine cervix, alimentary tract, or vocal cords.

PSORIASIS

Chronic, occasionally acute, recurrent skin disease of unknown cause, characterized by thickened red skin patches that are covered with whitish shiny scales. Psoriasis usually affects the scalp, elbows, knees, back, and buttocks.

PULMONARY EDEMA

Usually an acute condition in which there is a waterlogging of the lung tissue, including its alveolar cavities. Respiration is impaired. If inadequately treated, it may lead to rapid death; it is often a complication of chronic heart disease.

R

RHEUMATIC FEVER

Disease characterized by initial sore throat, chills, high fever, and painful inflammation of large joints. Frequently cardiac complications follow, leading to permanent organic heart disease.

RICKETS

Generally a disease of infants and young children caused by a vitamin D deficiency. There is defective bone calcification that causes skeletal deformities, such as bow legs, knock knees, and pigeon chest.

S

SCIATICA

A severe pain along the sciatic nerve, which extends from the buttocks along the back of the thigh and leg to the ankle. It is caused by mechanical pressure on the nerve at its spinal origin (from injury, local disease, or tumors).

SCOLIOSIS

A marked lateral curvature of the normally straight vertical spine, which may be caused by disease or mechanical deviation of the bones or muscles of the spine, hips, or legs.

SEPTICEMIA

Presence of bacteria or bacterial toxins in the circulating blood. This condition results from breakdown of local defenses, permitting the spread of a circumscribed infection to the bloodstream and rest of the body.

SILICOSIS

Occupational disease, usually chronic, causing fibrosis of the lungs. It results from inhalation of the dust of stone, flint, or sand that contains silica (quartz). Called "grinders* disease," it is observed in workers who have breathed such dust over a period of five to 25 years.

SLIPPED DISK

An acute or chronic condition, caused by the traumatic or degenerative displacement and protrusion of the softened central core of an intervertebral disk (cartilagenous disk between the spine bones), especially of the lower back. Symptoms are low back pain, which frequently extends to the thigh; muscle spasm; and tenderness.

SPASTIC PARALYSIS (CEREBRAL PALSY)

A condition probably stemming from various causes present since birth. Associated with nonprogressive brain damage, cerebral palsy is characterized by spastic, jerky voluntary movements, or constant involuntary and irregular writhing motion.

STROKE (CEREBRAL APOPLEXY)

A sudden attack of paralysis, with disturbance of speech and thought. It is caused by the destruction of brain substance, as the result of brain hemorrhage, vascular damage, intravascular clotting, or local circulatory insufficiency.

T

THROMBOPHLEBITIS

Condition caused by the inflammation of a vein complicated by the formation of an intravascular blood clot (thrombus). Circulation is obstructed in the affected area, usually the legs.

THROMBOSIS

Formation, development, or presence of a blood clot inside an artery or vein. This condition can be serious, if it affects the blood vessels of vital organs, such as the brain, heart, or lungs.

TUMOR

A swelling or growth of new tissue; it develops independently of surrounding structures and serves no specific function of its own.

U

UREMIA

Toxic clinical condition, caused by renal insufficiency resulting in the retention of urinary waste products in the circulating blood.

URINANALYSIS

See: LABORATORY PROCEDURES

V

VARICOSE VEINS

Abnormally distended and lengthened superficial veins caused by slowing and obstruction of the normal blood backflow. Varicose veins are most commonly observed in the legs, anus and rectum (hemorrhoids), and scrotum (varicocele).

www.ingramcontent.com/pod-product-compliance
Lightning Source LLC
Chambersburg PA
CBHW082033300426
44117CB00015B/2464